To War with a 4th Hussar

To War with a 4th Hussar

Fighting in Greece, North Africa and the Balkans

Peter Crichton

Pen & Sword
MILITARY

AN IMPRINT OF PEN & SWORD BOOKS LTD.
YORKSHIRE ~ PHILADELPHIA

First published in Great Britain in 2019 by
Pen & Sword Military
An imprint of
Pen & Sword Books Ltd
Yorkshire – Philadelphia

ISBN 978 1 52675 510 0

Printed and bound in the UK by TJ International Ltd, Padstow, Cornwall

Pen & Sword Books Limited incorporates the imprints of Atlas, Archaeology,
Aviation, Discovery, Family History, Fiction, History, Maritime, Military, Military
Classics, Politics, Select, Transport, True Crime, Air World, Frontline Publishing,
Leo Cooper, Remember When, Seaforth Publishing, The Praetorian Press,
Wharncliffe Local History, Wharncliffe Transport, Wharncliffe True Crime and
White Owl.

For a complete list of Pen & Sword titles please contact

PEN & SWORD BOOKS LIMITED
47 Church Street, Barnsley, South Yorkshire, S70 2AS, England
E-mail: enquiries@pen-and-sword.co.uk
Website: www.pen-and-sword.co.uk

Or

PEN AND SWORD BOOKS
1950 Lawrence Rd, Havertown, PA 19083, USA
E-mail: Uspen-and-sword@casematepublishers.com
Website: www.penandswordbooks.com

'Mindful of Former Valour'

In memory of the author's friends in the 4th Hussars
whose companionship he missed until the day he died.

Contents

Foreword

My father loved Egypt. The climate suited him – he hated the cold and wet – and I think that he and my mother were happy to return to the country not long after the war. By the end of 1951 they were back in England. They never spoke about their experiences in Cairo as the city's authorities lost control of the streets in the closing months of that year. It may be that they had left before the worst of the anti-British rioting and bloodshed. The quiet streets of Bourton-on-the-Water in the Cotswolds, where they settled on their return, must have seemed strange to this cosmopolitan couple, now accompanied by their 4-year-old son.

It was in Bourton-on-the-Water – at South Lawn, the small house they bought not far from the River Windrush and the centre of the village – that I first stumbled across some evidence of my father's wartime adventures. I must have been old enough to be left alone in the house and bored enough to explore the unremarkable cupboard under the stairs. At the back, past boxes of cleaning materials and the Hoover, I came across a great shaggy sheepskin coat hanging on the wall. It was too long to hang clear of the floor and its lower edge was draped over a small box and a pile of papers tied up with string. To my great excitement, the box contained a revolver and an automatic pistol, each with a few rounds of ammunition. The papers, once released from their string, turned out to be a collection of maps of Yugoslavia, what appeared to be telegrams and documents thrillingly marked 'Top Secret'.

I think that I was wise enough not to admit my discovery at the time. Over the following years, though, my father told me a little of his time first with the 4th Hussars and then, towards the end of the war, with Tito's partisans. No doubt he was encouraged by my decision to follow in his footsteps and join his old regiment.

I am not sure what prompted him to dust off the papers and write down his story. He began in 1969 when he was living in Naunton, a small village in the Cotswolds. I had just left Cambridge and had been posted to Singapore, so was finally off his hands. He had retired so had the time. He had written a couple of plays, and maybe the enjoyment he found in the process of writing induced him to start. He had no diaries and, apart from a few photographs and the papers and maps that had survived from his attachment to the Yugoslav partisans, had only his memory to aid him. Research from the isolation of a small rural village must have been difficult. There is evidence that he spoke to some of his contemporaries to check his facts. He was certainly in touch with the Imperial War Museum, which provided some of the illustrations that he wanted to include. He sent drafts to his 4th Hussar friends for their advice; General John Strawson and Brigadier John Paley had offered their comments at some stage in the process. Rear Admiral Morgan Giles provided details of Royal Navy operations in the Adriatic. A neighbour, Ralph Grey, Baron Grey of Naunton, encouraged him to publish, and Sir Fitzroy Maclean – the Head of '37' Military Mission in Yugoslavia during the war – suggested publishers and agents. He got as far as having his manuscript typed for publication and choosing the photographs, maps and diagrams he wanted to include. But in the mid-1970s his health began to deteriorate and his energy left him. Maybe he felt that it was time that his son picked up the baton; belatedly, that is what I have done, and this book is the result. I hope the reader enjoys it.

Robert Crichton

List of Maps

Part I

Chapter 1

Introduction to the Regiment

The Colonel was livid with rage. His knuckles showed white as he gripped the arms of his chair behind his desk.

The only other occupants of the room in the private house, which served as regimental headquarters, were the Adjutant, standing embarrassed in a corner, and myself. I was on the mat.

'I understand', said the Colonel, 'you have applied for a transfer to the Queen's Own Hussars; your application is refused; that is all.'

I managed a salute, turned and left the room. Tears of anger and frustration welled in the corners of my eyes as I made my way to my billet.

The outbreak of war had released me from a life I hated. My reactions had been ones of extreme excitement, heightened by fearful incredulity, but my enthusiasm had since been dampened by many months of playing at soldiers in England whilst the German armies had overrun Europe. The final blow had come when we had learnt that the armoured cars of the 2nd Northamptonshire Yeomanry, in which I served, were to be taken away and given to some other regiment.

A few weeks previously, whilst on leave in London, I had learnt from a friend that the 4th Hussars were going out to Egypt, where the desert war was in progress. Extolling all my virtues and great experience, I had written at once asking to join, and had had a promising reply. Now all my hopes were dashed by the Colonel's choleric decision. Of course, he was right, since no regiment wants to lose a reasonably competent officer.

However, the next day, the Adjutant presented me with a posting order to report forthwith to the 4th Hussars at Husbands Bosworth in Leicestershire.

My powerful, second-hand eight-cylinder Ford took me to London in record time. I parked it in the underground garage of the Dorchester Hotel in Park Lane, taking the best room I could get, high up in the building overlooking the Park. That night's air raid was but music to my ears. After a visit to the regimental tailor and a spending spree at Fortnum and Mason, which included amongst my purchases a large cabin trunk filled with every conceivable gadget for an arduous overseas adventure, I sped north to Leicestershire.

The officers' mess of 'B' Squadron, to which I had been posted as a troop leader, was accommodated at Welford Grange, an attractive country house belonging, by coincidence, to the Saviles, who were friends of mine.

No sooner had I arrived there than the new recruit was ordered to Regimental Headquarters for a night's duty officer. The Regimental Quartermaster Sergeant welcomed me, and I bedded down on a camp bed in front of a glowing coal fire. I felt thoroughly at home and fell blissfully asleep.

The next day, I took up my duties with my squadron. The squadron leader was a tall cadaverous Irishman, Major Clem Clements, whose main interest in life was the hunting field. I don't think he knew the difference between a sparking plug and a magneto. He and the rest of the officers were wonderful company.

Our tanks and vehicles had already been despatched on the long sea voyage to Egypt. During the weeks before embarkation we had nothing to do but enjoy ourselves as best we could, and the hospitality of the countryside was lavish.

John de Moraville, the squadron second-in-command, as a parting gesture of extravagance hired a huge black Daimler car, complete with uniformed chauffeur, which transported us to the various conferences and lectures we had to attend. The top brass, arriving in their far less comfortable military vehicles, were rather put out by this display of opulence on the part of 'B' Squadron 4th Hussars.

Welford was in the middle of the Shires, still at this time the best hunting country in England. The Master of the Fernie lent me his daughter's expensive jumping pony. It was scarcely fifteen hands high, and as I am six feet two, we were ill matched. But it was a veritable ball of fire, fairly flying over its fences.

I had been brought up with a love of horses, dogs and guns, but my father, a regular soldier and a handsome and arrogant man, having been in trouble of one sort or another for most his life, was unable to pay for me to finish my expensive education. I was therefore on the labour market of the depressing 1930s at an early age. In those days one had to work six days a week to earn a living, and I had neither the time nor the money to follow the country pursuits of my childhood. Now I found myself, by a trick of fate, in an utterly congenial situation.

Many kind people entertained us royally. We were invited to shooting parties and went racing. We had a splendid squadron dance at Welford Grange, which we decorated with a mass of potted chrysanthemums sent up from London for the occasion by Moyses Stevens, the Berkeley Square florist.

It was astonishing to reflect that only a few months previously, the German armies had conquered Europe, the miracle of Dunkirk had saved the British Army from its worst defeat in history and the Battle of Britain had saved the country from the immediate threat of invasion. There were no 'blood, sweat and tears' at Welford. The realities of the war had not yet struck home.

We sat at dinner on the evening before our departure from this happy situation. There was a meet of the Pytchley Hunt nearby the following day. As we were not due to entrain before nightfall, there was a last opportunity to go hunting, but I was desperate for a mount. I spilled my difficulty at the dinner table, and Clem Clements, in his usual abrupt manner, told me to telephone Major Peter Dollar who, he declared, was sure to fix me up. I thought he was pulling my leg. Peter Dollar was second-in-command of the regiment, a post traditionally held in awe by subalterns. Goaded by the rest of the company, I did as I was told and, to his eternal credit, instead of a flow of invective in reply, Peter gave me instructions to collect a horse from the mansion of some friends of his.

I arrived at the imposing stables in the early hours of the following morning as it was a long hack to the meet. My mount was ready for me, a little dark brown, thoroughbred gelding, with a bright eye, a plaited mane and a smart full tail. The bridle and saddle were supple and well fitted as they should be. I climbed aboard and we set out gaily. The little horse's hooves cracked the thin ice at every step. There was a light covering of snow. Very soon the sun shone through the mist. The countryside was quiet and undisturbed. I carried my great aunt's whip, with her initials on the silver band below the horn handle.

The Pytchley huntsman was mounted on his famous tubed chestnut gelding. It was restless, blowing steaming breath through the outlet in its neck [a permanent tracheotomy] into the frosty air.

Several of my regiment were out. Clem Clements, seeing my horse's antics because he was very fresh, and fearing no doubt to have to deal with a casualty before battle was joined, cautioned me that before long I would find myself on my back. But although I was kept busy in the saddle I was quite happy, as I was sure the horse had no vice.

I cannot say we had the best hunt ever, but as we hacked homewards I was absolutely content. It was fifteen years before I rode to hounds again. That night, we entrained for Liverpool. It was 2 October 1940.

Chapter 2

The Journey to Egypt

It was a ghastly journey in an unheated train, and in the murky, urban gloom of a cold morning, the regiment started its long march to the docks from the station. The farewells of the previous day had taken their toll and there was hardly a clear head in the ranks. The troops carried everything with them; even wireless sets tied with string were slung around the neck. Farewell gifts festooned their webbing equipment. The good-hearted people of Liverpool, turning out of their houses, ran alongside almost forcibly shouldering the burdens of the soldiers.

A great liner, the SS *Orcades* of 22,000 tons, lay in the dock to receive us. She was to carry the entire regiment thousands of miles across the ocean to Egypt in a voyage lasting nearly six weeks. The Mediterranean was closed to us by the Luftwaffe and the Axis fleet, as yet relatively intact at Taranto. We had therefore to sail in convoy all the way round Africa, through the Red Sea to the Suez Canal. Six great ships put to sea that night from Merseyside carrying 12,000 troops.

We were destined to reinforce General Wavell's army confronting the Italians in Egypt. Britain still stood alone against Germany and her Fascist ally. After the division of Poland, the Russians appeared content with their non-aggression pact with Hitler. American support was limited to Lend Lease and moral endorsement of our continued resistance. Even the French in North Africa and Syria were potentially hostile under the Vichy government. The Italians were undefeated in Abyssinia, and Rashid Ali in Iraq was consorting with the Germans. Wavell had to look to every point of the compass. This was the theatre of war to which we were bound.

Soon we left the overcast skies and grey seas of the North Atlantic behind us. The farther south we got, so an attack by U-boats grew less likely. The sun shone, life on board was almost luxurious. The *Orcades* was a well run ship, with excellent food and plenty of drink. The troops were well content.

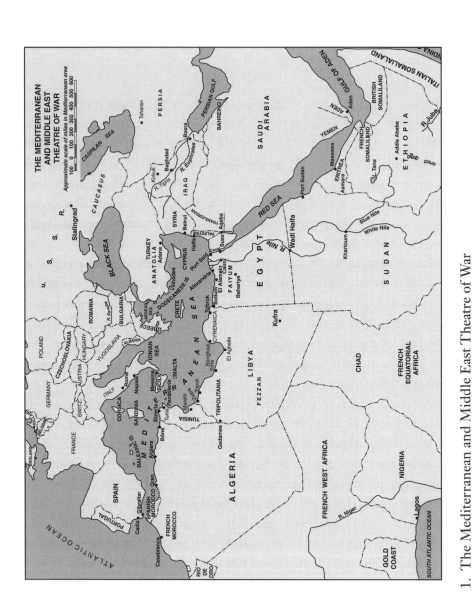

1. The Mediterranean and Middle East Theatre of War

In the mornings we did physical training and took apart and put together again our Vickers machine guns ad nauseam. In the afternoons we sunbathed and swam in the ship's swimming pool, and various deck games were organized.

Day after day, the six great ships plied their way across the ocean, shepherded by their fast escort of destroyers, whose slim grey hulls almost disappeared in the troughs of the great swell of the South Atlantic. At night, phosphorescent flying fish glowed in the spume of spray from the bow wave.

Every evening after dinner we played poker; I was a novice but found it the most fascinating card game ever invented. My squadron commander had a flair for it, his lugubrious expression and languid manner concealing his shrewd play. We struck up a partnership, and I have never enjoyed cards so much since.

On a boiling hot afternoon we were due to put in to Lagos to re-victual. Still far out from the port, out of sight of the African coast, on a great oily swell, we passed a flimsy native outrigger canoe, its two-man crew naked to the sun and the sea, their naturally hazardous lives as yet untouched by civilization or war.

Durban was our next port of call. The old Boer leader, General Smuts, had given us the unqualified support of the South African nation. The inhabitants of Natal were largely of British extraction. The troops were given shore leave and were splendidly entertained in many households. We hired a car to drive through the Valley of a Thousand Hills to the races at Pietermaritzburg, and got rather drunk in the first-class hotels of the principal city. It had a suburban atmosphere, in spite of the colour of the sun and the sea, as if Surbiton had been transported to Africa.

After a week's respite ashore, our great convoy set sail once more for the Indian Ocean on a course through the Mozambique Channel for the Red Sea. We passed through the straits of Bab-el-Mandeb into these strange waters. To the south-west lay the shores of Eritrea, and to the north the eternal sands of Arabia, the setting of *Seven Pillars of Wisdom*, which I had devoured page by page with romantic zeal as a boy.

On our final evening the *Orcades* was winched into a makeshift berth at El Kantara in the Suez Canal, where the regiment disembarked. By nightfall we were drawn up on parade on the sand whilst we waited for transport to take us to our camp at Tel-el-Kebir. Hour after hour in the bitter cold we waited. The troops started the age-old chant of the British Army when it gets impatient: 'Why are we waiting?' The sound swelled into a lusty chorus across the desert.

Tel-el-Kebir was a tented camp, 50 miles from Cairo to the west of the Delta. In a few days we were reunited with our tanks and vehicles, and strenuous training started in earnest. I got well acquainted with my three Mark VI B tanks. They were armed with two Vickers machine guns, of .303 and .50 calibre, and were powered by six-cylinder Auzani overhead camshaft engines, which would have brought a gleam to the eye of a sports car enthusiast. By careful retuning of the vernier couplings on the magnetos I got the maximum speed out of them. The guns, however, were a headache. They were mounted so that the breech was only a few inches from the top of the inside of the turret. The magazines were fed by webbing belts, whose efficiency varied with the temperature: if they got very dry, the rounds were apt to fall out as you jerked the belt through the breech. Moreover, in this operation the knuckles of one's left hand were generally bleeding from contact with the rough casting of the interior metal. The best cure for a stoppage was to call to the driver for a hammer. The tanks were at least five years old and twenty-five years out of date, but fortunately they were quite fast.

I was absolutely fascinated with Egypt. To the west of our camp lay a vast wilderness of desert, to the east the lush fertility of the Nile Delta, reeking of ancient history, where the way of life in the villages had scarcely changed since the days of the Bible. Against a huge red setting sun I saw a wedding procession in progress led by dancing girls with tambourines, the bride hidden from view within a decorated canopy mounted on a camel, followed on foot by the groom and the wedding guests. Even the twentieth century had not totally obscured the old city of Cairo. The scars on the stonework of the Citadel, where the cannon balls of Napoleon's Army had failed to penetrate, showed white as if they had been cut only yesterday.

I am sorry to relate that many of my friends were not as intrigued with our situation as I was. They were too far from the racecourse, the hunting field and sophistications of Europe. Nevertheless, we were not without sport. One day, on an exercise in the Delta, we came across some lakes upon which, to our astonishment, there were literally thousands of wild duck sitting on the water and flighting in from the north. We sped back to camp to tell of our exciting discovery, and a regimental invitation soon went out to the Brigade for a duck shoot. As it turned out, we had our day's sport at the expense of the British Ambassador, whose privileged shoot it happened to be. Sir Miles Lampson was not amused, and the following day our shotguns were impounded for the duration of our stay in the neighbourhood.

We went on leave to Cairo, dined at Shepheard's Hotel and Mena House, visited the Pyramids and sampled the nightclubs. Good food and wine were plentiful, and social life was very much in full swing. Back at camp, we still changed into blue patrols for dinner.

Meanwhile, not 40 miles away to the west, Wavell's army was poised for its assault on the Italian positions in Egypt and Libya. It struck with devastating effect on 6 December. We were not to take part in this great victory, which resulted in the virtual collapse of the Italian Army in North Africa. Churchill now took his decision to go to the aid of Greece, which had valiantly fought off the Italian assault on her frontiers from Albania. It was a political decision, having in mind the adverse effect upon Turkey and the Balkans if Greece were left to her fate. Thus he took from Wavell his powerful strategic reserve of two high-class colonial divisions and the 1st British Armoured Brigade, which included my own regiment.

Chapter 3

A Greek Adventure

W e were the first to go. Loading our tanks and vehicles on to transports at Alexandria, we boarded the *Gloucester*, one of the fastest cruisers in the Royal Navy, bound for Piraeus, the port of Athens. We crossed the Mediterranean in broad daylight. The great flat steel after deck of the ship seemed to drop below the level of the waves as her powerful engines thrust her at high speed across the sea, her churning wake welling out astern. No trooper could complain that he was not seeing the world, yet our travels had scarcely begun. It was a great adventure, and I had no premonition of the disaster that would so shortly befall us.

There were few signs of war in Athens. The Greek Army was far away in the north, and the ancient city went about its daily life unhindered. We camped amongst the olive trees of Glyfada, close to the shore, sorting out our equipment and getting organized once more after our swift transhipment. I explored the staggering beauty of the Acropolis by moonlight with Kenneth Caldwell, a young Canadian officer seconded to my squadron. As the gate was shut, we had to climb the protective iron railings to gain entry.

It had not rained on us since leaving the Atlantic only four months before. Now, just as we were due to entrain for the north, as we lay that night sleeping under the trees, it sheeted down. I woke to find my bedding sodden. One of my precious tanks had been under repair for a leaky radiator, but the Light Aid Detachment, who had promised to get it ready before morning, had left it partially dismantled. Furious, and with freezing fingers, I struggled to get the pieces together again to be in time to load it on the flat cars of the train.

The long journey to the north was extraordinary. The coaches reminded me of those one sees in Western movies; they had verandahs projecting to the rear on which one could stand in the open air to view the scenery. The antiquated engine could only pull its heavy load at 25mph on the flat, whilst uphill our speed was reduced to walking pace. The line ran past Thermopylae to Lamia, from where we could see the great range of the Pindus mountains; over the plains of Thessaly to Larissa; across the river Aliakmon into the mountains to Kozani, where the branch line led to Ptolemais; thereafter, through the pass to Edhessa on the eastern slopes of the Vermion mountains.

The journey took two days and covered about 250 miles as the railway ran; almost the entire length of Greece.

At Edhessa we got off the train, completing the journey to our destination at Yianitza by road.

Strangely, we had seen very little of the Greek Army. Evidently, they did not believe in base troops. It seemed that every Greek was a front-line soldier, in contrast to our own Army, which had ten men in the rear for every one at the sharp end. It was true that the conflict with the Italians was at present confined to the Albanian front many miles away to the west, but our isolated position at Yianitza was odd to say the least of it. We looked east across the Vardar river to Salonika and the Bulgarian frontier, and south to the deadly malarial swamps, so well known to many British soldiers of the First World War, but now drained by an elaborate system of canals and dikes.

Yianitza was no more than a primitive village. Our squadrons were dispersed about it in the countryside, living under canvas. Tortoises crawled under our tent flaps to keep us company; the village dogs were savage, wearing spiked collars to help them combat raiding wolves from the mountains to the north.

It was a strange and interesting land. Alexander the Great, King of Macedon, was born here at Pella, not five miles from our camp. Here he assembled his cavalry from the plains of Thessaly for his great conquests. Here General Mahon, commanding an Allied army of 300,000 men, had faced the German Eleventh Army and the Bulgarians only 25 years before, just within my lifetime. This was the ancient battleground of Greeks and Turks over the centuries.

Now the 1st British Armoured Brigade faced the German Twelfth Army and its old ally, the Bulgarians, awaiting their assault. Three Greek divisions were supposedly across the Vardar River watching the Bulgarian frontier, but we saw no evidence of their existence. A squadron reconnaissance as far as Salonika had seen no troop reserves, no military installations, no fuel or ammunition dumps, no military transport.

If we had to withdraw, our only line of retreat was over the mountains at our back, through the pass at Veria. The most vulnerable characteristic of our little tanks was their friction clutches. They would not stand up to the frequent application of the steering gear on mountain roads. The cruiser tanks of the Royal Tank Regiment, which made up the other regiment of our brigade, although much bigger and armed with two-pounder guns, were notoriously unreliable.

The Greek Army was spread out over a great distance, with a yawning gap between its Albanian front and its watch on the Macedonian border. The line of communication with Athens over hundreds of miles of bad roads and tortuous slow railway lines made coordination between the two armies improbable.

I think we all had an uneasy feeling that someone had blundered. Never having been trained as a soldier, I had no conscious sense of military appreciation, but a Boy Scout with a knowledge of fieldcraft would have known that our dispositions were wrong. I had had a highly developed defensive sense ever since, years ago, I had poached game on Mr Arkwright's estate in Essex from my grandfather's house, pitting my wits against Keeper Stanham and his son. You use the ground as best you can, the woods and the hedgerows for cover. You listen for the snapping of a twig or the low call to a dog. It is a far cry from poaching to warfare, but the same principles apply. A rise in the ground can correspond to a mountain, a stream to a river, a covert to a forest.

Here some of the principles of war had certainly been broken. There had been no proper reconnaissance since the decision to aid Greece had been taken.

It was ironic that we should be in the homeland of one of the greatest generals of all time, who had been dedicated to reconnaissance, going out alone often in disguise or with a local guide to see for himself the lie of the land and determine the strength of the enemy or the competence of his allies. There was no favourable interpretation of any of these factors with our present deployment. Neither was our intention clear-cut. It was inconceivable that we could venture to attack such a powerful enemy with our small force with any prospect of even limited success. And we had badly chosen positions for defence.

General Wilson would have found it difficult to emulate the King of Macedon. His portly British figure would have been hard to disguise as a

Greek peasant wandering harmlessly about the mountains in the twentieth century. But decisions had been taken in London, Cairo and Athens without proper information and, on his own admission, Wilson did his reconnaissance in a Wagon Lits train complete with restaurant car. Only Francis de Guingand, at that time on the joint planning staff, had seen the pitiable state of the Greek Army on the Albanian front, but even he had stood mute in a corner whilst the British Foreign Secretary, Anthony Eden, held forth to the Greeks with his ill-judged optimistic appraisal.

The Commanding Officer, Colonel Edward Lillingstone, who already surely suspected that his military career was about to be sacrificed to political expediency, told us of his fears with the utmost frankness. The New Zealand Division, which had followed us to Greece, was shortly to take up a position on the Aliakmon Line. In General Wilson's appreciation this was a natural defensive position, from the river of that name northwards along the Vermion mountains to the Yugoslav frontier. But it assumed that the Yugoslavs would resist if attacked. If they did not, then the gateway to Greece would be open and our left flank would be turned.

Meanwhile, Clem Clements, our squadron leader, had reverted to his favourite pastime. He had found a mare in the village with a saddle and bridle and was out riding. No doubt she was a direct descendant of Alexander's cavalry, but she had a sagging belly, a full udder and a foal at foot. We ragged him mercilessly.

On 6 April the German Twelfth Army struck at Yugoslavia and Greece.

Chapter 4

The Germans Attack

The regiment moved forward to take up battle positions in the hills overlooking the Vardar River. All that day, I peered in vain through my field glasses from the turret of my tank for a sight of the enemy.

The German Twelfth Army was a colossus compared to the forces which opposed it. There were fifteen divisions, of which four were armoured. The Bulgarians facing the Macedonian frontier were also under its command.

The British Expeditionary Force consisted of two divisions and one armoured brigade. The 6th Australian Division had arrived within the last few days. That was our total complement. The almost mythical Greek Army, which we had scarcely seen since our arrival in Greece early in March, commanded by General Papagos, was so split by distance and topography, and so worn by its hard five-month struggle with the Italians in Albania, that its ineffectiveness against a fresh, professional German Army was in no doubt. The divisions which had been promised for the defence of the Aliakmon line had never arrived.

Events turned out exactly as our Colonel had feared. Before we even sighted the enemy on our front, and towards evening of that same day, General Wilson ordered our withdrawal back over the mountains through Veria, in order to hurry north with all possible speed and plug the gap at Monastir.

The road to Veria was now choked with refugees fleeing from the Bulgarians, and our progress was slow. The dreadful spectacle of poor people leaving their homes had been already a familiar sight all over Europe, but it was new to us. A bullock cart had overturned to the side of the road, and its peasant owners were weeping at their sudden awful predicament. Captain 'Loopy' Kennard, our second captain, who always took great pains to make out he was less responsible than he really was, turned to me with a furious remark about the imbecility of war.

As we reached the mountains the weather worsened. It grew bitterly cold and began to snow. I could not help but notice, as we passed through Veria, that the blossom was out in the orchards. It was spring.

The Yugoslavs, under their vacillating Regent Prince Paul and under strong German pressure to follow the example of Bulgaria, had wavered too long. The militant Serbs, who had freed Monastir from the invader so many years before, had no time to organize. Too late, they seized the Royal Palace in Belgrade, forcing the Regent to abdicate. The German Twelfth Army swept through the country. The Luftwaffe bombed Belgrade without mercy for three days. The gateway to Greece was open and our flank threatened.

By the night of 7 April the regiment, having crossed the mountains, had reached Kozani. The Brigade had lost almost a third of its tanks due to mechanical failure on the tortuous mountain roads, but my troop was still in good working order. We slept that night in below zero temperatures and woke stiff with cold. It was agony to shave in the freezing morning air.

I was ordered to move out to a vantage point above the town, which lay in a ravine below the mountains, to watch the approaches. It looked quiet and undisturbed in the sunshine. The narrow road ran between tall, substantial, stone-built houses, and the river sparkled in the frosty air. There was no sign of movement, no people in the streets or the fields. The cold wind had died. There was an air of expectancy over the place.

Suddenly, with little warning or sound, a huge black German bomber swung low over the mountain tops, swooping on the town. I looked down upon its back, its wingspread enfolding the houses. It seemed almost to hover before releasing its bombs. A tremendous crash echoed in the valley. Thick clouds of dust and debris rose in the air. I was appalled. It was my first sight of the enemy. The realities of war struck home with dramatic impact. My tank crew fell silent, and I searched through my field glasses to see if the road was blocked. Thick power cables sagged between the buildings, debris littered the streets. I reported through my radio what I had seen, and our sappers were quickly at work to clear our only route to the north.

As we passed through the town, it was evident that the population had already taken to the mountains. Doubtless they had heard on the radio of events in Yugoslavia, of the holocaust on Belgrade and the advance of the German army. War was nothing new to the people of these regions.

The road from Kozani ran through a rocky defile, broadening out at Ptolemais into a narrow fertile valley. The scenery was harsh but beautiful. To the east and west of us, snow-covered mountains rose to 6,000ft. We were before Ptolemais on 8 April.

A brigade group from the 6th Australian Division, having arrived before us, had already taken up defensive positions. They were ill equipped to withstand the bitterly cold weather. It was probable that many of the soldiers had never seen snow before in their lives. They had arrived straight from the sunshine of Egypt as we had done, but whereas we had been brought up to English winters in cold houses, they were used to the wonderful climate of the southern hemisphere. It was a very adverse factor. A cold soldier finds it harder to fight. It pays to read history.

On 9 April the tanks of our brigade were deployed across the valley, with observation over the plain stretching in front of us for about 4,000yds. The road from the Yugoslav border emerged through a gap in the hills to the north. This was the gateway through which we expected the onslaught of the enemy.

On the 10th the Germans entered Monastir. Our first battle of the war was imminent.

'B' and 'C' Squadrons were deployed to hold the line of hills on the west side of the road, 'A' Squadron and the 3rd Royal Tank Regiment on the east. Our flanks in each case were protected by the steeply rising mountains. The Australians were digging in their machine gun pits, and behind our line the Rangers (1st Rangers, King's Royal Rifle Corps) were taking up their positions in front of the Royal Horse Artillery and the Australian batteries.

Meanwhile, on the other side of the frontier, five German motorized divisions and four Panzer divisions were assembling for their conquest of Greece.

The battlefield was once the estate of a Macedonian nobleman, whose soldier son, Ptolemy, was the founder of a fabulous dynasty. Perhaps he was looking down with a wry smile upon the scene unfolding. He would marvel at the modern apparatus of war, but bright steel was sheathed in the bayonet scabbards of the Rangers, the Australian Infantry and the German Twelfth Army. In two thousand years things had not changed so much after all.

It was the quiet on the evening of 11 April. The snow had reflected sunshine all day. There had been no sign of the Luftwaffe since the single attack on Kozani. Night fell. At eleven o'clock we posted troop guards and crawled inside our small canvas bivouacs to shelter from the cold wind. The ground beneath our bodies was hard from the frost.

With the dawn, there was still no sign of the enemy as we stood at the alert. All eyes were trained upon the gap in the hills 4,000yds away.

Quite suddenly in mid-morning the SS Adolf Hitler Division, the vanguard of the Twelfth Army, came into the plain, streaming down the road in a black column, fanning out on each side at the base of the hills in battle array, with no attempt at concealment.

I was ordered to the extreme left flank at the village of Mavro Pege, from where I could look down upon the battlefield.

A scouting patrol of four yellow Messerschmitts flew in at high speed over our lines, climbing suddenly in a steep turn for a better view of our positions. The Royal Horse Artillery opened up on their massed black target. There was answering fire from the enemy lines, their gun flashes clearly visible. The artillery duel now started up in earnest. The enemy's arrogant lack of concealment broke all the rules.

Shells burst in front of our gun sites but short of our positions, most of the fire falling harmlessly into a marsh.

The yellow Messerschmitts continued their high-speed reconnaissance flights unhindered by flak. I could see the line of the enemy spreading out to the west until their extreme flank was hidden from my view by the mountainside.

For hour after hour the artillery duel continued, yet there was no attempt by either side to move forward into battle.

The villagers and children of Mavro Pege came out to see the drama, gathering about my troop tanks. In vain I waved them away, but they appeared unconcerned about the danger they were in. An old man approached me, in his hands a loaf of bread and a flagon of wine, which I gratefully accepted, pleading with him to get the children into the houses under cover. He spoke in broken English with an American accent, telling me he had lived for years in Brooklyn and had returned to his native village with his savings. Without emotion, he said his son had recently been killed in Albania fighting the Italians. It was a chilling piece of information.

As the day wore on without a move by either side, I began to wonder at the hesitancy of the Twelfth Army, but towards evening their tanks advanced boldly across the plain, firing at us with their 50mm high-velocity guns. Our forward troops were engaging them at a range of 1,000yds. Alan Micholls was killed instantly as a shell went clean through the turret of his tank. Kenneth Caldwell reported he was engaging at close range.

We answered with our machine guns, but the bullets simply bounced off the German Mark III tanks. By nightfall we were under heavy attack. Tracer shells from the enemy tank guns showed like balls of fire, moving quite slowly past us. It was a vivid optical illusion, almost as if we could catch them and throw them back.

As the light began to fail we were ordered to withdraw. We simply could not fight off German armour with machine guns. Dusk saved us from utter defeat. There was great confusion on the road as the squadrons gathered in the darkness.

Due to the inexplicable hesitancy of the powerful German force to press home their attack on our lightly defended stand at Ptolemais, we had delayed their invasion of Greece by one day at least.

During the dark night we retreated slowly down the road. It was impossible to get off it due to the mountainous nature of the country on either side. At about midnight the Colonel called a halt where there was sufficient open ground to assemble the regiment; but when dawn broke we found ourselves leaguered in squadrons on the top of a hillside absolutely bare of cover. The rest of the Brigade group had continued their night march south towards Grevena. The road was now empty, and we were in a rearguard position.

I set about with my troops knocking up the pins in the tank tracks which needed constant attention. The sound of aircraft made me look up from my work. There, high up in the sky, was the Luftwaffe in strength. A flight of twenty-four Stukas flew serenely in formation above us like huge birds of prey looking for a kill. For some seconds I stood spellbound, then the formation leader gracefully pulled away in a dive straight for us. We were powerless to protect ourselves. We had no anti-aircraft guns, the Vickers machine guns in our tanks could not be elevated sufficiently to fire at an angle of more than 45° and the manual operation of the turret was too laborious and slow even to follow the pace of a running man. I bolted for the bed of a stream, where I was joined by my troop and our squadron commander. A dead cow lay in the shallow water, upturned with distended belly, her legs sticking straight up in the air.

For the first time I heard the hideous scream of Stuka dive bombers which had struck terror all over Europe. In a second the ground shook and heaved with the crash of bombs as we flattened ourselves against the protective bank of the stream. The smell of cordite was in our nostrils, dust and debris hurtled over our sanctuary.

When the bombing ceased, and the screams of the dive bombers had died away, we crawled out, muddied by the stream, expecting to see a tangled mass of wreckage. There was surprisingly little damage and casualties were light. Our tanks were for the most part scarred but unharmed. A few trucks were on fire. Kenneth Caldwell was wounded in the leg. The casualties were quickly got away down the road, and very soon we left our exposed position to continue on our way towards Grevena.

As we neared the Aliakmon river, Clem Clements ordered me to attempt to go across country and reconnoitre the bridge. With my troops following my lead, as I was speeding past the regimental headquarter tanks, I saw the Colonel signal to me from his turret to approach. Our way lay over an open gravel clearing amongst the rocks.

Getting out of my tank, with an ostentatiously professional wave of my arm I signalled my troops to disperse. To my consternation, they obeyed with an exaggerated interpretation of my order, speeding far from me in a shower of gravel and dirt. At that very moment, as I was about to bring up my arm in salute, the Stukas dived upon us again. The Colonel's head quickly bobbed down inside his turret, and I was left standing there in a fearful quandary. Having been summoned, was I now to run for my troop, 150yds away, or was I to seek the nearest cover under the Colonel's tank? Both courses seemed undignified. My total inability to resolve this dilemma froze me rigid to the spot, whilst the bombs burst all around. As the dust settled, the Colonel's head bobbed up again, and at last I got in my salute and told him of my mission.

Chapter 5

Guarding the Bridge

The river ran through a shallow, rocky gorge. The ancient, solid, arched stone bridge was intact. I deployed my troop astride the road on the northern approach, directing my squadron on the radio by the cross-country route I had taken. The troops were tired and hungry. I told them to brew up their eternal tea and to cook a meal. By some miracle, we were still supplied with the essentials of life.

At midday the regiment passed through my lines, where I was joined by my squadron commander, who stationed his tank by mine. At his invitation I climbed into his gunner's seat. The moment we began to discuss the situation, the Luftwaffe dived upon us yet again. I jerked the belt into the .50 Vickers gun, depressing the breech as far as I could and firing a continuous burst with maximum elevation on a fixed line in the vain hope that one of the enemy pilots would fly into my line of fire. There was no such luck.

I noticed that the Stukas made no attempt to bomb the bridge. Evidently, they wanted it intact.

The Royal Air Force now made its first appearance on the scene. The pilot of a Gloucester Gladiator, entirely alone, hell-bent on death or glory, flew over our position. This was a splendid biplane with a radial engine, very manoeuvrable but no match for a Messerschmitt. The red, white and blue roundels cheered us up tremendously but, sad to relate, this was the only one of our aircraft that I saw during the entire campaign. The Luftwaffe had 800 aircraft available. Our air force based on Athens and Larissa, originally of seven squadrons supporting the Greek Army in Albania, had already worn out its strength.

For the first time since our arrival at Piraeus we now saw the Greek Army. After five months of a hard and successful campaign in the mountains, the advance of the German Twelfth Army had broken its spirit, and it had completely disintegrated. Columns of weary soldiers streamed through my troop lines, many without boots, their feet bound with rags and string.

The remnants of a cavalry division came down the road, their horses in a dreadful state, flanks sunken in between their ribs, their heads hanging low to the ground. These were troops of the 12ᵗʰ and 20ᵗʰ Divisions from the Kastoria region, who were supposed to have closed the gap between our left flank and the Greek Western Army on the Albanian frontier. There was no order in the columns, no officers amongst the ranks. They were fought out, finished, in utter disarray and going home. A beaten army in full retreat was indeed a terrible sight. Some of the troops sadly waved to us in greeting as they passed. Probably our presence astride the vital crossing gave them some assurance.

All day long, we watched this sorry spectacle. A little Renault tank, manned by two Yugoslav officers, made its appearance. Towards evening, the columns began to thin out, the numbers began to dwindle and presently only a few stragglers came wearily down the road. As dusk fell, the last one crossed the river, and now there was silence as we listened for the enemy.

I was ordered to hold the bridge during the night. No one had apparently thought to blow it up. Three Bren gun carriers from the Rangers were placed under my command. I asked a young sapper officer who arrived in a truck if he could not destroy just one of the arches. He rummaged amongst his tangle of equipment but declared he had not enough explosive to damage the solid stonework. It was a great pity, because the gorge, although shallow, was very steep, and the river was impossible to ford with mechanized vehicles. However, he set about mining the road, assuring me that he would not fuse his mines until after I withdrew my small force from the northern bank.

It was still bitterly cold but a brilliant moonlit night with millions of stars. The Rangers' carriers were fast and manoeuvrable, so I posted them on the northern approach with orders to withdraw over the bridge if attacked. Together with my three tanks, we now had a fair amount of firepower to resist an infantry assault. After the sapper left us on our own, I walked up the road on to the heights above the gorge to look back along the line of our retreat. There was neither sight nor sound of the enemy. There was no wind, and the stillness of the night was only disturbed by the rushing waters of the river tumbling down from the mountains of Albania on its long course to the sea.

I walked back to my tank to stand alert in the turret, but it was hard to stay awake and my eyelids felt like lead curtains. I woke stiff with cramp and cold, tangled about the steel controls, which had failed to wake me as I dropped asleep on them. My watch showed an early hour in the morning. It was still dark. Only the Rangers' section commander and my own troop guard were awake on the other side of the river. None of us had had much sleep for the last 48 hours.

Suddenly I heard the unmistakeable sound of a horse's hooves in the distance. This was no worn out animal. Its pace was a crisp, sharp, confident walk. The troops sprang alert. All guns were trained on the road.

Into the moonlight rode a Greek cavalry soldier, a rifle slung across his back, mounted on a magnificent dark brown horse, its ears pricked and its head held high. The Rangers let him through. As he came over the bridge he reined in. I called out to him enquiringly, '*Tedeschi?*' (Italian for German); with a sweep of his arm and a laugh he pointed back up the road. I waved him on his way.

That cavalryman was in command of his own destiny. He would not run with the crowd or waste his horse. He would lie up by day, grazing his animal in the foothills under cover of the scrub, and ride by night at a steady, even pace until he reached his village.

Dawn broke, and still the Germans did not come. The Rangers were withdrawn, and in their stead I was given a troop of the Northumberland Hussars' anti-tank guns. The troop commander, the Duke of Northumberland, being too vulnerable a hostage to enemy propaganda, had been sent out of harm's way down the line. The two-pounder guns were mounted on high chassis trucks. I was given the doubtful honour of conducting the rearguard, whilst the retreat continued to Grevena.

The sappers fused the mines on the road, leaving the bridge solidly intact, regretfully, for the enemy's convenience.

The dirt road ran through broken hill country. On either side scrub and hardy trees grew where there was soil between the rocks. It would have been a wonderful country to hide up in. We were many miles from habitation in the wilds of Northern Greece, where roads were scarcely more than tracks, the few villages marked on the map separated by a day's march. The terrain was too rocky for cultivation, but countless streams flowed through the gulleys and the scrub. It was grazing land for hardy sheep and goats and a natural harbour for a fugitive. Before we left the bridge I told my troop to fill their small packs with food and to see their water bottles were filled to the top. I knew that if the Twelfth Army's vanguard caught up with us, the result of a fight was a foregone conclusion, as one German Mark III tank could shoot us to pieces. In that unhappy event, and if we lived, I determined to take to the hills for refuge.

We had hardly travelled a few miles when first one and then another of the Northumberland Hussars' gun carriers broke down. We towed them behind the tanks, but this put a severe strain on the clutches. The main body of the regiment had long since disappeared southwards, and I had lost contact on the radios, which were extremely unreliable, having in any case a very short range. Our progress was slowed down by towing the heavy carriers. I was now in a great quandary as to whether to abandon the guns to save the tank clutches. To make matters worse, a German Fieseler Storch spotter plane made its appearance, circling round us to keep track of our progress. We fired at it hopelessly with our machine guns. It was flying so slowly and with such contempt that I would have given anything even for a Lee Enfield rifle, a weapon with which I had been very familiar as a schoolboy at Bisley. With enough lead off I might very well have got in a lucky shot, as the Storch was a much bigger target than a pigeon and was flying no faster.

I decided to abandon one of the guns. We took out the breech block and I fired a burst from the Vickers through the radiator of the carrier into the engine casing. It was hardly a prize to be left for the enemy. My troop hitched the second carrier to my own tank, which was in better order than the others.

We now felt extremely isolated to say the least of it, having no idea how far behind the regiment we were. I simply could not understand the failure of the German vanguard to catch up with us, but perhaps the mines on the approaches to the bridge had held them up or made them wary lest our pathetic rearguard were busily sowing mines all along our retreat. Our frequent stops to deal with the broken-down carriers may have misled the Storch pilot into a belief that we were laying all kinds of deadly booby traps. If there was such a deception it was entirely unpremeditated.

Towards evening, when I was still towing our one remaining gun, the familiar sight of a solitary Mark VI B tank by the roadside spurred me on. Clem Clements had remained behind to find out what had befallen us. My rearguard duties were over, and we were still some miles from Grevena.

Meanwhile, the complete collapse of the Greek armies on our left flank and on our right in Macedonia meant that the British Expeditionary Force was now fighting alone. The Australian Brigade Group, which had withdrawn from the battle at Ptolemais, had gone southwards towards Larissa and had joined with its main force and the New Zealand Division in an attempt to hold up the German advance at Mount Olympus and the Tempe gorge.

We knew nothing of this as we slowly withdrew towards Grevena through the Stiatista defile, continually harassed by the Luftwaffe. As we neared the Pineios river we learnt that the bridge had been destroyed by the Anzac sappers; this meant that we had to turn north towards Tirnavos, now threatened by those German divisions which had swept through Macedonia and broken through the Vermion mountain pass at Veria. As we neared Tirnavos the shell fire on all sides was completely confusing. We had no idea whether they were our shells or the enemy's. The incessant bombing by the Luftwaffe added to the chaos. Larissa looked as if it had been completely destroyed by bombs and shell fire. (It was not until twenty years later that I learnt it had been destroyed by an earthquake a few days before. Even the gods had joined in.)

On 15 April the airfield at Larissa was put out of commission by a massive air raid, which finally finished the gallant efforts of the Royal Air Force in our defence. They had been outnumbered by twelve to one in any event. Hereafter, the Luftwaffe with its 800 fighters and bombers owned the skies over Greece and could hunt us down in their own time.

We crossed the Pineios river, through the Anzac lines, past their gun sites, where their batteries thundered out an answer to the enemy's fire. Progress on the road was slow, there were constant halts as vehicles broke down or were set on fire by dive bombers. It was difficult to get off the road due to the rocky terrain on either side. However, when we came upon a small plain, I led my troop on to open ground. At that moment a single Stuka pilot, seeing our move and thinking no doubt he would teach us not to stray from the herd, dived upon us. We jinked across the plain and I ducked down inside the turret as the pilot pulled out of his dive over my head. The wretched fellow withheld his bombs. He was coming around for a second run. The bombs missed my tank by a few yards and I could smell the cordite inside the turret. (I discovered later that my bedroll, strapped on the back of the tank, was full of bomb splinters.) These incessant air attacks by the screaming

Stukas were beginning seriously to worry the troops. During a temporary respite whilst we sought cover amongst some olive trees just off the road, my troop corporal came over to me, saying that he did not think he could stand much more of it. I assured him that we were all just as frightened, and that it didn't matter how afraid he was as long as he did his job. Our frustration at having no weapon with which to hit back was demoralizing. The Mark VI Bs should have been fitted with an external machine gun on a swivel mounting on the turret.

We now began to lose our remaining tanks through mechanical failure and our trucks as a result of the incessant bombing by the Luftwaffe. The Colonel issued orders that every man should make his own way to Glyfada if his transport was destroyed or broke down. It was a long way to go and nearly impossible to maintain an effective regimental command in the chaotic conditions on the road. We were mixed up with the 6th Australian Division and the New Zealanders. For some time my troop was tailed by a truckload of Australians. Every time we came under attack from the Stukas, they leapt out, and using my troop tanks as cover, supplemented our Vickers guns with rifle fire.

On 16 April General Wilson finally decided to withdraw to Thermopylae. Up to this time he had evidently not been convinced of the total collapse of the Greek armies on all fronts. In fact, his intelligence of the situation had broken down, due to the disruption of communications and General Papagos' failure to admit his final loss of all control. To those of us who had witnessed the sorry spectacle at the bridge over the Aliakmon there was never any question of effective support from the Greeks from that moment on.

Meanwhile, the Australian 17th Brigade, which fortunately had not arrived in time to reach our main force in Northern Greece, and had therefore not yet been engaged, was now available to cover our withdrawal across the plains of Thessaly by a deployment south of the Metsovon pass, whilst a rearguard of the Anzac Corps was still holding off the enemy's advance guard north of Larissa.

My three little tanks, which had now covered more than 200 miles, mostly over tortuous mountain roads, since 6 April, were showing signs of their ordeal and suffering from the effects of towing the Northumberland Hussars' guns. The steering clutches were giving up and the drivers were finding it increasingly difficult to keep their charges on the road. I doubted if we should reach Thermopylae intact. As we came into the mountains at Domokos the strain increased, and the drivers now struggled to prevent the tanks from plunging down into the ravines. First one and then another finally gave up the ghost. We smashed the radios, took out the breech blocks and dropped a grenade inside the turrets; the crews climbed on to the nearest trucks. Only my own tank was still in running order. We had long ago lost our Light Aid Detachment and, in any event, it was a major operation to fit new clutches even had they been available.

On the night of 17/18 April the Australian 17th Brigade and the rearguard at Larissa withdrew through Domokos, where two battalions and a battery of the Australian Division took over the rearguard action.

On 18 April Alexandros Koryzis, the Greek Prime Minister, following the example of Count Teleki of Hungary, killed himself. I have never understood this tragedy. There was no shame to Greece, which had so valiantly fought off the Italian attack upon her; there was no shame to Koryzis. It was a negative act, and I can only suppose it was prompted by utter despair and a conviction of German invincibility.

My little tank staggered up the mountains on to the very heights of the pass at Thermopylae before deciding it could go no further. My crew put it out of its misery in the same manner as its two companions. It was an ignominious act upon the scene of so famous a battleground.

Behind us was a three-ton truck loaded with tank crews of my regiment, and in the driver's cab sat the two sophisticates of my regiment, Captains John de Moraville and Olaf Wijk, in glum discomfort and depression. I took over from the driver and started out for our regimental rendezvous at Glyfada. There were still a hundred miles of mountain roads to our destination. I took the way to Thebes along the coast between the mainland and Euboea. The deployment of the rearguard at Domokos and now Thermopylae had thinned out the fearful congestion. Moreover, the way south to Athens divided at Lamia, and the bulk of the traffic had taken the shorter route through Brallos. More by luck than judgement, we soon found ourselves almost on our own. It was mid-April and we had left the cold and the snow of northern Greece 200 miles behind us and entered a warmer climate. It was a glorious spring day, the Luftwaffe were concentrating on the main road to Athens, leaving us alone, the three-ton Chevrolet was in excellent order and I began almost to enjoy myself at the wheel as we mounted one crest after another, with now and again a tantalizing view of the deep blue sea of the Talanti Channel. South of Livanatais we descended from the mountains to the shoreline itself. The sea looked so inviting that I pulled up into an olive grove to rest and to allow the troops to get out and stretch their legs. For nearly two weeks we had lived in our tanks, never taking off our clothes, with only a few hours' sleep at a time, eating bully beef and biscuits and the scant rations we had left. Nevertheless, I do not remember being greatly tired. The calm blue sea lapped gently on to the shores of the little cove and the sun shone through the branches of the olive trees.

A little way from us an ambulance pulled off the road for a sad ceremony. The crew got out their spades to dig a grave for a dead soldier. It would be hard to imagine a more beautiful place to lie forever at rest. (I meant one day to go back there, but I never have.)

General Wilson had established his headquarters at Thebes, 50 miles south of Thermopylae, and even now was assuming that the Greek Army in Epirus might still be an effective force; yet although we had now travelled from central Macedonia to Thermopylae we had seen nothing but the pathetic remnants at the river crossing. There were no depots of arms or transport, no base troops, no installations. All the way from the Yugoslav frontier southwards the British Expeditionary Force had been entirely alone. The Greek Army had days ago gone home or taken to the mountains for refuge.

The Germans were incredibly slow to follow up their attack and to complete their conquest of Greece, considering their overwhelming power on the ground and in the air.

I drove the truck towards Athens across the mountains, and as night fell the headlamps lit up the rocks and the deserted sandy road, twisting and turning along the defiles, its ill-defined verges scarcely marking the drop into the dark ravines below. My companions were asleep in the cab and there was no sound from the troops under the canvas canopy behind. The rhythmic note of the engine's exhaust as I constantly changed gear against the gradients and corners, and the pool of light in front of the truck, produced an almost soporific effect upon me after the hectic days gone by.

We reached Athens late into the night. The streets appeared deserted as if there was a curfew, and there were no lights in the houses. There was no sign of war, no troops or transport. It reminded me of London in the early hours of the morning after a late party. No explanation has ever been forthcoming for this extraordinary phenomenon. General Papagos had moved his headquarters out of Athens, already anticipating a capitulation, but the total absence of any British troops puzzled me as I sought my way through the city towards Glyfada.

The author's route
through Greece
April 1941   - - ->- - -

2. The Author's Route through Greece, April 1941

Chapter 6

The Colonel's Runner

I drove straight into the camp we had left in March. The Colonel had already arrived with regimental headquarters, and the greater part of the regiment were sleeping under the trees, exhausted after their ordeal. Rather fortunately, as it so happened, our echelons which had left northern Greece several days before us had arrived almost unscathed, with reserves of rations, arms and ammunition; but we had few tanks left. My cargo tumbled sleepily out of the three-tonner to join the prostrate bodies on the ground.

The morning of 19 April dawned with brilliant sunshine. After washing and shaving and a breakfast of fried tinned bacon, tomatoes and steaming tea, my morale was much restored, and I felt no trace of fatigue.

The Colonel sent for me almost at once, to find the Army Headquarters in Athens and to bring back any information I could get. I took a motorcycle, setting off along the coast road towards the city. In contrast to the utterly deserted appearance of the previous night, the Athenians were going about their business as if there was no war in Greece. The streets were thronged with civilians, and no casual observer would have guessed that the invader was so close. I found Army Headquarters in a modern block of flats behind the King George Hotel, where I had taken the precaution of leaving my expensive Fortnum and Mason cabin trunk more than a month before. The Headquarters occupied two or three flats, which were almost bare of furniture except for steel filing cabinets, hard chairs and trestle tables. There was only a small staff. I announced my mission to a staff colonel, who merely told me to wait. After an hour he returned with a sealed envelope which I was to deliver to my Colonel in person. I sped on my motorcycle back to Glyfada. The Colonel looked grave after he opened this ominous package and sent me back to Athens for any further instructions.

The Greek Army in Epirus had surrendered to the Adolf Hitler division, which had reached Yannena, and other divisions of the German Twelfth Army were now approaching our rearguards only 40 miles to the north.

General Wavell himself had arrived in Greece to evaluate the position of his small battered force, which was now so clearly out on a limb. But Churchill, with his eye for classic drama, was still hoping for an epic stand, 'one more undying feat of arms' at Thermopylae.

The King of Greece was at his palace at Tatoi outside Athens. General Mazarakis, the leader of the Republican party, had been called in to succeed Koryzis and, at a conference with Wavell on 20 April it was agreed that the only possible solution was the total evacuation of the British army in Greece.

Although it was obvious to everyone that we were in a desperate situation, the remarkably effective security arrangements prevented this decision from leaking out. I was not to know of it for several days, although it was undoubtedly contained in the sealed orders I carried by motorcycle to my Colonel.

Remembering the maxim that any fool can be uncomfortable, instead of hanging round Army Headquarters I took a room at the King George Hotel, where the hall porter sent up my trunk from the basement. I had a luxurious bath in my private bathroom and an excellent lunch in the dining room, where the food and service were totally unimpaired by the desperate events of the last two weeks. The hotel faces south across Constitution Square and was but a few hundred yards from the Headquarters building, where I left my telephone and room numbers.

Meanwhile, at Glyfada the squadrons were reorganizing into motorized infantry supported by the few tanks we had left. We were short of automatic weapons such as Bren and Tommy guns, but the Colonel did the best he could under the circumstances to organize an effective force.

On 22 April I carried orders that my regiment were to move to the Peloponnese the following day. The Colonel posted me as his personal contact with Force Headquarters, and I was to remain behind. My batman, Trooper Hyam, joined me in Athens and was quartered by the hotel staff of the King George in fair comfort.

On the afternoon of the 23rd I received an urgent summons and another sealed document for delivery. My regiment had started for Corinth early that morning, and I wondered how far they would have got before I could catch them up. I kicked my motorcycle into life and started off along the road to the Acropolis, past the port of Piraeus and on to the Corniche. It was a beautiful day. To my right the mountains rose above me, and to my left was the glittering blue sea of the Gulf of Aegina far below, beyond vineyards and olive groves. There was no traffic on the road and I opened the twist grip of the throttle to its fullest extent. Within the hour I overtook the Colonel's staff car halfway to Corinth. Little did I guess that the orders I carried were to seal the fate of so many of my friends for the duration of the war.

After the irrevocable decision to evacuate had been taken at the King's palace, General Wilson had now to consider the most practical means to do so. He withdrew the rearguard from Thermopylae after heavy fighting, leaving only two New Zealand brigades to block the roads to Athens at Erithrai and south of Thebes, and ordered my regiment to defend Corinth and Patras in the Peloponnese from a possible attack across the Gulf.

The main places of embarkation were selected beaches on the south-east coast of Attica and others between the Gulf of Aegina and Corinth near Megara, as well as the ports of Nauplion, Monemvasia and Kalamata in the Peloponnese. The Greek government, the Legation Staff and a large number of civilians were the first to get away. Thereafter, the evacuation of troops, particularly from the beaches on the south-eastern shore of Attica, proceeded quickly and smoothly without interference from the Luftwaffe.

It is incredible to reflect that I knew nothing of all this as I returned quite gaily to Athens on my motorcycle. The security arrangements had been wonderfully effective, and I had passed close to Megara on the Gulf of Aegina without suspecting that thousands of troops were lying low in the olive groves to await embarkation under cover of night.

In Athens the pavements were thronged with civilians, and all the shops were open for business as usual. At Force Headquarters I exchanged my motorcycle for a 15cwt truck complete with one of their drivers. My regiment was now 50 miles away from Athens, making the round trip a total of 100 miles. The following morning, I was given another message, this time to deliver to Corinth, and I set off, taking Trooper Hyam with me.

We had hardly left Piraeus when the Luftwaffe turned up in force, bombing and machine-gunning the road. My driver swung his truck into the cover of the trees and we ran down the hillside desperately seeking sanctuary among the rocks. We started off again when the Stukas had gone, Hyam standing in the back watching our rear. The truck had an enclosed cab, and it was difficult to keep a good lookout across the sky. West of Megara we came across a terrible sight. Someone in authority had sent a mule contingent along the Corniche towards the Peloponnese. It had been caught by the dive bombers, and dead mules lay all over the place, while wounded animals were struggling to escape up the mountainside and down the steep slope to the sea. They had been deserted by the muleteers; indeed, except for these poor creatures, the road was strangely empty.

Then a shout from Hyam through the rear window of the cab warned of another attack, and once again we got off the road into the trees. It became clear that the Luftwaffe were hunting down anything that moved, much as a hawk will watch for the movement of a mouse amongst the grass in a field. Apart from our solitary truck, there was no other traffic whatever. I discovered later that all unnecessary movement in daylight had been forbidden by order, not only to prevent casualties, but also to conceal as far as possible the use of the evacuation beaches.

I do not remember how many attacks were made on our truck before we reached the relative safety of Corinth, where I found my regiment busily digging slit trenches, an unfamiliar and undignified occupation for a cavalry regiment. It was a relief to see half a dozen anti-aircraft Bofors guns sited at strategic points manned by troops of the New Zealand Division.

The canal at Corinth is about two miles long, cut deep into the rock of the narrow neck of land which joins the Peloponnese to the mainland of Greece, thus providing a seaway between the Gulf of Aegina and the Gulf of Corinth. Sappers had mined the road and railway bridge across the canal. Provided the bridge was blown, the position, which was bare of cover, was only vulnerable to a seaborne or airborne assault.

The defending force was hardly formidable. A cavalry regiment without its tanks, with which it has trained, is hard to convert at short notice into effective infantry, and we were supported only by a company of the New Zealanders and their Bofors anti-aircraft guns.

The Colonel was worried about a shortage of water and petrol and told me to ask Athens headquarters for the location of the supply dumps which were supposed to be somewhere in the Peloponnese. I dreaded having to run the gauntlet again of that beautiful but terrifying road, now pitted with bomb craters, every mile of which was under observation by those black, faceless aircraft. I dreaded witnessing again the result of the massacre of the mule contingent and I cursed the fool who had so pointlessly sent them along the Corniche, where they had no chance to escape.

To supplement Hyam's watch on the sky, I stood on the footstep of the driver's cab as we crossed the bridge over the canal. Our return journey was no less hair-raising; the Germans were using Messerschmitts as well as Stukas, and they were flying low, suddenly appearing over the mountain ridges without much sound or warning.

It was a glorious evening as we reached the suburbs of Athens. The appearance of the city was almost uncanny in its apparently calm acceptance of the situation. The port of Piraeus had been heavily bombed and put out of action, and shipwrecks fouled the harbour only a few miles from the city centre; yet there was no panic or outward show of apprehension at the terrible fate which had already overtaken the country.

The staff at Army Headquarters had dwindled to a handful. Filing cabinets were open and charred papers cluttered the grates of the fireplaces in the rooms. Cigarette butts and refuse lay on the unswept floors and dirty tin mugs on the window sills and trestle tables, as order and discipline began to give way. I could get no answer to any of my questions and left at nightfall for the King George Hotel and my civilized quarters. The staff began to look at me with curiosity, as I was the only military guest.

It was now clear to me that the end was inevitable. The extraordinary contrast between the unaffected luxury of the high-class hotel, one of the best in Europe, and the fierce conflict now raging just outside the city limits produced a sense of complete unreality.

The following day, before leaving for Corinth, I changed into my service dress which I had ordered at such vast expense from the regimental tailors only seven months previously, and which I had no intention of leaving behind.

The second journey to Corinth was no better than the first. The road was getting marked every few miles with bomb craters, and the dead mules at Megara were becoming grotesque, their bellies distended and their legs sticking straight out with rigor mortis. Hyam and I were constantly on the lookout for aircraft, and our luck held.

I think the Colonel was in two minds whether to send me back again, but he had no radio communication with Athens. Halfway back, we were nearly caught by a sudden attack from low over the mountains. Neither Hyam nor I had seen the danger. The driver swung his truck off the road as the bombs fell, and we were lucky to escape destruction. The dust settled,

and we scrambled out from the crevices of the rocks where we had dived for
shelter. I stood on the road to direct the driver as he backed his vehicle up
the steep slope. But then he swung his tailboard in the direction of Athens,
and slamming the truck into gear, started back towards Corinth, his wheels
spinning in the dirt of the road.

For a second I could not believe what he was doing. Hyam stood with his
mouth open, his rifle held across his chest. I rushed to seize it and kill the
deserter with a shot through the back of the cab, but Hyam held his rifle
close shouting at me, 'No, sir! No, sir!' In a moment our transport had gone.
We were 20 miles from Athens and on our feet.

There was nothing for it but to start walking along the dusty road
towards the city. All our kit had gone. We had nothing now but the
uniforms we stood in, Hyam's Lee Enfield and my Webley pistol. For an
hour or more we trudged along, ducking for cover as aircraft flew overhead
searching for prey. Suddenly behind us an old motorcycle and sidecar
came clattering on to the road from a track leading into the foothills.
The tough-looking Greek rider pulled up as he approached and without a
word indicated the pillion seat and the empty sidecar. We quickly climbed
aboard the ancient vehicle, which jumped forward with a jerk as the
clutch was let in. Within the hour this splendid fellow had delivered us
right outside the imposing porch of the King George. The Luftwaffe had
evidently been ordered to consider Athens an open city, as they kept well
away even from the suburbs.

I walked round to Force Headquarters to find only a warrant officer in
charge busily burning papers. He could tell me nothing and held out no
prospect of providing me with transport. I ran down the concrete steps into
the street; there, across the road, as if by providence, was my salvation in
the form of a Ford 15cwt open truck with no driver's cab. It was of a type
I knew well: tough and fast, powered by exactly the same V8 engine as my
own car now stored in a garage in Leicestershire. I rushed to it. The engine
started with a powerful, healthy note, the twin tanks were full of petrol, and
I drove it triumphantly around the corner to the front of the hotel, shouting
for Hyam to show him my prize.

The hotel staff looked at us in some astonishment; passers-by on the
pavement gaped at Trooper Hyam sitting impassively erect in the driver's
seat of the truck, his rifle pointing skywards, the butt resting on his knee, the

shining regimental badge glittering on his black beret. I went to my room to have a bath, ordered a whisky and soda and went sadly through my beautiful cabin trunk, which I was shortly never to see again.

By morning we had slept, eaten well, bathed and shaved, and our morale was much restored after these simple needs had been fulfilled. The hotel manager approached me in the foyer as I was about to go out into the sunshine of Constitution Square. He asked me if I knew that Greece had formally capitulated to the Wehrmacht on 24 April.

I hurried angrily round to Headquarters. It was totally deserted. No one had sent me word. I was furious, but perhaps I was now paying the penalty for my sybaritic self-indulgence. There is sometimes a price to pay for independence, but I have always hated standing in a queue.

With the collapse of authority in Athens it was now high time for Hyam and I to depart. I had to inform the Colonel of my failure to get any useful information on the supply dumps, and I wondered if he knew of the latest turn of events in the capital.

We had no supplies of food in the truck, and I was short of clean underclothes, so I set off through the crowds to search for provisions. The shops seemed busy and were all open. I was returning with my purchases when I heard the unmistakable sounds of a crowd cheering.

The Royal Horse Artillery came dashing through the square, their beautiful 25-pounder guns trailing behind their armoured portees. They were covered in grime and dust, tin hats on their heads, stubble on their chins, camouflage nets flapping in the wind. The Athenians lined the pavements, people came running, women threw flowers and men stood waving their hats. The people knew of their country's capitulation and realized full well that these British soldiers were the last of the rearguard, yet they were giving them a victor's acclaim. It was a very moving spectacle, and one which I shall never forget.

My solitary duty as the Colonel's runner, and the strict security precautions, had kept me right out of touch with the situation. In fact, the Royal Navy had been evacuating the Expeditionary Force under cover of the darkness of the last few nights, and more than 36,000 men had already been safely embarked from the beaches of Attica and the five points in the Peloponnese; but even now I knew nothing of this. Only at Nauplion had disaster struck. The *Ulster Prince*, coming into the channel, had run aground, giving away our deception to the Luftwaffe. Two destroyers and a merchant ship were sunk the following day with the loss of 700 men on their way to Crete, and another 1,700, including my cousin, Major Dick Austin, were left ashore to hide in the olive groves and scrub with no more than a faint hope of rescue.

Chapter 7

Escape from the Peloponnese

Having stowed our provisions on the truck, we took leave of luxury to set forth once more and run the gauntlet to Corinth. With my own hands on the wheel of the powerful truck, and with no cab to obscure our watch on the sky, I felt more confident. The Luftwaffe did not catch us unawares although we had constantly to dive for cover. I had to grit my teeth to drive through the dreaded spectacle at Megara, where clouds of flies now rose from the stinking carcasses of the mules.

Now, for the first time on my journeyings up and down the 50 miles of this nightmarish road, I saw a British military truck approaching in the direction of Athens. As it got nearer I saw it was a water tanker, just exactly what I wanted. What was it doing going the wrong way? I drove straight at it, forcing the driver to pull up. A Greek officer sat alone at the wheel, but no explanations were possible as I spoke no word of Greek. I indicated to him to turn around and drive in front of me to Corinth which he readily agreed to do.

Peter Dollar greeted me as I drove over the bridge. He had seen the empty truck arrive the previous day with the deserter at the wheel. Presumably noticing our kit in the back, he had questioned the man, whose answers were so dubious that he had put him under arrest. The wretched creature had absconded during the night and, I suppose, unless he died in his bed, he is a free man to this day. If so, he owes his life to Trooper Hyam's scruples.

Meanwhile, the Colonel had been given the location of the elusive supply dumps, which were supposedly near Nauplion, 40 miles to the south.

So far I had been lucky in my almost personal vendetta with the Luftwaffe, but to start in daylight for a search over the deserted roads seemed to me to be giving away odds. Therefore I decided to wait for nightfall before setting out once again. The regiment's position at Corinth had so far been unmolested by the enemy, who had other plans, which they were shortly to put into devastating effect.

I left at dusk southwards. No one had anticipated the extent of the disaster which had now overtaken the campaign, and we had therefore long ago run off our maps. I thought that surely I would see some sign on the roadside indicating a supply dump or the location of other formations from whom I might get the information I sought, but the headlamps lit only the deserted countryside. For most of the night I drove along every byway as far south as Lerna.

Unknown to me, as I passed within a mile or so of the beaches at Nauplion, the 1,700 troops left there after the disaster of the previous night were hiding under what cover they could find, all lights extinguished, in complete silence with only a faint hope of rescue, anticipating at any moment an attack. But it was not until the evening of the following day that my cousin, Major Dick Austin, was to lose his life gallantly but hopelessly defending the beach in the turret of a Daimler scout car.

So far as I could tell, the whole of the Peloponnese was deserted but for my regiment and the handful of New Zealanders at Corinth. I was finding it almost impossible to stay awake, and Hyam was rolling about in the passenger seat beside me, his chin on his chest, so I pulled off the road, we ate some of the food I had bought at the store in Athens and slept for an hour or so by the side of the truck. The drone of aircraft at dawn woke us to the perils of another, but more fateful, day. It was now 26 April.

There was nothing for it but to go back to Corinth to report the total absence of any dumps, at least to the south. Passing near Myloi, I suddenly saw a number of vehicles scarcely hidden in an olive grove and drove through the trees for a closer inspection. A group of staff officers were standing near several armoured command vehicles. I got out of the truck to walk towards them.

General Freyberg was talking to a Greek officer [probably Prince Paul of Greece], who was very smartly dressed in tunic, breeches and shiny black riding boots. I had never met Freyberg and had only seen him once before. I had already lost my awe of senior officers and politicians, but the General was a very special person, a holder of the Victoria Cross, wounded many times in the First World War, a front-line soldier always, as I was to witness when next my regiment came under his command in a great victory.

I went up to him directly and told him of the plight of my regiment, short of water and petrol. He listened to me silently, apparently deep in thought, but at that moment a number of German bombers appeared overhead. The smartly dressed Greek officer took off his gold braided service cap and exchanged it for a British tin hat which he had been holding all the while in his hand. I waited in vain for the General's reply and, not wishing to interrupt his train of thought, turned to walk away, but suddenly he called after me, 'Where are you going?'

I replied that I was going back to Corinth.

'You can't do that', he said, 'Corinth has fallen.'

A senior staff officer beckoned me away to the armoured command vehicle and told me that the Germans had attacked Corinth at dawn with an overwhelming force of parachute troops after heavy bombing, and that the rest of my regiment which might still be at Patras was to withdraw to the beaches immediately. Only Monemvasia and Kalamata were still serviceable, as the channel to the beach at Nauplion was blocked, and it was doubtful if the Navy could venture there yet again.

With the unreasoning overconfidence of youth, I found it impossible to believe that such disaster had overtaken my own regiment. That kind of thing happened to other formations and to other people, but not to me or mine.

With difficulty I persuaded the staff officer to give me one of the scarce maps which I spread out upon the bonnet of the truck. I gasped when I worked out the distance to Patras as more than 100 miles. As Corinth had fallen we had to go by way of Tripoli. My vendetta with the Luftwaffe was about to start again.

The weather was now perfect; it was hot, and the brilliant Mediterranean sun blazed down on the white rocks and dusty green olive trees of the home of the Spartans of ancient times, as Hyam and I took once more to the road.

As we came within 15 miles or so of Tripoli, our way lay dead straight across a plain bare of cover into the foothills of the mountains in the distance. A warning shout from Hyam made me turn my head. The sharp nose of a Messerschmitt was right behind us on our tail coming down in a shallow dive for a kill. The muscles in my back tightened involuntarily, and I could almost feel the bullets smash into my spine as I put my foot hard down on the accelerator. A solitary tree stood not 200yds away, and as we drew level I slammed on the brakes, shouting to Hyam to run for the slim protection of the tree trunk. The pilot swooped low over the truck but my sudden stop had made him overshoot his target. I feared he would turn for another attack, but he made off in search of a richer prize.

I sighed with relief as we got off that plain into the hills, but suddenly a Heinkel bomber skimmed low over the crest to our left. It was so low that it looked huge, and it was flying so slowly that I saw the rear gunner in his transparent tail cupola swivel the twin barrels of his guns to bear before we dived from our seats down the steep hillside into the scrub. In a second there was burst of fire.

We lay under cover for some minutes, bruised by the rocks and shaken by our narrow escape. When the coast was clear, we scrambled up the bank. The body of the truck was riddled with bullets and one of the twin petrol tanks was holed, the precious liquid spilling on to the road, but the engine and controls were apparently undamaged.

We were past the New Zealand machine gun emplacements before we saw them. Tripoli was now garrisoned by a battalion of the New Zealand division, which was manning defences on all the approaches to the town as a protective rearguard to the southern beaches.

The senior British officer in the town was the military attaché from Athens who, I suppose, like the captain on the bridge of a sinking ship, considered it his duty to remain until the end. He told me that if I passed the New Zealanders' barricades and continued on my way to Patras over the sixty miles of mountain roads to the north, then I would surely run into the enemy, and suggested instead the marvellously simple expedient of using the telephone.

Captain Taylor, who was in charge of a party of about six officers and eighty-five men from the regiment and had followed me up from Freyberg's headquarters, now arrived in Tripoli, and the three of us went to the telephone exchange, to find the line to Patras open. To our great relief we learned that all British troops had left for the south that morning and the Germans had not yet entered the port.

A column of my regiment, after losing their way, arrived in Tripoli, but the remains of our two squadrons had gone on to Kalamata. Captain Taylor set off with the column to Monemvasia. The military attaché told me there was an officer of my regiment in the hospital, and I drove there directly to see if he could be moved.

The sun blazed down, I was pouring with sweat and covered in dust; it was in my eyes and nostrils, and I could taste the grit about my mouth. My entrance was an affront to the cool, clinical interior of the little hospital set in a pretty garden on the edge of the town. Lieutenant Henshaw had been terribly burned after his scout car was shot up by aircraft as he was attempting to get away from Corinth. He was lying on an iron bed in a small ward. His face was unmarked, but otherwise he was heavily bandaged. He was quite lucid and cheerful, but when I asked if he could be moved, the nurses shook their heads. I decided to leave him in the sanctuary of the hospital as in any event my own future was uncertain to say the least of it. (It is sad to relate that he was never seen or heard of ever again.)

The New Zealanders were now pulling out of Tripoli, and Hyam and I joined them on the road to Monemvasia, where Freyberg had now established his headquarters. A number of officers and men of my regiment, including my friend John Vaughan, who had been lucky or resourceful enough to escape from Corinth, had joined Captain Taylor and the column from Tripoli. John had defended himself from the mouth of a cave at Corinth with a rifle until his ammunition was exhausted, upon which he had been taken prisoner; but when his captors in turn had come under fire, he had seized the chance to make his escape.

When I went to report our arrival and the squadron's withdrawal from Patras, Freyberg was grave and silent and was writing a message on a signal pad. Turning to the small company about him, with the written message in his hand, he asked, 'Will somebody try to find the naval party? I would go myself but I cannot leave here.'

It was an irresistible appeal.

The General was looking tired, as if overburdened by the heavy responsibility thrust upon him for the last stages of a disaster which was now inevitable. Wilson had handed over his command two days earlier at Myloi.

I took the message from him. It read that unless we were evacuated by the Royal Navy that night then we would be lost, and it called upon God to save us. It was addressed to Admiral Baillie-Grohman, who was supposed to have been landed by a destroyer during the night somewhere on the shoreline north of our position; so far, however, he could not be found, and without him our communication with the ships at sea did not exist and our chance of salvation was gone.

I set off through the olive trees in the direction of the beach and on my way came across a small farm, where in the yard there stood a mule, saddled and bridled, tied to a tree. The farmer was standing in the doorway of his house, and seeing my intention, set me willingly upon his animal, which for all he knew he might never see again. But no sooner had we reached the sandy shore, gently lapped by the deep blue sea, than the Luftwaffe once more appeared overhead.

We were terribly exposed. I kicked the mule in the flanks, but to my horror he resisted all my efforts to get him into a trot, let alone a canter, by bucking like mad. We must have appeared an extraordinary target to the Luftwaffe pilots. Desperately I urged the mule to the cover of the scrub, where I took off the saddle and bridle and turned him loose to find his own way home. I was safer and faster on foot.

With luck and by the grace of God I found the Admiral and his party amongst some boulders beneath a cliff face and delivered my dramatic message. An able seaman was cooking a meal over a primus stove, and I gratefully accepted a share before I set off on the return journey with Baille-Grohman's reply in my pocket.

On my way, there in a secluded cove lay a large broad-beamed Greek caique, her heavy brown sails furled on her massive boom. I had taught myself to sail on the Norfolk Broads as a boy and had graduated to the Solent, where I had crewed on a Solent Sunbeam and a Dutch barge belonging to a friend of my uncle. I had read every book on sailing I could get and in a burst of enthusiasm had nearly become the possessor of a Dragon lying in the Hamble river which had been for sale at £170! I thereupon determined that, if the worst should happen, I would set sail in that caique for Crete. There was no wind, but I was sure she would have an auxiliary to get us out to sea. (This was not as improbable an idea as it might seem, since my friend Roy Farran of the 3rd Hussars, who only a few days later was to be wounded and captured in the defence of Crete, was to escape from Piraeus with the aid of the Greeks in an open boat of half the size; although nearly dying of thirst, he was picked up by a destroyer off the African coast to fight again with extraordinary distinction.)

Approaching the headquarters, I came upon a brigadier of Freyberg's staff. It is strange how the mind works on occasions, but I was greatly concerned to reward the farmer for the loan of his wretched mule and for the abandoned saddle and bridle, and so asked the brigadier if he had any money for the purpose. Although I received an irritable answer, to his credit he produced from his battledress pocket thousands of drachmas, which I exchanged for the Royal Navy's optimistic reply and trudged back to the farmhouse to discharge my debt.

All that night and the next day, the 4,000 troops at Monemvasia lay hidden in the olive groves, the scrub and the rocks, their motor transport camouflaged with elaborate care with branches torn from the trees, grass and herbage heaped upon the engine covers and on the nets. Movement was forbidden, and the men were silent. The Luftwaffe constantly prowled overhead looking for a worthwhile target, and the Twelfth Army's vanguard approached ever nearer.

But the Royal Navy came to the rescue. During the night their ships' boats put into the shore by a wooden jetty running out into the sea. The embarkation was carried out as efficiently as if it had been rehearsed over and over again.

We climbed the scrambling nets on to the deck of the cruiser *Ajax*, who was to distinguish herself yet again in the Battle of the River Plate. A midshipman approached me as I stepped over the gunwale with the most wonderfully cool invitation I have ever received – 'Would you care for a whisky and soda?'

Alas, there was a different story to tell at Kalamata, where 8,000 British troops and 1,400 Yugoslav refugees awaited rescue. Ironically, this was considered the safest beach, where evacuation had proceeded smoothly on successive nights. Sadly, the senior officer had failed to organize any proper defence. When the Navy came in that night they found a small force of Germans in command of the beach. Many of my friends were taken prisoner, condemned to spend the next four years in camps in Germany. My great friend Francis Romney took to the hills with some of his squadron, but resistance for long was hopeless against such odds. I am glad to say that all of them were to survive the war, with the exception of one gallant officer [Lieutenant J. Hornby] who was shot dead while attempting an escape in broad daylight.

The decision to go to the aid of Greece will remain a matter of controversy. If we had not done so we should have been accused of forsaking her in her hour of need. Turkey might have questioned our willingness to aid our allies. All over the world, those many nations not engaged in the conflict were watching and weighing in the balance our motives and our military capability against the might of Germany. Our motives were now seen to be indisputable, but our power to be lacking.

General Wavell's acquiescence in the use of his only strategic reserve in this disaster is strange since, if his two high-class mobile colonial divisions had been available to back up and consolidate his remarkable victory over the Italian Army in the Western Desert, it might well have been impossible for the Germans to have built up a force in Africa. Rommel had landed only one division at this time, the forerunner to the Afrika Korps which was so nearly to conquer Egypt.

The political decision having been taken, we failed to make the best use of the Expeditionary Force. All the principles of war were broken. As I have described in my narrative, there was virtually no reconnaissance, therefore our information was faulty, our intention ill-defined and our method hopeless.

Our military intelligence must have been non-existent, or too overawed by the Imperial General Staff to state that the Greek Army was nearly fought out even before our venture.

The topography of Greece is favourable to a defence in many places by a small determined force against odds in carefully chosen positions, but the assumption that the Greeks were still effective led Wilson and his staff to deploy his two divisions over far too wide an area. The lines of communications were tortuous, of nearly 200 miles and impossible to secure from attack by the Luftwaffe.

It is interesting to conjecture where we might have made one last epic stand, which would have so delighted the dramatic imagination of Winston Churchill and perhaps have provided a rallying point for the Greek people. There were several possibilities, but alas the opportunity had gone, and it can only be of academic interest to students at the Staff College to work out where they would have deployed two high-class infantry divisions and one ill-equipped armoured brigade for such a purpose.

It is easy to be wise after the event, but you cannot ignore the age-old principles of warfare without paying the penalty.

The German Army had conquered Greece and were to remain in occupation for nearly three years. In the end, it did them no good at all, and I was myself to take part in harassing their line of retreat.

Part II

Chapter 8

The Return to Egypt

The *Ajax* landed us at Heraklion on Crete. We were standing on the quayside in some sort of regimental order when a harassed looking staff officer arrived. Without examining our badges he asked who we were, and when he discovered we were armed as tank crews with pistols and a few rifles he told us to get back on board the cruiser, which we were delighted to do. Twenty days later, Crete was invaded and lost to the enemy. We reached Alexandria on 1 May, and I took a luxurious room at the Cecil Hotel overlooking the sea. That night, there was an air raid alarm, and I resisted a strong inclination to crawl under the bed. In the midst of war on all sides Egypt remained unscathed. I had returned from Macedonia, the birthplace of Alexander the Great and Ptolemy I, to the scene of their conquests in the valley of the Nile, where the temples and pyramids still held some of the secrets of one of the most ancient cultures in the world, and where the glorious head of Nefertiti had been unearthed for all to marvel at.

Now, after so many centuries of subjugation to foreign invaders, the 20 million inhabitants of the fertile Delta had become polyglot. King Farouk, the descendant of an Albanian mercenary, whose father was a tobacco merchant of Kavala [in Macedonia], owed his throne to British patronage but was surrounded by Italian sycophants, spies and lackeys. Diplomatic intrigue in the embassies and consulates of many nations was in full swing. A German agent with a radio set lived for months inside the wooden mock-up of a Perrier bottle which served as an advertisement on the road to Mena. A silky-skinned Egyptian dancer took her admirers to a luxurious villa on the banks of the river at the direction of German intelligence.

The splendid hotels of Cairo and Alexandria did a roaring trade. Countless restaurants, cafés and nightclubs were thronged with British troops. The old red-lamp districts of the cities saw again the scenes of the First World War, and the Military Police were kept at full stretch. At the Gezira sporting club, on a green island in the middle of the Nile, officers played polo with the pashas and the diplomats, swam in the pool, sunbathed and drank on the terraces, played tennis and golf; at Heliopolis they went to the races under a temperate, almost perpetual sun. Romance flourished. The beautiful daughters of rich Egyptians, Copts, Greeks, Jews and Armenians chose their escorts from any regiment in the Eighth Army. Even the English Cathedral was full on Sundays. And yet, not far away in the Western Desert, two armies faced each other in a conflict which was to prefigure the final defeat of Germany in the Second World War.

The remnants of the regiment reassembled at the camp at Tel-el-Kebir, whence we had started out to the disastrous Greek campaign. Lieutenant Colonel Dick Sheppard took over command. He was a distinguished and experienced officer of the 7th Hussars, who had just made a name for himself and his regiment in the victory over the Italian Army by leading raiding columns, probing fast, far and deep into the very heart of enemy-held territory.

I went on leave to Cairo, staying at the famous Shepheard's Hotel in the centre of the city, formerly the palace of Elfi Bey. Its Moorish domed interior had tremendous atmosphere. It had scarcely changed since the days of Kitchener, Cromer, Samuel Baker, Stanley, Burton and Speke and Rudolf Slatin – all of whom long ago had surely taken their drinks on the wide verandah looking down upon the street thronged with the populace.

The *fellaheen* of the Delta still passed by in their *gallabias*, fezzes or turbans on their heads, leading camels and donkeys into the market laden with produce from the farms and contrasting so strangely with the shiny Cadillacs and Packards of the Pashas and the Beys, the stream of cars and taxis and the city suits of the more prosperous urban population.

Meanwhile, almost at the same time as the Adolf Hitler division had appeared through the gap in the hills at Ptolemais in Greece, a German army had arrived in North Africa to come to the rescue of the remnants of the Italians, to threaten the Egyptian frontier and the Nile Delta itself.

It is strange to reflect that the decision to send an expeditionary force to Greece had been taken in the knowledge that the Afrika Korps had been landed at Tripoli, and that the German warrior, Erwin Rommel, had arrived with his staff as early as 12 February.

The British Eighth Army was tired and worn after its victory. The 7th Armoured Division, which had led the attack, had been withdrawn to the

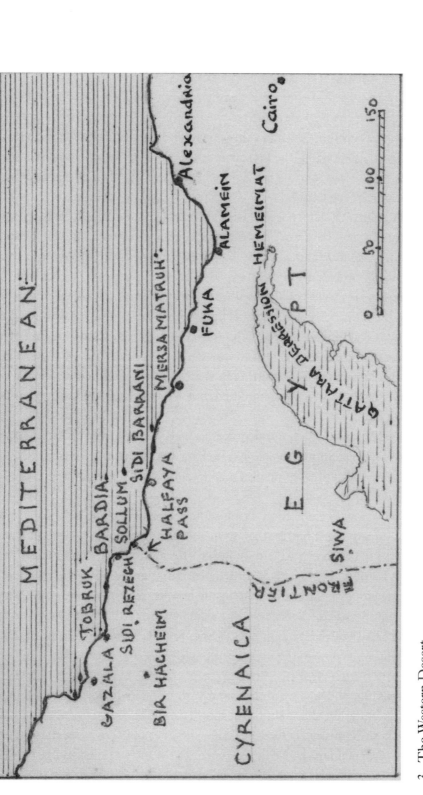

3. The Western Desert

Delta to rest and re-fit and was short of tank replacements. Wavell was now faced with a fresh, formidable enemy, without the resources for a counter-attack, having lost his strategic reserve in Greece. Moreover, simultaneously there was a revolt in Iraq and a threatened German infiltration into Syria. As if his cup was not full, the Germans attacked Crete with powerful airborne forces on 20 May and in ten days of hard and bloody fighting had taken possession of the island.

On 2 July 1941 General Wavell gave up his command of this complex theatre of war. There was a mystique about him which had filtered through the ranks; soldier and poet, he had won victories with inadequate arms, continually pressed by political expedients and ill-informed directives.

He was succeeded by General Auchinleck. For months there was to be a lull in the fighting, whilst Rommel built up his power over hazardous supply lines and Auchinleck waited. The immediate threats from Iraq and Syria were resolved, but at the cost of our strength in the Western Desert. The Italian colonial armies in North-east Africa had surrendered by 5 April, and at least the issue was now simplified, but we were short of tanks, guns and trained men.

On 22 June Hitler invaded Russia and we were no longer fighting alone. This incomprehensible blunder by the German nation, in defiance of history and all the principles of war, convinced many of us that the last victory would be ours.

There now began a most extraordinary and almost entirely satisfactory period of my life. I had lost all my personal possessions in Greece, having arrived in Alexandria with nothing but my best service dress uniform in which I stood. The National Provincial Bank, going about its business as usual at Holborn Circus in spite of the bombs, sent me money with which to re-equip myself. I also bought an ancient American Reo two-seater car, which I had noticed parked outside Shepheard's Hotel. In a little while the regiment moved from the desert camp to the Gezira racecourse.

Reinforcements of officers and men arrived, but slowly. I shared the stewards' room below the grandstand with Captain Taylor. We dined in the open air under the starry sky on the mown turf of the members' enclosure. We swam in the club pool before breakfast, and I began to enjoy, for the first time in my life, an almost sybaritic existence. The stables of the Cavalry barracks at Abassir were well stocked with the polo ponies of those regiments which had served in Egypt immediately before the outbreak of war. Government-owned horses, also stabled there, were on hire to any officer who cared to pay a nominal charge of 14 shillings a month (known as the 'fourteen bobbers'). They were looked after by Sudanese *syces*, who were traditionally first-class grooms. A few of us quickly took advantage of the situation to ride at exercise round the splendid racecourse in the cool of the early mornings.

The flame trees were in full bloom along the avenues, and in the evenings the air was full of the smell of jasmine. Kites wheeled above us in the clear sky with their mewing cries, white ibises strutted in front of our horses' hooves on the green turf, and the muezzin called out the hour of prayer from the minarets of the mosques.

The polo grounds of the Gezira club were most probably amongst the finest in the world. In the almost total absence of rainfall, they were irrigated by a system of shallow flooding. Whilst one pitch was in play, the other was under water, and years of good management had produced an incomparable turf, never too hard for the ponies' legs, or so soft that it was cut up or the game became slow.

There were quite a number of very high class players of international standard who turned up regularly, including several Turks and Egyptians. I had never played before, but the temptation was too much for me. I took over two of the 7th Hussars' regimental match ponies and one government horse, giving me a string of three. It was a simple matter to kit oneself up with gear from the local shops.

Our Brigade Major, Gerald Grosvenor, who was himself an experienced player, kindly took me in hand, shouting directions during play and teaching me the fundamentals of the game. Eventually, we shared six ponies between us. It was the most exciting game in the world. Although I never became what is called a good striker, I was a lightweight in spite of my above average height and I had one of the best and fastest ponies in Egypt which belonged to Captain Pip Watson of the 7th Hussars. It was a great thrill, whilst playing back, to stop an international player as he was on the point of scoring a goal. Few of my fellow officers joined in this wonderful game, but in the end we managed to get up a regimental team.

I cannot say at this time that I had much thought for world events or apprehension about the future of my country or myself; I lived only for the moment, like many of my contemporaries.

This happy situation was to continue for many months whilst the strength of the regiment was brought up to its full complement. Extra-regimentally employed regular officers returned to the regiment, and fresh troops arrived from the Royal Armoured Corps depots in England by the long sea route round the Cape. We were soon supplied with new American light tanks, popularly known as 'Honeys', armed with a 37mm gun, a coaxial machine gun and, much to my delight, a reliable Browning anti-aircraft gun mounted on a swivel on top of the turret. They were relatively fast, capable of speeds of up to 40mph. We moved out to a desert camp at Mena, within a few miles from the great Cheops Pyramids and the Sphinx, where training started in earnest.

On 18 November 1941 the Eighth Army struck back at Rommel to relieve Tobruk and drive the Axis forces out of Cyrenaica. The first objective was achieved, but now the German Afrika Korps, with their far superior tanks and anti-tank guns and the brilliant generalship of their commander, made it all too plain that they had not lost the initiative. After a withdrawal to the west of Tobruk, Rommel carried out a fast, daring raid across the Egyptian frontier, outflanking our positions, to attack the rear formations of our army, before breaking off the action to retire to Agheila, where he was to stand until once again he was ready for the offensive.

All this time, the Royal Navy and the RAF from Malta had been harassing the Afrika Korps' supply line across the Mediterranean to Tripoli, seriously affecting its offensive ability. The Luftwaffe had been drawn away to support the invasion of Russia, and already Rommel was fuming at the evidence of Hitler's incredible folly.

Auchinleck's counter-offensive, Operation Crusader, had caused the Afrika Korps very heavy losses and further demoralized the Italians. Many thousands of German prisoners of war were now behind barbed wire in the Egyptian desert.

The German general staff was now fully occupied with the Russian front, failing to appreciate that what they had intended merely as a gesture of support to their Axis partner in North Africa had suddenly developed a staggering strategic potential due to the brilliance of their commander. Rommel now realized that, with only a little more power and a supported line of communication, he could break through the thin defence in front of Egypt to open up millions of square miles of territory to German conquest, even to the Black Sea and the Indian frontier. It must have been a tantalizing prospect.

But on 7 December the Japanese attacked Pearl Harbor, the Americans came into the war with their vast military potential and the ultimate fate of Germany was sealed. Within five months we had gained two mighty allies at the cost of one efficient and dedicated enemy, and the balance of power was once more in our favour, although we had to take the immediate consequences in the Far East.

I was far too busy playing polo and enjoying the delights of Cairo to concern myself greatly with the strategy and consequences of the greatest conflict the world had ever seen. I had left nothing behind in England to which I particularly wished to return.

It is astonishing to reflect upon the geographic spread of our military effort. Historically, it was not a new phenomenon. In the last century our island nation had conquered and administered a quarter of the world's surface and had fought and defeated great empires with massive resources and populations so far exceeding our own that a comparison would be absurd. But since that time Bismarck had created the German nation and Garibaldi had welded together the Italian principalities which Mussolini had turned into a Fascist state. Our victory in the First World War had only served to strengthen our enemies. Japan had profited by its industrial revolution to become the greatest military power in Asia, bursting at the seams, pressing hard for living space. But still vast areas of the world's surface were coloured red on the map, and among them were Malaya and Singapore, now threatened.

The regiment came under command of the 1st Armoured Brigade, and Gerald Grosvenor asked me if I would join the brigade headquarters as Intelligence Officer. Although I was reluctant to leave my regiment, it meant promotion to Captain. Colonel Sheppard was not much pleased at this proposal but reluctantly gave his consent. It was a very happy staff. Gerald was one of the most charming men I had ever met, universally popular with the regiments under command. Captain Bill Van Namen and Captain Lord Haig (the son of the famous Field Marshal of the First World War) were staff captains, and Captain Max Wise of the Middlesex Yeomanry was signals officer. There was only one fly in the ointment; a big one: I did not get on with the Brigadier. Nevertheless, we had great fun in otherwise delightful and amusing company.

One day, as I was driving my old Reo back to Mena from Cairo, a car passed me in which were several officers and a young woman with striking golden hair and a very fair skin. I envied her lucky companions, but I was to get to know her very well indeed.

My first duty as intelligence officer was to serve for the first time as an advocate at a court martial. A trooper of my regiment had been charged with deserting his post whilst on sentry duty, having been found by the guard commander during the night in his tent. The charge appeared indefensible, and I told the man that my chances of pleading successfully were almost non-existent and that if he wanted another officer to defend him, who might take a more optimistic view of his chances, he had better tell me at once. However, he was resigned to his fate.

I searched frantically for hours through the Manual of Military Law for any possible loophole. The troops always considered that this famous book, which had stood the test of time, laid down principles which were much fairer than those of civilian law. As I turned the pages relating to sentry duty, four words stood out: 'Definition of a post'. Sending at once for the guard orders, I discovered with a thrill that there was no proper definition of the man's post.

Nevertheless, waiting outside the tent to be called in to the court martial was nerve-wracking.

The prosecuting officer was first to examine the witnesses and the accused, proving conclusively that my client was found in his tent, where he said he had gone to look at his watch. But I sprang to my feet to protest at the leading question, 'You do smoke don't you?' My objection was upheld, and fortunately the prosecuting officer failed to rephrase the question, so he got no answer.

When it came to the turn of the defence, I produced the guard orders, reading them out very deliberately in detail, questioning the guard commander. There was no clear definition of the post. The man was not a sentry at all, he was a 'flying picket'. The prosecution had been unable to prove that he was not properly dressed and armed. He was entitled to go to his tent to look at his watch; the area of his picket duty included the whole of regimental lines, as no clearer definition had been produced.

Outside the court martial I waited in great suspense. When the verdict of 'not guilty' was brought out, my satisfaction was out of all proportion to the achievement.

I told Dawyck Haig of the exciting apparition I had seen on the road to Mena. The scarcely perceptible smile with which he listened to my tale made me suspect that he knew who she was. There was surely only one woman in Egypt with such glorious golden hair. A few days later, Dawyck gave a large party at Shepheard's Hotel and, to my great excitement, I found myself sitting at dinner next to the object of my admiration. Brita was the daughter of Ivan Danielsson, the Swedish Minister to Egypt. Thereafter, I was a constant guest at the Swedish Legation on the banks of the Nile. We dined and danced together in Cairo and Alexandria and had a wonderful time. We were to be married in London after the war, but much was to happen before then.

The whole world now came to the boil, from the River Plate to Shanghai. The Japanese struck in all directions: across the Pacific Ocean; southwards through Malaya to threaten Australia, where cattlemen in the Northern Territory drove their herds thousands of miles south for safety; to the west against China and Burma, even to the Indian frontier. From Europe the German armies spread east towards Leningrad and Moscow, and in the Atlantic their submarines hunted the shores of the American continent from Newfoundland to Cape Horn. Finland, which had been savaged by Russia, had understandably thrown in her lot with Germany against her old enemy. Sweden alone in Scandinavia stood neutral, held tight in her predicament. Spain, after bitter years of civil war, balanced on the brink.

If I had grasped the magnitude of these staggering events I might not have been so easy in my mind as I drove my old Reo along the banks of the Nile to the Swedish Legation or to the polo grounds at Gezira.

It seemed a very long time before the Brigade was ready and equipped for war. There was ample justification for Churchill's angry criticism of the enormous ration state of the army in Egypt, but it was misdirected. What we wanted were high class weapons, not a surfeit of men. Few commanding generals or senior officers had much concern for ballistics; a tank was tank, whether it had a 37mm or an 80mm gun, and whatever the velocity. The German armaments industry was far in advance of anyone else in this field. Their Mark IV tank and 88mm gun were the best military weapons in the world in 1942.

Someone had accurately stated that a hundred American Sherman tanks could have finished the war in North Africa in April 1941, but even these were only armed with a 75mm gun of relatively low velocity. As it was, all the armour which the Eighth Army possessed were the little Mark VI Bs, the fast but unreliable Cruiser tanks armed with a two-pounder and the ponderous I tanks with their thick skins and maximum speed of 5mph. It was very demoralizing for our tank crews to know they were constantly outgunned.

On 19 January, after only a brief respite at Agheila, Rommel struck again at Cyrenaica. The German high command, belatedly realizing the danger to his supply routes, brought back sufficient of their air force from the Russian front to ensure the safety of his reinforcements. With only a light force, he drove the Eighth Army back to a line from Gazala to Bir Hakeim, where this thrust to the east was successfully resisted and where the two armies were to face each other in this sea of sand for nearly two months, with only minor skirmishes disturbing the uneasy status quo.

A good friend of mine, Tony Philpotts, had become PA to Auchinleck and was now a brigadier. When I heard that he was ill I went to see him. An enormously tall, cynical and academic member of a famous literary West Country family, he had been general manager of the *Evening Standard* for some years before the war. He was in bed with a fever in the Commander-in-Chief's fine villa just by the Gezira club. His huge feet stuck out from under the sheets, and his naturally humorous cynicism was entirely unaffected by his high temperature. Although he could never be serious, he gave me a review of the military situation as he saw it.

General Auchinleck was reluctant to commit his reserves to the Western Desert, and even now was not convinced of the direction of the strategy of the Axis powers. He foresaw a possible enemy advance from the Balkans. The revolt in Iraq, the militancy of the Vichy French in Syria and the uncertain neutrality of Turkey made him hesitate, but in a very short while he was to be left in no doubt whatever where the threat lay. Moreover, the outbreak of war in the Far East had resulted in the recall of two Australian divisions for the protection of their homeland, thus seriously weakening his reserves. He now had no intention of taking the offensive again before the Eighth Army had time to build up its strength, although he was being pressed hard by Churchill to do so, in order to relieve Malta, which was now under heavy attack and facing famine.

About this time, two troops of my regiment were detailed in the utmost secrecy for an extraordinary duty. Sir Miles Lampson, the British

Ambassador who had impounded our shotguns for poaching on his preserves before we had left for Greece, had formed the opinion that King Farouk of Egypt was playing politics to our disadvantage by favouring pro-Italian politicians. He had decided to present Farouk with an ultimatum: that either he accept Nahhas Pasha of the Wafdist Party as premier, or he must abdicate. The ultimatum was delivered at the Abdeen Palace and backed up by force of arms. Our tanks were at the gates, truckloads of infantry surrounded the grounds and a destroyer waited at Alexandria to carry away a royal passenger. Not a shot was fired, the king signed the document and Nahhas was installed; but the insult to the Egyptian people has never been forgotten and this drastic expedient was never justified.

The consequences of war were brought home to me with sudden and sickening reality when I lost one of my best friends, Kenneth Caldwell. He had been posted to the Western Desert simply to gain a little experience, but within a few days of his arrival at the battle front he had been killed instantly whilst commanding a tank in a skirmish with the Afrika Korps. We had been constant companions since sailing from England in 1940.

Rommel's extraordinary success in Africa had now created a sudden enthusiasm in Germany and Italy, and his imaginative and forceful representations to the German high command had begun to strike home, and even to fire the Italian dictator with ambitious dreams of riding into Cairo on a white charger. At the end of April the General decided it was time to destroy the Eighth Army and to conquer Egypt. He had now assembled the complete complement of his famous Afrika Korps, the main elements of which were the 15th and 21st Panzer Divisions and the 90th Light Infantry Division. He had put new heart into the Italians, whose armoured division, the Ariete, and the Trento Motorized Division, were also under his command.

He attacked our positions on the Gazala/Bir Hakeim line by moonlight on the night of 27/28 May, and my holiday was suddenly brought to an abrupt end.

Chapter 9

War in the Desert

I packed up my belongings not required for the battle into my Reo and hurriedly drove it into the garage at the Swedish Legation for safe keeping to await my return. The Brigade had been ordered up to the Western Desert without warning, and without predetermined intention, as the furious onslaught of the enemy and their initial success had forced Auchinleck to use his reserves, which he had been so cautiously holding in the Nile Delta.

My transport as Brigade Intelligence Officer was an armoured car of South African manufacture, crudely made of welded armour plate, spacious inside but as an effective fighting vehicle of less value than my light tank which I had destroyed at Thermopylae. We left the Sphinx and the Pyramids behind us as we took the desert road to Alexandria which runs for 100 miles across the melting tarmac strip west of the Delta to Damanhur. It was now the Egyptian summer; the sun blazed down upon the sand and we said goodbye to the palm trees and waters of the great Nile valley for a harsher landscape of almost unending sameness, of dust, heat and flies.

The Brigadier called a halt for the night at Damanhur, by the salt pans at the junction of the coastal road to the west which was to take us to the front. A railway, painstakingly extended by the Royal Engineers, ran parallel to the coast almost to the 200ft escarpment at Sollum on the Egyptian frontier with Cyrenaica, 300 miles away. Before us lay the chosen battleground upon the great deserts of North Africa.

As we made our way along the coastal strip to Mersa Matruh, the debris of an army littered the sand on either side of the track and the wheelmarks of thousands of vehicles led in all directions to nowhere. We traversed the escarpment by the notorious Halfaya Pass, known to the British Army as 'Hell Fire Pass' after the fierce battles with the besieged German garrison in January. The Brigade halted across the Egyptian frontier on the sands of Cyrenaica after a 370-mile journey from our camp at Mena.

We were immediately attacked by the Luftwaffe, and I heard once more the now familiar scream of the dive bombers, but our anti-aircraft guns were rapidly in action in our defence.

At dusk, when the grinding noise of four-wheel-drive trucks and the metallic clank of tank tracks had ceased, a silence settled over the place. There was a curious sweet smell as of almonds in the air which puzzled me and my companions. It was the smell of the dead of Halfaya, hastily buried in hundreds in shallow unmarked graves in the sand.

The following day, I drove to General Ritchie's headquarters 20 miles east of Tobruk in my armoured car to find out the situation. There was undoubtedly an air of confusion and uncertainty, and I could feel instinctively, as I vainly sought some coherent information, that already disaster was imminent.

Still the Brigade was not engaged, and we listened to the sounds of battle and saw the great dust clouds rising in the air to the west. The Desert Air Force was constantly overhead, heavily engaged in its own combat with the Luftwaffe, and occasionally we saw the fearful result of these aerial duels as a trail of black smoke plummeted to the ground, ending in an orange flash as the aircraft exploded on contact.

The front, defended by extensive minefields, stretched for 40 miles due south from Gazala, the Free French holding the extreme left flank, the South Africans the right on the coast, and our two armoured divisions the centre, with three Indian brigades in support.

Rommel had attempted to turn our flank at Bir Hakeim but had been initially repulsed in a gallant action by the Free French which has gone down in history. However, his two powerful panzer divisions were destroying our armour in the centre in fierce battles.

Whilst all this was going on, an incident occurred which has scarcely left its mark on world events. The Brigadier had sent me again to Army Headquarters for a situation report, but also to fetch his gold pencil which he had left in the operations tent. I was so excited by the news I received there that I quite forgot to carry out the last part of the order, and I am ashamed to relate that I excused myself by declaring that I had had more important things to consider. That did it. Nature has endowed me with above average height and a rather long nose, and my friends have always told me that I am quite unable to conceal my feelings, a characteristic which had also bedevilled my father. Evidently, I was not cut out to be a staff officer. I walked home to my regiment across a few hundred yards of sand. The Colonel was highly amused at my abject appearance at regimental headquarters and posted me immediately to relieve Captain Tony Johnson as second-in-command to 'A' Squadron.

But at once, before I had a chance to take over my duty, the squadron was ordered into battle to reinforce the 2nd Armoured Brigade, now heavily engaged. Within twelve hours the squadron had ceased to exist, shot to pieces by the German armour, and Major Knight and Captain Johnson were taken prisoner with two thirds of their men. So the die is cast.

With my posting to Headquarter Squadron, there now began a strange partnership which was to last for many months, until long after the Battle of Alamein. The squadron was commanded by Major Archer, one of those extra-regimentally employed officers who had rejoined after the Greek campaign. We had absolutely nothing whatever in common and were opposites in almost everything, but in many ways I believe we were to prove complementary to one another in the business of warfare. His unglamorous nickname was 'Porgy', indicating his bulk.

I took a convoy of trucks into Tobruk to load with supplies. Invested by the Afrika Korps seven months before, the aftermath of the struggle for possession of this strategic port was everywhere in evidence. Forlorn graves of soldiers, crudely marked by a helmet or a tin hat and defiled by barbed wire and empty tins, were unevenly scattered over the sand where the fighting had been fiercest. The black skeletons of burnt-out tanks and trucks scarred the desolate landscape, and the beastly flies were everywhere.

The following day, General Klopper commanding the South African garrison was to surrender to the Afrika Korps with over 30,000 men, leaving intact hoards of badly needed supplies to sustain Rommel's pursuit of the retreating Eighth Army for 300 miles to Alamein.

Poor General Ritchie, faced by the efficient, compact professional German Army and finding himself outgunned by the high-velocity weapons of Rommel's two Panzer divisions, had no alternative but to withdraw.

During these last days the confusion of the battle was increased by severe sandstorms, which restricted visibility to a few hundred yards on occasion and prevented the employment of our two remaining squadrons, which therefore escaped almost inevitable destruction by the German armour, to fight another day.

This war of movement upon a sea of sand depended upon quality of armament to a greater degree than a naval battle. It was impossible to disable a Mark IV tank with a 37mm or two-pounder gun in the same manner that a daring destroyer might cripple a battleship with a lucky shot below the water line. However much you closed the range, no penetration was possible, and a Mark IV even with its tracks shot off would not sink.

Churchill, in his *History of the Second World War*, wrote that this excuse freely put forward after the event needed closer examination. It certainly did, but not with the inference that lay behind his comment. Even the Italian tanks of the Ariete Division had a 47mm gun.

The retreat of the Eighth Army now began, and tens of thousands of weary men made their way towards Sollum in what remained of their tanks and transport along the desert tracks to Egypt. The columns were four abreast at times, but the Desert Air Force flew protectively overhead keeping away the bombs of the Luftwaffe. There was great confusion but no panic as units lost their cohesion, extricated themselves from the hazards of our own minefields in the rear and streamed themselves towards the east in great clouds of dust.

Auchinleck's caution had made him prepare a defensive line only 70 miles from Alexandria at Alamein, where the topography favoured a defence. Here his left flank was protected by the Qattara Depression, 35 miles to the south, a vast area of supposedly impassable soft sand below sea level.

The staff in Cairo were even preparing a plan to defend the Delta itself with base troops as a last contingency, the consequences of which could not have been thought out to a conclusion. We had over 200,000 supporting personnel in the Nile Valley. Where were they to go in the event that Cairo fell? Was there to be another expedition to the source of the White Nile in the heart of Africa, or were they to retreat into the parched deserts of Sinai? The questions provide an interesting hypothetical exercise for the military mind. General Wilson was to command this last ditch stand, but very shortly two officers with more aggressive instincts were to take over the conduct of affairs.

Modern warfare in the densely populated area of the Nile Delta would have produced scenes of indescribable horror and chaos.

Nevertheless, the British Fleet left Alexandria, areas of the desert were flooded with the Nile waters and static defences were erected on the approaches to the capital city of Egypt. The 51st Highland Division recently arrived from England, instead of engaging in the defence at Alamein, was spread out west of the Delta. Personally, I saw no sign of these somewhat desperate precautions and I would have been astonished had I done so.

I had been brought up in the waning shadow of the Victorian era, in which Great Britain had attained such power in the world that a belief in ultimate defeat was unthinkable. We were surely bound to triumph in the end. And so we did.

Therefore, on the long retreat from Tobruk I had no depressing thoughts, only hope that with any luck I might shortly find myself once more in the company of an attractive young woman at the Swedish Legation. At any rate we were going in her direction, and the pestilential flies, clustering about the moisture in the corners of my eyes and on my lips, were only a minor irritation. General Freyberg came to the rescue with the New Zealand Division. Although Churchill had asked Auchinleck to commit them earlier, fortunately they had only just arrived fresh from Syria and had dashed across the desert to confront the vanguard of the German Army now pressing hard upon our heels. The leading units of the 15th and 21st Panzer Divisions were brought up with a jolt south of Mersa Matruh by the New Zealanders' anti-tank guns and infantry. Two warriors of the First World War, who were personally known to each other, were almost face to face: the Victoria Cross of England against the Iron Cross of Germany.

A fierce battle took place in which Freyberg was wounded yet again and Rommel nearly captured. This check to the Afrika Korps gave Auchinleck time to deploy what forces he could muster on the Alamein line. He had taken over command personally. Our own 'B' Squadron was detached at Alamein and sent 20 miles south to join in the defence. Major Taylor, who had escaped with me from Greece and had been promoted to command the squadron, and Captain Eric Jones, his second-in-command, were both killed in action within a few days. Together with the loss of 'A' Squadron, the Regiment was again reduced to a skeleton of its full strength within seventeen months of sailing from Merseyside.

We halted in the open desert five miles from Mena and fifteen miles from the Swedish Legation. Whether by generous design or not, I do not know, but I was selected to collect the regimental pay from Cairo. It has struck me as remarkable that the organization of an army at war, hard-pressed and even facing disaster, can still function efficiently in such mundane matters as regular financial reward. Each man received a few foreign notes of doubtful value which he could not spend unless on leave or at the NAAFI, but pay day was still all-important.

The Legation was deliciously cool and civilized after the fierce heat and harsh realities of the desert war. It is a wonderful thing for a soldier to have a young woman waiting for him on his return from the front. I was lucky. Many men of my regiment had left behind them sweethearts and wives and children whom they were not to see again for several years, in contrast to the troops of the German Army who were given far more generous leave to their homeland. By the end of the war most of my companions and I had been away from England for more than four years. Later on, it was to prove a factor adversely affecting the morale of even the steadiest veteran.

There was considerable panic in Cairo on my arrival, particularly at General Headquarters, where the staff were busily engaged in making huge bonfires of secret papers and files. The charred remains carried upwards by the thermal currents over the hot streets rained down again like black confetti all over the city. Rich Egyptians sent their chauffeurs with heavy black boxes loaded with jewels to the neutrality of the Swiss and Swedish Legations for safe keeping.

Even Brita asked me what she should do with my old Reo should the Germans arrive. I told her that in the unlikely event she could drive it into the river over the embankment, as I should have no further use for it. She herself had been approached in a rather amateur manner to act as a spy for British Military Intelligence if we were forced to evacuate Egypt, but I did not know this until many years later.

We were rapidly re-equipped with new Stuart tanks and were joined by the remains of 'B' Squadron after their gallant but tragic fight on the Alamein line. We still had enough crews to man two squadrons and a few days later left again for the front. We retraced the line of our retreat to Damanhur and thence westward once again. A few miles before Alamein, the Colonel ordered me to navigate the regiment 25 miles south to a point where we had a rendezvous with a battalion of the 60th Rifles.

The ordinary oil compass was thrown out of accuracy by the mass of metal of a tank, but someone had invented a marvellously simple substitute called a sun compass, which worked on the principal of a sundial. I had become reasonably competent in the use of this instrument, but above all it required faith. We turned off the well-worn tracks and the coastal road across virgin desert, unmarked except for the pad of the camel, the dainty feet of the gazelle and the little jerboa, which had given its name to the Eighth Army. The North African desert is seldom flat. Sand dunes blown into odd shapes by the winds and sandstorms rise in irregular patterns to heights of 30ft or more, whilst little depressions where the dew has settled provide enough moisture for the camel thorn to grow, to provide sustenance for the few animals which can survive in this barren land.

The sun compass was mounted on the crossbar above the fascia board of the 15cwt Morris truck, and the slim needle cast its shadow on the circular disc as I took a bearing towards the Qattara Depression. It was impossible to navigate a straight line because of the dunes and the patches of soft sand which bogged down the three-ton trucks, and it was therefore necessary to make constant deviations to the right and left, which required careful reckoning and correction, but only by one's own estimate. I hoped my eye for distance was not too far out, and that the balance of error would result in an accurate arrival at our destination.

The desert had been apparently empty since we had left the coast, but after hours of grinding over the sand, by my reckoning we had arrived. However, there was absolutely nothing to be seen. The rendezvous had been simply a spot marked on a map as there were no features to signify the end of our journey. The Colonel called a halt. There was absolute silence and no sign of allies or enemy.

'Are you sure', said the Colonel, 'that we have arrived at the right place?'

I found that question very difficult to answer but suggested that he should send out a scout car a mile to every point of the compass from our position, as the dunes prevented observation for more than a few hundred yards in any direction.

The King's Royal Rifle Corps were only 500yds away. Thereafter, I always had great faith in a compass. It is easy to doubt your direction by instinctively feeling that you are too far this way or that, but as I have related, you must have confidence in the instrument. The great single-handed sailors might be amused at my uncertainty, but they have a sextant and a horizon on which to fix their position; there is no certain horizon on land, especially in broken country, neither do the sailors have a mass of moving metal to deflect their instruments.

With the 1st Battalion of the Kings Royal Rifle Corps we moved into position at the southern extremity of the defensive line, in which we were to remain for such a long time that I would know the country even to this day like the back of my hand. A hill called Himeimat stood out like an enemy sentinel surveying the desert to the south and east. It could not have been more than 200ft above sea level, but in that landscape it had the appearance of a mountain.

Rommel's rapid advance, having been blunted by the brilliant action of the New Zealand division at Mersa Matruh, had run out of steam. His line of communication was being constantly harassed by the Royal Air Force, he had suffered casualties and mechanical breakdowns of his tanks and transport, and in spite of the booty he had collected at Tobruk he was running out of petrol. Alexandria was but 65 miles away, almost within his grasp, but the glittering prize of the conquest of Egypt was never to be his.

Both sides now paused for breath after the Eighth Army's somewhat costly and desperate efforts to counter-attack in July, which only history has revealed very nearly succeeded in driving the enemy back to the Egyptian frontier.

We were now joined by the remaining squadron of the 8th Hussars, which was all that was left of this regiment after the fierce battles on the Gazala/Bir Hakeim line. We now had a full regimental strength of three squadrons of Stuart tanks. (This temporary amalgamation of our regiments was to become permanent long after the war to form the Queen's Royal Irish Hussars).

We settled down in this bleak locality, watching for any movement, looking to our left flank particularly, not trusting to the supposition that the Qattara Depression was such a sure protection; nor did we know what force was deployed over the 35 miles between us and our army's right flank on the sea. Before dawn our forward troops would move out as far as they dared, and at night we would collect in to a closely guarded leaguer, our positions being taken over by the infantry. As day followed day and week followed week, the procedure became a routine, but there was no move by the enemy against us as we gazed through the shimmering heat haze across the sands.

Mealtimes became a welcome break in the monotony. After first light, when the whole regiment was alert, we stood down and then we cooked tinned bacon and tomatoes and brewed the tea without which the British Army could never function. At midday we ate Maconochie's tinned stew and bully beef, a disgusting diet, lacking essential vitamins. Some of us contracted what had become known as desert sores, mainly on the backs of the hands and on the wrists, where the skin peeled away, exposing suppuration which was immediately attacked by the millions of ever-present flies. Later on, as there began to be casualties on this account, we were issued with American vitamin pills to make up for the dietary deficiency.

But on the whole, the dry air and the sun prevented any other outbreak of sickness except for sand fly fever, and the troops were tolerably fit and certainly free from the common diseases of populated areas. There was a saying that we were 'tank fit', which signified that if we had been ordered on a long march on foot we should have been in trouble. Being naturally of spare build, I now had a waist measurement which was the same as my hatband, but I felt extremely well, as the heat never bothered me and we were not required physically to exert ourselves beyond our ordinary duties. Even a standard form of physical training would have been out of the question. Of course, there was no fresh meat of any sort and no bread or fruit and vegetables, except those out of a tin.

We slept in the open without tents. There was usually a heavy dew at night, and it was necessary to fold our clothes in groundsheets, with another spread over our blankets, before we settled down to sleep.

At dawn the air was so pure as to be almost exhilarating, and our appetites for our simple breakfast were sharp. Tinned bacon and tomatoes surely never tasted so good. Each tank or truck crew would cook for themselves by the simple expedient of placing a small tin filled with sand saturated with petrol inside a larger perforated tin, the sand acting as a wick for the makeshift stove. Doubtless, it was an extravagant use of petrol, but it was quick and wonderfully effective. We were never short of water, and there was always enough not only to wash and shave but also to wash our scanty clothes, which dried thereafter within minutes in the blazing sun. Any waste food had to be buried immediately, and if you wanted to go to the lavatory you always took a spade with you. It was considered an unforgiveable sin not to do so, and anyone who sneaked off in the night to a slit trench failing to comply with this unwritten precaution forever lost the respect of his companions.

It was certainly a strange existence, but for many of us the desert held a peculiar fascination, and most of the troops were remarkably content. Only occasionally were we attacked by aircraft, but we now had reliable Browning machine guns on every tank with which to answer back. We lived in a world of our own, so far from the coast and with the vast expanse of Africa stretching thousands of miles to the south. The desert was at times very beautiful, particularly at sunrise and sunset when the light had many colours.

To the officers and men of the regiment so cut off from world events in our isolation there was only one theatre of war of any consequence, the one in which we were engaged. Little did we know that the battles before us were indeed to be of such extraordinary significance.

At this time, in the autumn of 1942, nowhere else was the British Army in action on land against the Axis powers. Only in Burma were our troops, who had been driven out of the country, preparing to counter-attack the Japanese.

The Americans were heavily engaged in the Pacific in the battle for Guadalcanal, having scored great victories at sea over the Japanese fleet.

The Russians were furiously resisting the German advance into their homeland by their stand at Stalingrad and their delaying tactics in the Caucasus.

The Royal Navy has always protected the lifeblood of England, and the Royal Air Force was engaged in its daily battle for the skies over Europe to threaten the enemy's war potential.

We knew little of all this as we watched the threatening feature of Himeimat directly in front of us.

Chapter 10

The Battle of Alam Halfa

A nother character now made his appearance upon this stage, an extraordinary little man, as spare as a sparrow, with a rat-trap mouth, a sharp nose and very clear eyes, a teetotaller and non-smoker, whose self-discipline went beyond the bounds of ordinary human behaviour, a dedicated and practical soldier with a confidence and a personality which infected those about him.

General Bernard Montgomery took over Auchinleck's command of the Eighth Army, and there now began a classic exercise of professional skill in warfare which was only the beginning of the end for Germany in the Second World War.

The antagonists were both hampered by their lines of communication across the seas. Malta, although still hard pressed, remained inviolate, harbouring the Royal Navy and the RAF, both attacking with marked effect the short but vulnerable supply routes across the Mediterranean to the Afrika Korps from French and Italian ports. On the other hand, the Eighth Army still had to wait for nearly two months for convoys to reach Egypt from England by the long voyage round the Cape, and there was to be no repeat of the desperate and hazardous runs through the Straits of Gibraltar which had proved so costly earlier in the year.

Whilst Montgomery enjoyed the complete support and confidence of the War Cabinet and was backed to the hilt by General Alexander, the new Commander-in-Chief of the Middle East, Rommel had to contend with the half-hearted Marshal Kesselring, the sickening futility of the Italian dictator and the competing demands for armament and air support from the Russian front, which had a much higher priority.

On 21 August 1942, Winston Churchill, the Colonel of my regiment, personally visited the Western Desert. He himself had made the sweeping changes in the Middle East command and for a long time had been very uneasy in his mind as to the conduct of our affairs in this theatre.

I was ordered to navigate a representative body of men to meet him near the field cemetery, 15 miles or so to our rear. We shone up our badges, washed the sand off our clothes and generally smartened ourselves up as best we could.

It was difficult to navigate to the rendezvous through the maze of formations and transport, which to my astonishment were now so numerous. We gaped at the new Grant tanks, which had just arrived with their 75mm guns, and at the brand new six-pounder anti-tank weapons, which we had never seen before and which looked so much more formidable and reassuring.

As we weaved our way through all this paraphernalia there were anxious moments when I thought we should be late for this important appointment, but we made it on time. Here in this cemetery were already buried officers and men of my regiment, mostly from 'A' and 'B' Squadrons which had suffered such heavy casualties.

I must admit that, as I stood rigidly to attention on parade with my small contingent of the Queen's Own Hussars, I was somewhat overawed at the approach of the stooping figure, who had so punctiliously handed his cigar to his driver before inspecting his regiment. He was dressed in his now famous siren suit with a pith helmet on his head and was followed by the Chief of the Imperial General Staff, General Brooke, General Alexander and, last but not least, the sparrow-like figure of our new commander.

Montgomery had an immediate effect upon the Eighth Army. He certainly swept out the house and opened the windows to let in a fresh hope of victory, but there have been exaggerated references by senior officers since the war to a previous lack of morale among the troops. There was never any deterioration of morale in my own regiment, although it had suffered such heavy casualties already in the two years since leaving England in the two campaigns in which it had been engaged. There was inevitably a certain criticism of generalship, and a creeping contempt for politicians who had failed to provide us with high class weapons. I continually marvelled at the acceptance by the troops of their situation; without complaint, day after day, they manned the tanks and settled down with good humour to their allotted tasks. But of course a cavalry regiment was a family affair. If you had to go to war, then it was a home far from home.

By the end of August both sides had built up their strength, and two highly professional soldiers were now intent upon the most deadly and fascinating game in which they had both been trained to excel. Montgomery decided to wait for his opponent's move and, with the most extraordinary foresight and confidence, deployed his forces in elaborate anticipation with deadly effect. But Rommel was ill with an infection of the nose and a liver complaint. Nevertheless, as reports reached him of huge convoys of reinforcements reaching Suez for the Eighth Army, with great courage he put out of mind his physical handicaps and decided to attack.

Air reconnaissance reported concentrations of the Afrika Korps in the south on our front on 31 August. We faced the advancing enemy across our wide minefield. Towards evening, they advanced apparently in a mass, nearly as black as the appearance of the German Twelfth Army at Ptolemais. Their sappers were walking forward, little dark figures against the sand, disregarding our gunfire, concentrating on their mine detectors, their bayonets prodding at the deadly hidden obstacles to their progress. It was an astonishing sight, and we could scarcely believe the reality before our eyes as the slow movement towards us continued without pause. Shells began to fall about our position, and our forward troops were replying with their tank guns.

But Montgomery was deliberately leading the enemy into his trap. Behind us to the north-east our armour had been dug in to defensive positions directly across the anticipated line of their advance on the Alam El Halfa ridge, a rising feature of sand, the northern extremity of which was only five miles from the coast. It was not a natural obstacle in itself but provided an opportunity, by its contour, to conceal our guns.

But as night fell, the brave sappers of the Afrika Korps had not succeeded in clearing a way for their armour. Massed behind them were the two now famous 15th and 21st Panzer Divisions, eagerly waiting to launch their assault through a gap in the minefield.

Within our regiment, the rank and file knew nothing of our remarkable general's subtle tactics, and we were therefore astonished when the 7th Armoured Division was ordered to withdraw to let the enemy pass and run headlong on to the hot reception so carefully laid on for them farther north.

Quite suddenly, and I believe without predetermined intention, my regiment was ordered south and thence westwards to attack the Afrika Korps' echelons on their flank. This sudden order giving us an independent role in the battle meant that we had to take with us a greater supply of reserve petrol and ammunition, since we should be divorced from the divisional supply columns on our solitary advance.

I was sent at once to collect together a convoy for this purpose with spare tanks, and to rendezvous with the regiment at yet another isolated spot marked on the map. Trooper Hyam and I set off in our 15cwt truck to the divisional supply area, where we were horrified to find on arrival that the vehicles had been dispersed against bombing attacks to such an extent that it took hours before we could assemble a convoy of our own trucks. I could only find one tank to take with me. The officer in charge only made his appearance just before we were due to set off, and I was so furious at his inefficiency that, although he was by far my senior, I let fly with a volley of invective. I was already many hours behind the regiment, and my responsibility to reach the rendezvous on time weighed heavily upon me.

I set off to the west with my small convoy of twelve trucks and one Stuart tank. As we approached Himeimat, now such a familiar landmark, we ran almost into the battle and came under shell fire. I shied away to the south with my valuable caravan and, taking a chance, made straight for the escarpment and down to the soft sands of the Qattara Depression for safety. It was quiet down there and undisturbed, and I was able to get out my map and mark out our course before night fell. The radio in our single tank failed to pick up the regimental frequency, and I was now completely out of touch with any formation and blind to events.

The sands of the great Depression are curiously dark in colour and there are countless billions of large round stones worn smooth as the pebbles on a beach. The ground is scarcely flat, but more resembles the surface of a sea with a huge swell upon it.

I slept little that night and was greatly puzzled by the absence of any sound of the battle, which could only have been five miles or more to the north, if indeed it was still in progress. But for all I knew, Rommel could have been in Alexandria by this time if our fortunes had failed us.

At first light we set off again on our course. Upon our way we came upon the wreck of a Messerschmitt, the burnt corpse of the pilot still slumped forward in the shattered remains of his cockpit. One of our trucks broke down, and I changed its cargo of petrol for shells and abandoned it.

By midday, by my reckoning we had reached our rendezvous, but there was nothing to be seen. The sands were unmarked by the tracks of vehicles.

I tried every combination of dials on the tank radio without success. In any direction there was nothing but the desert, and no sound but the eternal buzzing of flies.

I could see no possible action I could take to relieve my anxiety. Desert navigation was never very exact. On the other hand, any vehicle in that dusty arena could be seen for miles, and to leave my charges on a personal reconnaissance in the tank without protection seemed out of the question. Having decided to stay where we were for at least the next 24 hours, I retired to the truck to continue my reading of Tolstoy's *Anna Karenina* which had been interrupted by the events of the last few days.

Hyam was sitting beside me in the passenger seat. Suddenly, he shouted at me as we heard the sound of aircraft and we simultaneously took a dive out of the truck as two Messerschmitts, flying low with their cannons firing, swooped down on us. I covered the back of my head with hands and ground my face into the sand as the shattering explosions pounded in my ears. In a second they were gone. I spat the grit out of my mouth and examined myself, expecting to see fearful wounds on my body, but there was not even a scratch. The truck was shot full of holes and one of the petrol tanks was leaking; a repeat performance for Hyam and me, reminding us of our narrow escape in the Peloponnese. The ground was pitted with the craters of the cannon shells all about where I had lain prostrate. I ran for the tank to man the Browning on the turret, expecting the pilots to turn for a second attack, but they were gone.

They had singled out the 15cwt truck on account of the pennant flag above it signifying the leader of a convoy. It was lucky they had not the wit to attack the precious petrol and ammunition trucks, which would have provided a much more profitable target. As it was, we had not a single casualty.

My book was now forgotten, and I stood in the turret of the tank searching the desert for movement, the comforting Browning gun on its well-oiled swivel close to my hand. In mid-afternoon, through shimmering haze, I saw a dust cloud directly to the south in the least likely direction for any approach by the regiment, which I expected from the north or west. Twenty-four hours had gone by since I had left on my solitary expedition. Anything could have happened within that time. Was it friend or foe approaching? I ordered the truck crews to man their vehicles and to assemble pointing east, with orders that, if they saw me fire, they were to move off with all speed towards the Delta. The tank gunner put a round up the breech and we advanced towards the unknown.

As the cloud of dust came ever nearer, I strained my eyes, but the shimmering haze distorted the mass in the distance into all sorts of fanciful images. Presently, however, I made out the unmistakable silhouette of a Stuart tank, and as it came nearer and nearer I saw a familiar figure sitting on the track cover. Lieutenant Stuart Fryer was navigating the regiment to the rendezvous with an oil compass on his knee.

The regiment had carried out their task by harassing the enemy's flank and running into their transport. There had been a considerable melee, in which two troop leaders had been badly wounded. My small convoy re-armed and refuelled the tanks for further action, but Douglas Nicoll, our regimental medical officer, was greatly concerned about our two casualties and transferred them from his ambulance to a three-ton truck of my convoy with a caution that they needed very urgent surgical attention.

I set off once more towards Himeimat, whither the regiment were bound, providing they had no further encounter with the enemy. The Colonel was concerned to know that we had been harassed by aircraft so far off the beaten track.

I turned away towards Himeimat with my convoy now empty save for the two wounded officers strapped to stretchers lying on the hard metal bottom of a three-tonner. It was a nightmare journey, and I felt every jolt over the ground as we made our way back. Bobby Beachcroft was very seriously wounded in the head and Lieutenant Hirst in the eye. Neither was conscious, but I stopped frequently in a futile attempt to see to their wants. I did not know how far I should have to go before I could get them to a field hospital, even if one still existed.

As I reached the vicinity of Himeimat, as if once again by providence, which was not my friend, I saw an ambulance entirely on its own in that desolation. The red cross was unmistakable. I put my foot hard down on the accelerator to intercept it. Of all things, it was a freelance American ambulance wandering without direction in the rear areas of the battle. Gratefully, I transferred my friends to professional care. (It is sad to relate that Bobby Beachcroft died of his wounds and Lieutenant Hirst lost an eye.)

In a little while the regiment reassembled in front of Himeimat in the positions we had occupied before the battle began. To our north the Afrika Korps was hastily withdrawing through the minefield gaps, pressed hard by General Freyberg and his New Zealand Division, and fierce fighting was taking place there. The two Panzer divisions and the Italian Ariete and Litterio divisions were desperately trying to extricate themselves and to disengage.

Whilst we had been carrying out our harassing role on the flank far from the main scene of battle, Rommel's Army had run right on to the guns of our 10th Armoured Division and 44th Infantry Division in the positions they had carefully prepared weeks beforehand on the ridge. Each individual tank and each gun had been dug in with allotted fields of fire.

But now the New Zealanders were strongly resisted by the determined German rearguard action and sustained such heavy casualties that they were forced to abandon their intention to close the minefield gaps. Thus the Axis forces were able to withdraw behind the defences of the Alamein line, and the status quo was once more resumed.

It was astonishing to reflect on Montgomery's incredibly accurate assessment of the enemy's intentions. It was almost as if he had Rommel's operation order in his hand; but history has not revealed that our military intelligence was so efficient, and our remarkable commander was thereafter credited with almost superhuman foresight.

What if he had been wrong, and the direction of the assault towards Alexandria had been only 20° more to the south? What if the Reconnaissance Group of the Afrika Korps had created a panic by making straight for Cairo across the Qattara Depression with their efficient half-tracked vehicles? Since I had travelled many miles across it with ordinary three-tonners, I now knew it was not as impassable as both sides assumed it to be.

Montgomery has written that if the Afrika Korps had sidetracked the Alam Halfa ridge making straight for the Delta, then he would have attacked the enemy's flank with 400 tanks, and that would have been the end of it. I do not think many regimental officers would have agreed with this facile assumption. Weapon for weapon we were still outgunned, and to reorganize rapidly for such an eventuality from static positions would have taken a great deal of time, during which the Afrika Korps could have wheeled left-handed to attack us in the rear, whilst their armoured Reconnaissance Group could have created havoc in our base areas and even entered Alexandria.

Neither side yet realized that the vast deserts afforded room for manoeuvre as in a naval battle; they were still wedded to the idea that a direct confrontation with each other was a primary essential to the final outcome.

Alam Halfa was a big gamble which paid off. For Rommel, now a sick man, it must have been a bitter blow. Egypt was so very near in distance but now so much farther from his grasp.

Chapter 11

The Tide Turns

Major Archer was now given command of 'C' Squadron, and I went with him as second-in-command. I had not cared for my responsibilities in Headquarters Squadron, which had proved defensive, dangerous and fraught with the anxieties of a full back in a rugby football game. It was much simpler to be a forward.

Montgomery now began a most elaborate deception in preparation for our own offensive. The El Taqa Plateau, a sharply rising feature stretching for ten miles east and west across the desert terminating in our direction in the hill of Himeimat, gave the enemy an advantage of observation over our activities, but our General made use of this very factor to his own advantage.

Every night as we withdrew from our daily watch on the front, truckloads of curious equipment, escorted by the King's Royal Rifle Corps, would move up past our tanks; and in the morning when again we visited our positions we would find huge camouflage nets pegged out on the ground, hiding absolutely nothing, merely providing a little cover for the lizards where they lay in wait under the canvas strips for an unwary fly to settle.

As Montgomery had already decided to launch his offensive in the northern sector he set about to deceive Rommel into a belief that an attack would be made in the south. Behind us, also, false supply dumps were set out and a dummy pipeline was laid; transport and tanks were constructed of any material which the specialists in deception could lay their hands on.

The watchers on Himeimat were so tantalized by these curious operations, which they could only observe through the shimmering light, that one day they could restrain their curiosity no longer and selected an adventurous officer from the Panzer Corps who, with half a dozen Stuart tanks which they had captured in the fighting at Gazala, was ordered to find at first hand out exactly what was going on. One day in September, the officer slipped off the El Taqa plateau with his little force to carry out his orders, no doubt with his heart in his mouth.

But one of our forward troops, fortunately very much on the alert, saw him as he attempted to sneak off towards the escarpment using folds in the ground for cover. But they could not identify the intruder; all they saw was a movement across their front as of some unidentifiable vehicles, which they immediately reported.

It was mid-afternoon, and the sun beat down on our positions as I lay under the belly of my tank for shade and some protection from the flies. My wireless operator called out to me urgently, and I climbed into the turret. The haze at this time of day frequently produced optical illusions and mirages in the middle distance, multiplying numbers of objects, distorting their shape and falsifying directions. Nevertheless, all my defensive instincts were alerted. We had occupied this position day after day, from first light to dusk, with no sight of the enemy, our left flank supposedly protected by the armoured cars of the Household Cavalry, but otherwise open across the vast spaces of the desert directly to the south.

Archer was away, having gone to regimental headquarters in the squadron jeep. I reported the movement which had been seen on our front but received the reply that the Household Cavalry would look after the situation. Nothing so far had been heard from them to indicate any enemy action. This was not as reassuring as it was meant to be, and I immediately ordered the squadron to stand by ready for battle. Our tank engines roared into life as we came off our positions to advance.

Suddenly one of the Household Cavalry's armoured cars came dashing in our direction at high speed, pulling up in a shower of sand a hundred yards away. Lord Roderick Pratt got out of the turret and, supported by his gunner, came staggering towards me. He was pouring with blood and pointed with outstretched arm desperately to the west, shouting, 'There they are, there they are!'

He collected himself sufficiently to tell me that his troop had been attacked by Stuart tanks.

Now it would be hard to distinguish between friend and foe, but I ordered our forward troops to stand fast where they were and to suspect anything that moved. Archer came racing up in his jeep; breathing hard, he heaved his portly figure into his tank and we advanced to find the enemy. Soon 'A' Squadron joined us in the hunt, and the quarry was sighted making fast for

Major Peter Crichton, 4th Queen's Own Hussars, after the Battle of Alamein.

The author's cousin, Major Dick Austin, killed defending the beach at Nauplion in the Peloponnese in 1941, in the full dress uniform of the 4th Queen's Own Hussars.

Kriegsgefangenenlager

Datum 30ᵗʰ Nov 41

Best wishes to you, John, Kenneth and all it was good
news to hear you all made it. I got ¾ way to Crete but
the opposition got there first. We are all together again
now but no news of Bill. Thank Ian for his letter, send
us what news you can. Some one sent me a parcel many
thanks. Remember me to all the old B. Hope you
got some polo. I am buying horses in readiness yo Clem.

Above: Prisoner of war postcard from Major Clements in Oflag VIB. He was the officer commanding B Squadron during the Greek campaign.

Left: General Erwin Rommel. (© IWM)

Above: Trooper Hyam with the author's old Reo car in the Egyptian Desert, 1941.

Below: Captain Hidden, Major O'Brian and Captain Carleton Patterson, Western Desert, 1942.

Captain Dick Hidden with a Browning gun, Western Desert, 1942.

General Montgomery at the Battle of Alamein, November 1942. (© IWM)

The author (right) with Major O'Brian and Captain Carleton Patterson at
El Adem, November 1942.

The author on an Egyptian Defence Force camel at Sakkara.

(L to R)The author, Brita, Douglas Nicoll and Captain Ozier at breakfast, Gezira Club, 1944.

Africa Star.

Ref: G/73.
6 Dec 43.

To: Os.C.: A, B, C & HQ Sqns.

Copy: Q.M.

1.   Urgent orders have been received from GHQ that every Officer and man of the Regt entitled to the Africa Star shall be wearing this Star by 1800 hrs to-day, Monday, 6 Dec 43.

2.   The ribbon will be drawn by the Q.M. this morning and a team of seamstresses is being despatched from GHQ in order to effect the necessary attachment.

3.   Seamstresses will be allotted to Sqns on their arrival.

4.   Sqns will return to this Office IMMEDIATELY the names of all Officers and men NOT entitled to the award of the Africa Star.

Capt.
Adjt., 4 H.

JC?

An important order before Churchill's inspection, December 1943.

4th Queen's Own Hussars on parade for the Colonel-in-Chief's inspection, December 1943. C Squadron in foreground with the author to the front.

Winston Churchill inspecting 'C' Squadron at Mena, December 1943.

Above and below: The full complement of C Squadron, 4th Hussars, 1944.

Reading left to right and down

C.C. Rouge... A Hickson. Brown... G Crichton. B Ayr.

ROBINSON 27, HARAN, BLACKWOOD, KEY, STANWELL, FENNELLY, ADLEY, KNIGHTS 94, BEER, POLLITT, BEGGS, ASHFORD, McGHY, MILLINGTON, STANLEY, LOVE, BALL, BRUNT, BARR, SCOTT, ROTHWELL, BATEY.

BOTTOMLEY, CARMICHAEL, KINCAID, SPENCER, WILSON, CLOWTHER, ALLAN, WELLS, HUTTON, ANKELLAN, GILLSON, HEARD, BOSWELL, CLAMB, DAWSON, CLOWDES, BARNES 50, KIRKHAM, WEYMOUTH, HOWARTH, ROBERTS, CLARKE, HOULOCK, WILKINSON, BLOWNE 27, BONE, STEAD, MOOGAN, GREGORY, YATES, SYKES, McNINCH.

CARTER, TONKLIN, BOWDEN, BOOTH, BARNES 59, PETRA, JONES O, McGOWAN, COOPER, COHEN, PATERSON, SMITH II, HUMPHRIES, CROFT, NYE, BLASH, LAW, BROWN 04, APPLEBY, GITSHAM, CORNELL, DICKER, FALCON, SLODGE, SHUCK, DAVIES, BISHOP, LITTLE, TYE, CURTIS, MILLAR.

EVANS, VALLANCE, EDDCOTT, HARRIS, AYRE, BURTON, BROOKSBANK, HARRISON, LEWIS, JACOB, PIKE, SMITH 15, CURT, BROWN 82, ROWARTH, DAY, BAILLIE, WHITE, EMMOTT, MOLLARD, FLETCHER, PENDEBURY, SEYMOUR, PETTITT, HILTON, JONES 54, NEW, DYKE, SCHWARTZ, PHILLIPS, GRANGER, CAMERON, WILKES.

Officers — Hedley, Hickson, Brown, Freyer, Crichton, Wheeler, Shawson, Thompson, Crawley, NN, ROGERS, DIXON, THOMPSON, POPE, LEES, SSM. — SSM'S POOLE, PEGGIE, MANSELL, DAVIES, IRONS, CAILEY.

STRAY, HOLDSWORTH, GRENAN, ROBINSON 46, GRIGG, HAMPTON, JONES 75, SMITH 91, BUDGE, RATURE, WATSON, PAGET, CREE, DALY, BLACK, WILLIAMS, LITTLE(A), BELL, JONES 19, MITCHELL, HYDE.

...ly, Well-Hedley, V. Paley, JM Shawson, G Palmer, B Hoyle SSM.

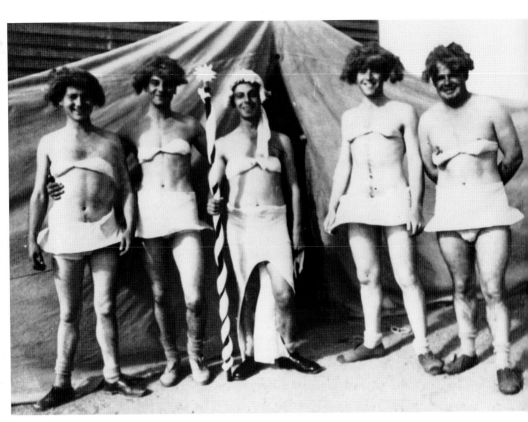

Members of 'C' Squadron at Mena Camp – the origin of the 'Drag Act'.

The author commanding 'C' Squadron in 1944, mounted in a Sherman tank.

Right: Trooper Brash (right) with friends in Cairo.

Below: 75mm Pack Howitzers of the Royal Artillery in action, in support of Yugoslav partisans. (© IWM)

Above and below: Typical partisans, the Yugoslav Army of National Liberation. Partisans resting in the hills near the Dalmatian coast. (© IWM)

Right: 4th Hussars
badge and colours.

Below: Partisan
vessels off Zadar,
April 1945.

Second Sector partisan gunners in action, 1945.

Kommandant Vulin, Commander of the Second Sector (right) with his Political Commissar, Major Mamula, 1945.

Above: Partisan gunners with a 17-pounder, 1945.

Right: Major Branko Mamula, Political Commissar Second Sector, 1945.

Above: Peter and Brita Crichton on their wedding day, August 1945.

Left: Husky, the mascot of the Balkan Air Force, and the author at play, 1945.

a bowl-like depression in the sand on the other side of our dummy minefield which reached almost to the edge of the escarpment.

The forward observation officer of the Royal Horse Artillery, always eager to seek a target, quickly brought his guns into action. We moved into positions for the kill as the 25-pounder shells burst into the bowl.

I heard the familiar slow voice of Major Terence O'Brian Butler, the battery commander, telling our Colonel over the radio, 'They are yours if you want them.' The adventurous panzer officer must surely have thought that he had not long to live. But inexplicably we stood fast and, as we waited, with a sudden rush our quarry got away to the west.

It was a bad business. The daring German tank commander had destroyed two of the Household Cavalry's armoured cars, probed our defences and escaped unscathed to report in triumph to his redoubtable General. We had been ordered to hold off for fear of exposing, by our tank tracks, the dummy minefield, part of the elaborate deception which had been built up so painstakingly over the last weeks.

We had been in the Western Desert almost continuously for over four months, and our environment was now completely familiar. Our tanks were our mobile homes, providing shelter and storage space for our water and food and a few personal possessions which were carefully stowed away in selected spaces between the shell racks, over the radio set and in any void not occupied by the turret mechanism. The designers who had drawn this engine of war had never anticipated that men would live in it for weeks and months on end.

Life was reduced to a very simple form. A rum ration was issued, but few of the troops liked the rather coarse salty alcohol, and I therefore enjoyed very nearly the entire ration of my crew. I have always been a heavy sleeper, and it takes me at least half an hour from waking to be fully conscious. In the cold before dawn, when I had to navigate the squadron to our forward positions, it was a great help to consciousness to get down a good dram of the fiery liquid. I took out a shell to accommodate the precious bottle in the metal holder close to my hand.

The evenings were the best time of day, and sometimes the sunsets were glorious. I must admit that, as I looked through the mauve light across the dark sands of the Qattara Depression towards the setting sun, with Cairo only 70 miles away, I saw only a golden-haired young woman with fair skin in a scanty printed cotton dress walking towards me as if on the air. It was a soldier's dream. Sometimes, when we were in leaguer at night, we would gather together, and the talk was often of what we should do when the war was over. Many were the extravagant ideas which were laughed out of court. On occasions I would go over to talk to our youthful regimental medical officer, who had become a close friend and who was so shortly to distinguish himself by winning the Military Cross. He held a surgery every night in his ambulance and had a remarkably effective manner with the troops who arrived for treatment for such minor ailments as desert sores, stomach aches, and so on. We had set out from England equipped with pith helmets, having been cautioned about the ill effects of hot sun on the scalp, but the helmets had been discarded immediately on our arrival, and the old fashioned idea of the dreadful consequences of over-exposure had long since been proved unfounded.

Meanwhile, Field Marshal Rommel was in hospital in Germany and General Stumme had taken over command of the German and Italian armies in Africa. Huge quantities of new weapons and supplies were reaching the Eighth Army from England, and Montgomery was massing his greatly improved resources on the Alamein line. Moreover, plans were now far advanced for a joint British/American landing in French North Africa which was to follow our offensive in the Egyptian desert. Thirty-five miles from the coast, in front of Himeimat, we knew nothing of all this, only suspecting from our occasional glimpses of the new Grant tanks with their 75mm guns that our situation had improved.

Thinking that if I stayed in the desert indefinitely I should surely be superseded by some lucky fellow in the affections of the attractive daughter of the Swedish minister, I summoned up my courage to ask for leave. It was charmingly but promptly refused. It was now September, and the scene was set for one of the great battles of the war.

Just as the Germans had decided to probe our defences, General Montgomery suddenly made up his mind that it would be a good thing if 'C' Squadron 4th Hussars ventured across the unknown hazards of no-man's-land toward the El Taqa plateau, to test the reactions of his opponent and to locate his gun positions.

We received our orders, which Archer and I studied the previous day with careful interest. They were simple in the extreme: we were to advance directly in a straight line to draw fire.

At dusk I developed a bad headache and was sure I had a fever. Douglas Nicoll checked my pulse, took my temperature and, giving me a couple of aspirins, pronounced me fit for action. I cursed him under my breath as I felt like death.

We moved on to our start line for this dangerous adventure before the sun was up in the morning. Fear had chilled my fever. We had two troops in front and two in reserve as we waited anxiously for sufficient light. The familiar sentinel of Himeimat gazed down into the arena waiting for the play. Archer gave the order to advance, and dust clouds billowed out behind the leading tanks as they sped towards the enemy.

Suddenly the horizon came to life as shells burst all around us. We watched urgently for gun flashes, and as we halted I had to climb out of my tank to walk some distance away from the mass of metal before I could get accurate bearings with an oil compass on the pinpoints of bright light flashing from the plateau.

A squadron commander from the 11th Hussars in an armoured car joined us, with patronising interest at our crude efforts at reconnaissance, which he clearly considered was his own famous regiment's prerogative. Our forward troops reported machine gun fire from dug-in positions in front of them. I held my breath as shell bursts from heavy guns narrowly missed the tanks jinking at high speed over the sand. This circus continued for an hour or more as the enemy came to life, exposing his positions, before we retired to collate our information.

We gathered about the Colonel's tank marking our maps, but a far-sighted German artillery officer had spotted our little conference in the open, and shells burst about us, forcing us to scuttle for the relative safety of our tanks and retire farther east out of range.

That night, I had a high temperature and went to hospital with sand fly fever. Not the bullets of a Messerschmitt, or a shell splinter, but the bite of a little fly sent me back to my heart's desire, but within a week I was in the line again.

It was now autumn, and flocks of migrating birds flew over this desolate battlefield. Skeins of wild geese in perfect formation at a great height made their way from Russia and Europe to the waters of Central Africa, having crossed the sea with still hundreds of miles to go before alighting on their chosen winter grounds. One day a bright red robin hopped at my feet and eagerly devoured the scraps of bully beef I threw in his direction. (I never knew the robin was a migratory bird, but there he was in all his glory; perhaps he was a pioneer in this hazardous experiment.)

The Fighting Free French Group now joined the 7th Armoured Division to settle on our right. They brought with them nearly all the comforts of life, erecting huge marquee tents, determined to make the best of their harsh circumstances. We wondered if, by their elaborate preparations almost within range of the German guns, they had not also brought some light entertainment from Cairo which they could share with us, but in a little while we were to be otherwise occupied.

The British Army with its long history of warfare over many centuries, even when taken by surprise and ill-prepared, had such a sure foundation that it had got into its stride at last after a slow and very inauspicious start, to such an extent that all the essential services were incredibly well maintained even over a sea route of 12,000 miles. We were fed and watered without fail, we had cigarettes and alcohol. The NAAFI truck was always somewhere in the rear with its cut price comforts. The postal service was sacred, and letters from home hardly ever went astray, being delivered with more certainty of despatch than modern days allow from one village to another only a few miles away.

Sometimes Brita sent me from Cairo tinned delicacies and books, which never failed to arrive, and even a special blue gauze veil which she had made to keep the flies away; however, it proved too hot to wear for long over my face.

But I doubt if we had as good a cellar as our new French neighbours with their conspicuous mess tent. Ours was a relatively spartan existence as we had been taught to be highly mobile, so that the whole regiment could move off within minutes leaving nothing behind.

We badly missed accurate news and English newspapers and, although we were scarcely kept in the dark, we had insufficient facts on which to assess the general war situation. The change in the Middle East command which had achieved such a notable victory at Alam Halfa did not really strike home with great significance, and we had no sense of the climax which was so shortly to occur. As I remember, General Montgomery visited us once, only the second time in my life I was ever to see him, and then at a distance. As I have already related, there was nothing wrong with the morale of a good regiment, and some of us had already had more experience of warfare than our commanders, so we were not easily impressed. All officers who could leave their front line duties were called to Regimental Headquarters on 20 October. This was an unusual occurrence, and now we knew that something of extraordinary importance was afoot. At least I found out why my request for leave had been turned down. A lot of impressive top brass were present, and we were addressed by General Horrocks commanding the XIII Corps, a most charming character with a breezy Boy Scout manner, who rather disarmed the regimental soldiers' usual cynical mistrust of general staff officers' pep talks.

In short, we were to attack and destroy the Axis in Africa. There was to be no doubt and no faltering. General Montgomery was certain of victory. We were to fight to the last man and the last round, and so forth. Personally, I never did respond to over-dramatic exhortations, for which I saw no necessity, and I think my feelings were shared by the majority of my fellow officers. Nevertheless, I suspect that we returned to our squadrons with a few more butterflies in our stomachs.

Chapter 12

The Battle of Alamein

Montgomery's opponent was now General Stumme, since Field Marshal Rommel was still in hospital in Germany. Nevertheless, even without their legendary commander, the enemy's battle array was extremely formidable. The hard core of the German Army still consisted of the three famous and redoubtable divisions, the 15th and 21st Panzer Divisions and the 90th Light Division, whose titles will never be forgotten by anyone who fought in the Western Desert. They were supported by the Ramcke Parachute Brigade and the 164th Motorized Division. The Italians had no fewer than eight divisions in the field, including the Ariete and Littorio Armoured Divisions. Whilst the Italian infantry, with certain notable exceptions, was always of rather doubtful value, their artillery was generally considered very efficient.

But the Eighth Army was more powerful than ever before. We had three UK Infantry Divisions, the 44th, 50th and 51st Highland, as well as the 9th Australian, the 1st South African, the 4th Indian and three armoured divisions, the 1st, 7th and 10th, and last but not least, General Freyberg's New Zealanders, probably the most formidable fighting formation in the world.

There was also another important factor. Poor Stumme, having doubtless tasted the fruits of life to the full, had a bad heart, which was to kill him within a few days, whereas our own abstemious, steely little commander was as fit as a flea, an advantage designed by him for just such an occasion as this.

Montgomery's plan was briefly to attack on the fronts of the XXX Corps in the north and the XIII Corps in the south during the night of 23/24 October, and to pass the 10th Armoured Division through two corridors which were to be cleared through the minefields on XXX Corps' front, whilst XIII Corps were to clear a way for our division, the 7th Armoured, on the southern sector. The Free French Group were to pass Himeimat and to take the high ground known as Nagh Rala on the enemy's right flank. But the main attack was to be made in the north, and fortunately for us, Montgomery had told

General Horrocks that our division was on no account to get so mauled that it would not be available for mobile operations after a breakthrough.

His original intention, to attack the *Panzerarmee* with his own Armoured Corps once it was through the enemy's static defences, was changed when he decided instead to attempt to draw the *Panzerarmee* upon our guns even before we were clear of the corridors.

The code name for the operation was Lightfoot.

On 23 October the Free French group took over our positions in front of Himeimat, and as dusk fell and the full moon cast its baleful light over the desert, we moved back into the rear to form up in line astern as part of XIII Corps armour.

The whole of the 7ᵗʰ Armoured Division was now formed in this way in order to be able to pass through the two enemy minefields called January and February, through the narrow corridor which we hoped would be cleared by our sappers just south of a feature called Munasib. Each tank followed the tail of the other, and we crawled slowly on to our start line. Zero hour was 10.00 pm.

Brita had sent me a tinned tongue, which I had open on the turret of my tank and crudely ate with the blade of a penknife as we clanked along at a snail's pace. Since the battle of Alam Halfa the Germans and Italians had been strengthening and adding to their minefields and defences, which stretched all the way from the coast to the Depression, and on our front were to a depth of about two miles.

General Horrocks' orders were to penetrate the enemy's position and to pass the 7ᵗʰ Armoured Division through towards Jebel Kalakh.

Towards 9.00 pm the whole column clanked to a halt whilst we waited tensely for the show to start. With the thunder and flash of a thousand guns the curtain went up upon the Battle of Alamein.

Some of our heavy batteries were close to the right and left of our column, and their gun flashes lit up in dark silhouette the figures of the crews at their rapid drill as they fired salvo after salvo in one of the most terrific artillery bombardments of the war.

At 10.00 pm precisely we started towards the enemy. In front of us our sappers, supported by our infantry, were desperately trying to clear a way through the first minefield. By the light of the moon the Royal Air Force were bombing the enemy's gun positions on the El Taqa plateau, some of which may have been accurately plotted by our crude reconnaissance weeks previously. Smoke screens were dropped to obscure the view of the Italian gunners of the Brescia Division as at midnight we entered the narrow lane already cleared and marked with white tape. Very soon we ground to a halt, and occasional shell bursts made us duck inside our turrets for safety. For hours now we waited, seemingly caught in the minefield, the leading sappers under heavy fire having failed to get our tanks out into the open ground beyond.

Suddenly the unmistakeable Boy Scout voice of our corps commander (another front line general) called out through the confusion, 'What's going on?'

With the protection of the anonymity of semi-darkness, one of our tank commanders behind me, recognizing the general, good-humouredly shouted an answer: 'You ought to know!'

But our efforts to get through the enemy's defences on that first night were to no avail. Some of the leading tanks of the Royal Tank Regiment which just managed to squeeze through met with such fierce resistance that they began to suffer heavy casualties, and Horrocks, under orders to maintain the division intact, decided to withdraw. It was easier said than done, because each tank had nearly to turn within its own length to keep within the safety of the white tapes on either side marking the mines, which could blow a track off.

By dawn we were out of the melee in the relative quiet of the rear area after the shattering sounds of the night, savouring our regular breakfast of bacon and tomatoes and tea. There is nothing like hazard to whet the appetite.

The sounds of battle still raging on the northern sector echoed across the desert, and the Royal Air Force were continually overhead seeking out the enemies' batteries and bombing the echelons of the Panzer divisions.

In mid-morning, not a hundred yards away from my tank, I spied an ambulance truck. It was a three-tonner fitted up as a dentist's surgery. What on earth it was doing there in the middle of one of the epic battles of the war I can hardly imagine. An aching tooth was hardly a casualty, and I can only suppose that the dentist, having got bored with his non-combatant role, thought he would see for himself what was afoot.

In any event, since I had not been to a dentist for years, and out of personal vanity more than anything else, I strolled over from my tank to take advantage of the situation. I think I must surely be the only soldier who, purely for cosmetic reasons, had a tooth stopped in the middle of the Battle of Alamein. But then I had good reason to look my best when and if I returned to Cairo, and I must admit that I had no serious doubts that I should do so.

In the middle of the afternoon, quite suddenly and without any preliminary briefing, we were ordered to advance to attack a salient held by the Italian Brescia Division, which was harassing our infantry and sappers in their attempt to get through the minefields.

The second-in-command of a squadron had to receive the orders from the colonel to translate them in intelligible form to the squadron commander. It is not an easy matter to direct the driver and the gunners and, at the same time, study the map and concentrate on the garbled orders crackling into headphones through interference from all the other frequencies in use.

As we advanced through the terrific bombardment it seemed to me that we were on a course which would inevitably lead us directly into the 'January' minefield. The code name for mines was 'Tomatoes'. I warned Archer of the hazard I was sure was in front of us, and he called a halt. But the 8th Hussar Squadron ran straight into the mines, their leading troops getting their tracks blown off. The Brescia Division, dug into their salient so low down that we could scarcely see them over the sand, started firing away with their anti-tank guns with deadly effect. We suffered heavy casualties at once. I saw Douglas Nicoll in his little scout car with its white cross dashing up to the rescue through shell bursts. I was sure he would be killed, but by a miracle he did what he could for the wounded and escaped with his life.

The infantry were in terrible trouble, pegged down in their open position under the artillery bombardment, without slit trenches or any cover whatever. Many of them ran to the tanks to seek protection, but many were killed.

We could make no headway, and shortly the order came to withdraw. About half of the 8th Hussar Squadron managed to back out on their track marks. The rest were lost, except for a trickle of survivors who made their way back to our lines under cover of nightfall. Now, again, we only had two effective squadrons.

After this fiasco we were sent north to come under command of General Freyberg. Now surely nothing could go wrong. The famous New Zealand Division was held in reserve to exploit the first breakthrough of the enemy's deep defences, and we were destined to be Freyberg's vanguard.

But the battle raged fiercely day after day whilst we waited for our opportunity. On the other side of the minefields and in the midst of the fighting, General Stumme died of a heart attack. Field Marshal Rommel left his hospital bed in Germany to come to the aid of his beloved Afrika Korps, and once again the two remarkable antagonists were locked in a duel.

As the days went by and casualties began to mount without any visible territorial gain by either side, even Winston Churchill became uneasy and began to question the veracity and confidence of his sharp-faced little general 2,000 miles from Downing Street. By 1 November we had suffered 10,000 killed, wounded and missing.

But Montgomery drove on his commanders with ruthless insistence, in spite of some protestations. Now the final phase of the battle was to begin with a tremendous infantry assault supported by over 300 guns according to the plan called 'Supercharge'. By 2 November a gap had at least been opened, and the 9th Armoured Brigade were ordered to pass through it and to hold it open at all costs in the face of the Afrika Korps' armour and their anti-tank guns. It was a fearful order, but the General declared that he was prepared to accept 100 per cent casualties if necessary.

The brigade went through and stood fast, fighting off repeated attacks by the 15th Panzer Division and the Afrika Korps' anti-tank guns. The 3rd Hussars, in particular, suffered appalling casualties amounting to two-thirds of their tanks and half their men, but their object was achieved and the 1st Armoured Division came to their support.

Now General Freyberg gave us the order to advance as vanguard to his New Zealand Division. The dust of battle darkened the sky, fine sand blew into our eyes and caked our mouths and nostrils as we charged at high speed through the gap, standing head and shoulders above the tank turrets. Long-range armour-piercing shot literally ricocheted from the desert surface. Suddenly we were truly out in the open, swinging northwards towards the coast in an attempt to cut off the enemy's retreat at Fuka, but we were too late.

On 7 November there was a heavy rainstorm which slowed down the infantry and our own echelons, and we pushed on alone. We reached the tarmac coastal road, which enabled our tanks to reach their maximum speed, and we now tore along to the west in hot pursuit.

We ran straight into the German rearguard at Sidi Barrani.

The Colonel's voice, distorted by the crackling headphones of the wireless, gave us the order to attack. Archer and I had agreed that we would hunt like a pack of hounds, closed up and as fast as we could, to exploit the speed of our tanks and to concentrate the firepower of our small calibre guns.

We swung off the tarmac road into the dunes to the south and turned west, heading straight for the enemy. Anti-tank gun shells smacked into the sand as we drove over one crest after another. Within minutes we were right into the enemy's position, all guns firing. German infantry were running hither and thither, some with their hands up, some still resisting. It was the confusion of close battle. What were we to do, kill them all? It was impossible from a tank to select one man over another for execution. I could scarcely answer the Colonel as I heard his voice on the wireless, and shouted for my pistol as Ramcke parachutists, many with their hands up, came within yards of my tank.

We were now right behind the enemy position and turned to attack their rear. Less than a hundred yards away, an anti-tank gun crew were desperately trying to turn their weapon to fire. They had almost carried the trail round and were dropping it. One of our troop leaders was just in front of Archer's tank and mine, and he was standing high up in his turret laying his gunner's aim as if on a practice shoot. My brain froze in fascination at the spectacle. Who would fire first? Then the small solid shot from the 37mm seemed to spit into the sand close to the gun trail, and the gunners' hands went high above their heads in surrender.

I called to the Colonel to bring 'M' Battery RHA into action, and within minutes their 25-pounders were laying a barrage of gunfire upon the defenders. However, by now we were isolated behind the enemy, and I was uncertain of the position of one of our troops and had to ask the RHA to hold their fire.

But the enemy rearguard were now broken, and those who had not surrendered were pulling out with their vehicles on to the road. 'M'

Battery opened up again, but within minutes, or so it seemed, the battle was over. Squadron Sergeant Major Hoyle appeared, his tank festooned with prisoners, some clinging to his gun barrel, excellent insurance against a sneaky hand grenade.

In this action we had suffered only relatively light casualties thanks to the speed of our attack and our concentration, but sadly we lost one of our best troop leaders, Lieutenant Tony Cartmell, who was killed; his crew were killed or wounded.

We continued the pursuit towards Sollum at high speed but we were getting short of petrol. The Colonel called a halt on the road, but Mark Roddick, the Brigadier of the 4th Light Armoured Brigade, turned up with a Royal Air Force tanker full of high octane fuel. He asked if our tanks would go on this super stuff, and we were able to assure him they would go all the faster.

Contrary to all custom, Archer and I were leading the squadron with one headquarters tank in front as in the late evening we arrived at the bottom of Halfaya Pass. Without a pause the Colonel ordered us to go straight up. We had got half way when there was a terrific explosion, which I thought at first was shellfire, and I wondered how we should fare if the enemy had such heavy guns on top of the escarpment; but it was a double Teller mine, which had blown the bottom out of the leading tank under the driver's feet. The man was badly wounded, and the crew carried him to put him on top of the engine cover of my own tank, crying out with the pain of his damaged legs. Although I have always had a horror of injections, I was forced to jab the needle of the morphine capsule into his arm which almost immediately quietened him. Douglas Nicoll, always somewhere close to hand, trudged up the pass in the dark over the mines with a stretcher party to collect the casualty.

We were now well and truly stuck, since we could not go forward or back. We knew not if the enemy were waiting for us on top of the escarpment, but there was no action we could take until the mines were cleared, so we attempted to sleep by the side of the tanks on the gravel of the road.

Some time during the night, I was woken from my uneasy slumber by a New Zealand sapper who prodded the ground where I had lain and passed on with his bayonet, shoving it in at an oblique angle rapidly in front of him as we walked. I would not be a sapper for a million pounds, and I have always thought they must have nerves like steel. We had undergone a course in the defusing of mines, and I had always prayed that I would not be called upon to put my lessons into practice.

With the dawn, Hell Fire Pass was apparently cleared of mines, and the New Zealand gunners hastened to climb the escarpment, passing the damaged tank which was blocking our way by using a narrow lane marked, as was the custom, by white tape. There was scarcely room to squeeze by, and as the first portee approached I stood in front of my tank to prevent the driver from fouling my tank tracks with the nearside wheel of his gun. As the hub narrowly scraped against the track, and I was furiously shouting at the driver, who had pressed away from the dangers marked by the tape, there was a terrific explosion. The wheel of the gun disappeared as a double mine blew it off. I was almost completely deafened. My driver, who had been standing at the rear, was wounded in the face by the sharp gravel blown sideways by the blast. I could scarcely believe I was alive; only the back of my left hand was bleeding.

The spot where the mine had been buried was the exact position where I had slept.

Archer asked me how I was after my narrow escape, to which I replied that I was white and shaking. It was a standard joke between us, but in point of fact not far from the truth on this occasion. I have been deaf in my left ear ever since.

Very soon we got the damaged tank out of our way and slowly we climbed the winding pass on to the flat desert on top of the escarpment, where I had first smelt the almond smell of death.

Again we resumed our pursuit, racing across the desert to the coastal road along the Via Balbia through Tobruk.

The retreating Afrika Korps had selected another rearguard position some miles before Gazala, where the road runs very close to the sea, with a steep rocky escarpment to the south. The leading tank exploded a mine, thereafter holding us up. Captain Dick Hidden, being considered more expert at dealing with these fearsome hazards than most of us, arrived in his tank to cope with the situation. I watched him with my heart in my mouth. He was a great humorist, and I do not know how frightened he was, but he put on a deliberate display of exaggerated terror simply to amuse us. I could not manage even to force a laugh, such was my anxiety, since I doubted if he had ever defused a live Teller mine in his life.

In fact there were only two or three which had been hastily set into the roadway and were clearly visible. As Dick took away the last fuse he kicked the metal discs out of the shallow holes into which they had been placed as a footballer will kick at a ball. It was the most dangerous piece of humour I have ever witnessed.

Just after this incident several German troops appeared from amongst the rocks of the escarpment, where they had been hiding, to give themselves up in surrender. It was lucky for us that they had decided their war was over, because they had been in an excellent position to pick us off as we stood waist-high in our turrets watching Hidden's extraordinary performance.

We had now covered over 400 miles from Alamein, far over the serviceable mileage of our tanks without overhaul, and many had broken down. We withdrew a little way to leaguer for the night close to the shore. The great battle was behind us; we were still alive and still young. The deep blue sea lay tranquil in the silence, and the mauve light of the evening spread over the desert. My thoughts went out to the great horizons of the world and the imponderable future which now seemed so limitless.

However, the following morning, I was quickly jolted out of my relaxed state of mind. The few tanks which remained in good running order were formed into a single squadron, to which I was posted as second-in-command to Major O'Brien. We were to get ready to cross the Cyrenaican desert to Agheila in an attempt to harass the enemy's retreat to Tripolitania. We accepted this order in disbelief, since the tanks were unlikely to last long enough to achieve our objective, and we knew it.

I must admit this sudden task which now presented itself was a bitter blow to me, as I had thoughts of getting back to Cairo after our victory; indeed, as can be imagined, my urgent application for leave had been paramount in my mind for a very long time.

However, almost at the moment of our departure, our orders were cancelled, and we withdrew to El Adem airfield. The following morning, as we were eating our breakfast on the perimeter of the field, the Colonel walked over to our lines. Knowing very well my state of mind and urgent desire, he told me I could go on leave if I could find my way back. Transport Dakotas were taking off regularly with wounded from the battle. In a moment, one of them with engines racing for take-off and its cargo doors open, came almost within a hundred yards of my tank. I raced for it and just managed to clamber aboard before the pilot released his brakes and opened his throttles.

Within two hours we landed at Heliopolis just outside Cairo, from where I got a taxi to Shepheard's Hotel. I was still covered in the dust of the desert, and my bush shirt and trousers were caked with the sweat and dirt of the battle.

I telephoned Brita to send me my decent clothes, which Spiro, the Legation chauffeur, delivered within the hour. After a luxurious bath I was once again in a civilised state, and my appreciation of all the good things in life was sharply heightened by the discomforts and dangers of my recent experience.

Chapter 13

Cairo Life

On the same day that I climbed into the Dakota on El Adem airfield, a great British and American force carried by an armada of 650 ships landed in French North Africa.

At first they were strongly resisted by the Vichy French troops, and fierce fighting took place at Oran and elsewhere. But the sudden invasion of unoccupied France by the Germans, contrary to their agreement with the Vichy government, gave the French Admiral Darlan a chance to turn his coat without, so he thought, losing face. He thereupon ordered the French forces in North Africa to cooperate with the Allies, and the French fleet at Toulon was scuppered on his orders.

Now the Americans had, for the first time since the outbreak of war more than three years before, joined us in an attack on the Axis partners on land.

Rommel was sandwiched between Montgomery's Eighth Army attacking from the east and General Eisenhower's British/American Army from the west; only now did Hitler send him those reinforcements he had begged for five months ago which, had they been supplied then, would have enabled him to conquer Egypt and the whole of the Near East. Instead, he now stood with his back to the sea faced with a hopeless task.

The prize for the Allies was mastery of the whole North African coast, from which to strike at what Churchill had called 'the soft underbelly of the Axis'.

My regiment, now sadly depleted, reassembled in a tented camp near the Sakkara Pyramids, close by a cemetery wherein were buried the mummified remains of those of Mark Antony's Roman legions who had died in Egypt when Cleopatra had graced the throne.

Again we awaited reinforcements of officers, men and tanks.

I was reunited with my old Reo car, which made me independently mobile, as we were not allowed to use Army transport for private purposes. In a nearby village in the green Nile valley I found an Arab entire [stallion] to ride in the early morning, and I rode into Memphis, the ancient city of Egypt, now no more distinctive than any other village in the Delta except for the colossal statue of Rameses II lying on its back with a wooden structure to protect it from the elements. It would indeed have been incongruous if once again it stood erect at full height to look down now on the collection of mud huts, the brackish waters of the canals and the impoverished disease-ridden inhabitants – all that was left of one of the great cities of the ancient world.

After the victory of Alamein, Cairo had quite recovered from its panic; the affair of the black confetti had almost been forgotten, the padlocked boxes were collected from the neutral embassies and valuables recovered from their hasty hiding places. Life resumed its luxurious hothouse atmosphere, but we were not to stay for long, since we were ordered to Cyprus.

The Royal Navy, which had suffered such fearful casualties in the Mediterranean since the beginning of the war, had by now gained mastery of the seas east of Malta, supported by the Royal Air Force, which could operate from secure bases on the North African coast after the victory of Alamein. Therefore our transhipment to Cyprus was uneventful, and we were landed at the port of Larnaca in this ancient British colony, which had harboured the crusaders and Nelson's fleet in years gone by. On a clear day you could see the mountains of Turkey across the blue sea.

A hutted camp at Kokini Trimithia, ten miles from the capital of Nicosia, was ready to receive us. Shortly after our arrival our Colonel came once again to visit us after his conference with the Turkish president at Adana, by which we hoped to bring Turkey into the war, if not actively engaged, at least as a benevolent ally. At this time also, in January 1943, the Germans in Russia suffered their worst defeat yet in Hitler's ill-judged enterprise when Von Paulus' Sixth Army was forced to surrender, and their General and his staff were taken prisoner by the Russians on the outskirts of Stalingrad. For Russia also the tide had turned at last.

Whilst these important events were taking place without our participation, I immediately set about making the best possible use of my time. The Cypriots of Nicosia were horse fanciers. There had been for many years a British government stud on the island supplied with high class stallions to breed from the hardy local ponies, with the result that there were many small horses of high quality in the backyards of farmers, grocers and even laundrymen, who would enter their animals in the local races on the course just outside the capital.

The National Provincial Bank at Holborn Circus sent to Barclays Bank in Nicosia £30 for my first purchase, but subsequently I found another beautiful little horse in the backyard of a laundry. It was a mouthwatering prospect, but when I attempted to purchase it, the Cypriot owner refused, saying he would lend it to me for as long as I should require. It was very high-spirited due to the practice of its owner who, with laughter, would untie it from its stall and encourage it to rear and buck, thereafter turning it loose and, with a stick, driving it over the fence enclosing his yard. When I ventured to sit upon it, it was almost unmanageable due to the fierce bit in its mouth. I had brought with me from Egypt two saddles and several bridles, one of which was a plain, beautifully made racing snaffle. When this was substituted for the savage local contrivance, the animal immediately became more docile. I accepted its owner's offer at once, and Major Harry Cowdell, who was a brilliant horseman and much lighter than I, agreed to ride it the ten miles to Kokini Trimithia, where Trooper Grocock took it into his care. I have never forgotten the wonderful time I had with my two horses riding over the plains of central Cyprus. As the spring arrived and the swallows started their migration to the north, they would surround me as I rode, catching the flies attracted by the horse's sweat.

Douglas Nicoll and John Vaughan also took advantage of the opportunity to acquire horses for our stay in the island, and we had great fun with them. Someone produced a magazine in which an article declared that a fast sprinter on foot could beat a horse over 100yds. We had in the regiment an athlete who could run the distance in ten seconds, and on a sports day it was decided to try out this supposition to see if it was true. My little horse was extremely fast and a quick starter, and at the pistol shot which started the race he nearly left me behind as he rushed off at a gallop. We beat the runner by half the distance, disproving without doubt the theory once and for all; but strangely enough, although there were several competent horsemen in my regiment, I could not take any bets against me. Douglas Nicoll tried out his large rangy animal against mine over a quarter mile with a ten lengths start, with a similar result, although Francis Blackett had declared that you could give away weight but not distance. Perhaps the little horse had capabilities which, alas, I was never to find out.

After a month in Cyprus I was sent on a course for squadron commanders at the tactical school near Gaza in Palestine, not far from Tel Aviv. On my way I put up at the King David Hotel in Jerusalem, where fortunately I ran into an attractive acquaintance, who is now renowned in the Arab world as a great actress and satirist. She had been a talented dancer in the nightclubs of Cairo and at that time went under the unimaginative pseudonym of 'Carioca', by which I understand she is still known.

I have always disliked hypothetical problems and what the Army calls 'tactical exercises without troops', but in the end, and much to my astonishment, I was passed out with an 'A' in every subject, which denoted above average. This was to stand me in good stead afterwards, but I am sure I owe it to Colonel Sheppard, who had a trick on these exercises which was most effective. When asked where he would deploy his troops, or where he would attack, he would never point a finger but would spread his hand in a vague but commanding gesture, so that thereafter no one really knew exactly where his point was. It needed some practice, but once perfected it was extremely impressive.

We did not only ride horses and enjoy ourselves during our stay in Cyprus, since there were many new recruits to train who had never seen action. Our facilities were somewhat limited, however, and we were short of equipment.

After three months or so on this beautiful Mediterranean island we were ordered back to Eygpt, attracted as if by a magnet to our pleasant camp near the Pyramids, where we were fully equipped with the new Sherman tanks armed with their 75mm guns. These were certainly the best weapons we had yet seen and a great advance on the Grant tank, which had the disadvantage that the gun in its sponson could not be traversed more than 80°, being mounted in the hull and not in the turret. The regiment had now also been reinforced to its full strength in officers and men.

Training in gunnery started in earnest in the desert, and I was fascinated with the accuracy of the new weapon, particularly with high explosive shells. Its velocity was not nearly as high as that of the German armour at this time, and its trajectory not flat enough to compete with a Mark IV tank, nevertheless it was a vast improvement, and the turret mechanism was fast and practical. Moreover, it was relatively comfortable after the sharp discomforts of a Mark VI B or a Stuart.

I had sold my old Reo car on leaving for Cyprus and, as it was essential to be mobile in view of the great attraction once more so near to me on the banks of the Nile, I bought an old Buick with wooden wheels. These creaked badly in the considerable heat and had constantly to be kept damp with buckets of water so that the spokes swelled into the sockets in the rim.

Discipline amongst the troops of many nations on leave in Cairo was becoming rather slack, forcing the military governor to call on regiments quartered near to the city to supplement his police with nightly patrols to keep good order. I think we were rather amused with this duty. One night, as I waited with two truckloads of my own regiment at the central police station, an urgent distress call came from the Sweet Melody café: an armed soldier was threatening the whole company of clients with a pistol. We tore round there at high speed through the streets, rather as the American police in a gangster movie of the 1930s. My sergeant and I burst through the swing doors into the dim light of the café.

A soldier sat in the middle of the room, his hand clasped firmly round the butt of a pistol resting on a table. The revellers stood around subdued, with their backs to the wall, gaping at him, but when we approached the man, with a heavy sigh he handed over his weapon and came with us like a lamb to the slaughter.

There were many similar incidents at that time which is hardly surprising. There were French, Polish, Greek, Australian, Cypriot, American, Indian and British troops on leave, with enough money to get well and truly drunk. A graver duty fell to our lot one day when we were ordered to provide a firing party to execute an Indian soldier who had been convicted of the murder of a comrade. I did not volunteer for this unpleasant task.

Two important events happened about this time. I became engaged to be married and was promoted to command my squadron. My existence was now entirely satisfactory. The dirty waters of the Nile looked as blue as the sky, there was surely a smile on the face of the Sphinx and every man was my brother. Meanwhile, my satisfaction at the state of my personal affairs was matched by a turn of events in all theatres of war, from the North Atlantic to the Pacific, which was to spell disaster to the Axis powers and Japan.

By 13 May 1943 all resistance by the Germans and Italians in North Africa had ceased. Field Marshal Rommel flew back to Germany to take over another command facing the English Channel and the white cliffs of Dover. Tens of thousands of prisoners of war were in our hands in barbed wire cages in the deserts from Egypt to Tunisia. General Montgomery invaded Sicily on 10 July, and the Eighth Army landed on the toe of Italy on 3 September, to begin its hard and long campaign towards the Alps. In the Far East the tide of war had turned decisively against the Japanese, and in Burma Admiral Lord Mountbatten was engaged already in effective counter attack. In China General Chiang Kai-shek, aided by the extraordinary American General Stilwell, who commanded the Chinese Fifth and Sixth Armies, was harassing the enemy wherever they were to be found. But there was a long hard fight ahead for all the combatants. Italy surrendered to the Allied command on 8 September after the Salerno landings.

Winston Churchill, Colonel of the Regiment, arrived in Cairo from his conference with Roosevelt and Stalin at Teheran at the beginning of December. He was accommodated in a villa near to Mena House Hotel and within a few miles of our camp; we were honoured to guard him with our tanks. Once again, for the third time in the war, he announced his intention to inspect his regiment.

When the General Staff discovered that we had not been issued with the Africa Star and the Eighth Army clasp, there was something of a panic, which resulted in a team of seamstresses hurriedly arriving in our camp to sew them on. Churchill had always been very insistent that medals should be worn, and I can only suppose that those responsible for the delay feared a blast of wrath if the great man found that his own regiment was parading without the distinction they had earned.

The actual notification to the squadrons was so amusing that I kept my copy, which reads as follows:

Africa Star   Urgent and Immediate

To: Os.C: A, B, C & HQ Sqns.

1. Urgent orders have been received from GHQ that every Officer and Man of the Regiment entitled to the Africa Star shall be wearing this star by 13.00 hours today, Monday 6 Dec. 43.

2. The ribbon will be drawn by the Q.M. this morning and a team of seamstresses is being despatched from GHQ in order to effect the necessary attachment.

3. Seamstresses will be allotted to squadrons on their arrival.

4. Sqns will return to this office IMMEDIATELY the names of all officers and men NOT entitled to the award of the Africa Star.

Signed

A. Downes

Adjt, 4H. Capt.

Churchill was joined at this Mena House Conference, as it came to be known, by President Roosevelt, Chiang Kai-shek and Admiral Lord Louis Mountbatten, whose responsibility it was to defend the Indian sub-continent and to drive the Japanese out of Burma. Together they could plan campaigns against a common enemy on behalf of nearly a thousand million people, excluding mighty Russia; and when one reflects on the colossal potential represented by these few personalities, the folly of the Axis dictators seems unbelievable. In a little while we left for Italy. Sadly I said goodbye to my fiancée, without knowing when we should meet again. Her father had left for Budapest to take up his duties as Swedish Minister in that dangerous capital, and she and her mother intended to leave for Portugal in a neutral ship from Alexandria after my departure.

And so we set sail once again for Europe in the spring of 1944 to land at Taranto where, on 11 November 1940, the gallant pilots of our Fleet Air Arm had launched their attack from HMS *Illustrious* to disable half the Italian fleet for more than six months. It had been sad to leave Cairo, of which I had such happy memories, but exciting to be once again on the Continent. For a week or two we encamped in the olive groves not far from the great port, before thundering north with our powerful Sherman tanks to settle in the hilly country near Altamura, which had such beautiful views across the Adriatic Sea.

The battle fronts stretching across Italy were 150 miles to the north, the Fifth Anglo-American Army on the left and the Eighth Army on the right, facing Field Marshal Kesselring's eighteen German divisions. Bitterly hard fighting continued over ground favouring the German defence.

At Altamura we lived in a tented camp on the spring grass in squadron areas, each squadron having its own officers' mess consisting of a simple,

rather scanty tent. We slept in two-man bivouacs in company with hundreds
of enormous, bright green cicadas, which were so slothful that it was almost
impossible to take a step without crushing them underfoot.

My squadron was a very happy one, and I was lucky enough to have
two of the best troop leaders in the regiment who had joined us after the
battle of Alamein, John Paley and John Strawson; both were to distinguish
themselves shortly and in later years were to command the regiment in
succession to each other.

I was in good company with my friends and, although strenuous training
in this different terrain soon started in earnest, we had many opportunities
to enjoy ourselves in this beautiful country. We went swimming in the clear
waters of the Adriatic at Polignano and visited the urban comforts of Bari.
Dick Hidden, our second captain, decided he would explore the bottom of
the sea with the aid of a home-made diving apparatus, which consisted of
a stirrup pump, originally designed as a fire fighting appliance, ingeniously
attached by a length of rubber pipe to a gas mask. In order to sink him we
tied rocks held in sacks around his waist. But we had forgotten one important
fact, that the outlet of a regulation gas mask consisted of a Bakelite disc
through which one's breath was expelled. Under 20ft of water, of course it
became impossible to do this, because the pressure on the disc was much
greater than the ability of Dick's lungs to exhale. It was very fortunate for
all concerned that he was tied to a lifeline, and when we saw his desperate
gesticulations on the seabed through the crystal clear water we pulled him
up before he finally expired.

On 6 June 1944 Allied forces launched the greatest amphibious invasion
the world has ever known upon the shores of France to strike at the evil
tyranny still dominating Europe, and we heard this news with the greatest
excitement. It was bold in plan but difficult in execution. All the ingenuity
and determination of the British and American people had been employed
to the full over many months to bring it about. It was stupendous in concept,
and even the inscrutable Russian dictator could scarcely believe it could be
done. But it was. And of course the victor of Alamein was there, unhurried,
steely and as abstemious as ever. I do not think any of us now doubted the
final outcome, but there was yet a long way to go and many more desperate
battles to fight, even though the ring of steel was closing in upon the German
nation.

I could not help but reflect at this time on the incredible efficiency of the German Army. On all sides they were outnumbered and overpowered by their enemies, yet almost a year was to go by before their surrender. Under a balanced leadership what could they not have accomplished in a purely military sense? And how was it that the German people had fallen under the spell of the little corporal with the Charlie Chaplin moustache, whose very oratory and gestures would have been an anathema to the British? What a fearful waste of talent it was.

Whilst we were thus relatively unemployed at Altamura, Churchill had written to General Ismay, the Secretary of the Imperial Defence Chiefs of Staff Committee: 'In any case it must be considered a most important objective to get a footing on the Dalmatian coast, so that we can foment the insurgents of Albania and Yugoslavia by weapons supplies and possibly commandos.'

This had not yet come about, except on the offshore island of Vis, and an attack in June on the island of Brac had been repulsed by the German garrison. Tito, the communist insurgent leader, had been promised a brigade of tanks, and a friend of mine at '37' Military Mission, the organization set up in Bari to implement Churchill's intention, asked me if I would join in the role of advisor on armoured warfare to the Yugoslav National Army of Liberation.

I was very reluctant to leave my regiment, which I had served almost continuously for four years; indeed, I think there were only three of us left of the original complement of officers who had sailed from Merseyside in 1940. But now I was faced with a familiar difficulty.

Before the Battle of Alan Halfa, Colonel Sheppard had been promoted and replaced by Colonel Kidd. Unfortunately we did not get on. I thought him indecisive and vacillating. Moreover, he was apparently wedded to the idea of maximum dispersal, whereas practice had taught me that concentration was essential to the effective use of so small a force as a squadron, particularly as communication from one tank to another was still so uncertain even at this stage of the war.

I had also become absurdly possessive of my regiment and I resented a commanding officer who did not identify himself with his new command sufficiently even to change the buttons on his tunic for the distinctive cherry-shaped ones of the 4th Hussars.

I was so upset by this situation that I even considered a trial of strength to be judged by higher authority, but the result would certainly have gone against me. I was an amateur and I was bound to lose against a professional, so with a heavy heart I accepted the invitation to go to Yugoslavia, and Trooper Brash decided to come with me.

Sergeant Major Hoyle presented me with a cigarette case inscribed by the sergeants of my squadron which touched me deeply. So Brash and I left for another adventure, which was to last almost to the very end of the war.

Part III

Chapter 14

Introduction to the Partisans

The Italian barracks at Gravina were built long ago on top of a hill overlooking the surrounding countryside of Southern Italy. The central block, a building four storeys high, looked more like a prison than a barracks, with symmetrical rows of rectangular windows. The whole structure was surrounded by a high wall built of hard grey stone. A dusty road led up the hill into the barrack square through forbidding grey stone pillars.

Trooper Brash drove the jeep into the square and shut off the engine. We were covered in dust. I got out and made for the huge doorway in the central block. Inside the building, the corridors rang with my footsteps. It was depressing. Suddenly a door slammed and a soldier appeared with a red star in his forage cap. He stood still in uncertainty, but when I called to him and asked to see his officer, he suddenly came to attention with a tremendous rattle, which resounded through the whole building, and beckoned me to follow him. We marched in step down the seemingly endless corridor, then my escort stopped before a double doorway, at which he motioned me to wait and diffidently opened it to disappear inside. A moment later, the door was flung open and I was invited to enter. The large room was full of Yugoslav partisan officers, the smell of garlic and thick tobacco smoke. I felt curious looks and knew I was being examined from head to foot.

I introduced myself as an officer of the Queen's Own Hussars sent by '37' Military Mission to teach them the art of armoured warfare and to help them to equip an armoured regiment. Here in Gravina were assembled hand-picked partisans, got out of occupied territory by various means to form a regiment of Stuart tanks. It was an improbable and ambitious undertaking at the outset, and Stuart tanks with 37mm gun were in any case out of date against German armour in the autumn of 1944.

My reception was lukewarm, the whole atmosphere heavy with suspicion and I felt homesick for the friendship of my regiment.

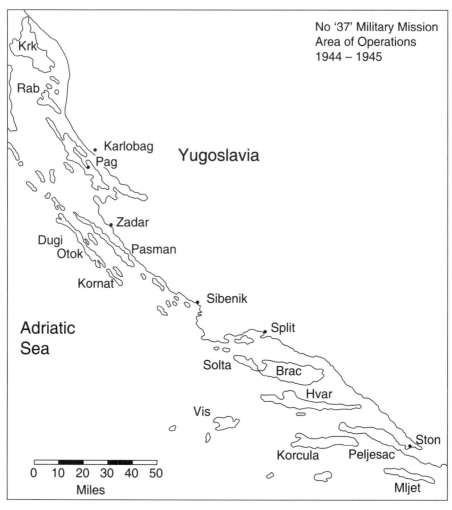

4. No 37 Military Mission Area of Operations, 1944–1945

During the next weeks I struggled single-handed in my bare barrack room with indent forms for equipment, tanks, guns, spares, ammunition, echelons and all the items which would make up a full complement for an armoured regiment. I doubted if even half the stuff was available. Every morning, I would lecture on tactics through an interpreter. It became clear, through many questions and answers, that nearly all the partisans had taken part in guerrilla fighting, with automatic weapons, rifles and grenades. Their success in this type of warfare had rather gone to their heads, perhaps with some justification, but I doubted if their experience would allow them to take kindly to the discipline necessary to the employment of a regiment in action.

One afternoon, as I was struggling rather hopelessly with the wretched indent forms, clouds gathered over Gravina. I looked out of my window at the bleak barrack square. The day became as night, the sky black with the approaching storm which broke with tremendous thunder and lightning, the like of which I had never seen before or since. The storm had the effect of jolting me into reality. This was an ill conceived idea. I wrote out a report which said that it would take at least twelve months to train and equip the partisans as an effective armoured regiment.

The very next day, Trooper Brash drove me to '37' Mission Headquarters in Bari, where I presented my report to Brigadier Fitzroy Maclean, Churchill's appointed envoy to Tito and head of the Mission. He showed no surprise, saying he would take it with him the following day when he was to meet Churchill in North Africa to consider future policy in Yugoslavia.

I sighed with relief, which, however, turned out to be very short-lived, for a few days later, I found myself on board the *Empire Roach*, an ancient cargo vessel bound for the island of Vis with twenty of the outdated Stuart tanks and their untrained partisan crews on the decks and in the hold. We sailed from Bari at night to avoid attack.

The hold of the vessel stank from years of filthy cargo and the sweat of unwashed bodies. At midnight we ate all together from rough tables erected in one of the holds, where I found myself sitting next to a youth whose age I guessed at seventeen. He had two medals hung on ribbons on his tunic, of which he was obviously very proud, and a large automatic in a leather holster was strung around his armpit. I must confess I was not impressed with the company, and I longed for the fresh face of Squadron Sergeant Major Hoyle and his forthright, down-to-earth character. I had been a regimental soldier too long to welcome this violent change.

At this time in 1944 Tito had a headquarters in Vis, which was heavily defended by partisans, British Commandos and the Royal Air Force. Otherwise the whole of the Dalmatian and Yugoslav hinterlands were fully occupied by the German Army. Tito and his Chief of Staff, Arso Jovanovic, later killed by his own countrymen [while trying to escape into Romania, having openly sided with the USSR], had their headquarters in a cave on the island. '37' Military Mission occupied a large villa on the eastern side, overlooking a small but beautiful bay of clear water. Lieutenant Colonel Vivian Street of the 60th Rifles and John Clark and Andrew Maxwell, both of the Scots Guards, were running this cloak and dagger outfit. The villa was staffed by local residents, all in khaki battledress, both male and female. It was remarkably comfortable. The food was excellent and the wine and spirits plentiful. Nevertheless, I had an uneasy feeling.

The atmosphere on the island was oppressive. Relations between the partisans and the Allies were clouded with suspicion. We had been aiding and abetting the Četniks led by Mihajlovic, formally Chief of Staff of the Royal Yugoslav Army. The Četnik movement was Orthodox Serb in its origin and its dream was the creation of a Greater Serbia. It was an ancient, militant organization, and its hatred of the Croats was traditional. Since Tito, the partisan leader, was a Croat and communist, there could never be any reconciliation, even in the face of the invader. The local Četnik commander was an Orthodox priest called Gjujic, and he was still holding out in the Knin region with his ragged and desperate followers.

The British government had changed horses when they found that the Četniks were less effective in opposing the common enemy than Tito's communist partisans, and in this they were correct. Tito was hunting down the Četniks with as much vigour as he applied to the foreign invader.

Moreover, yet another force had to be reckoned with. The Italians had earlier set up an independent state of Croatia under Ante Pavelic, whose policy of survival was to throw in his lot with the Germans. He was now assisted by the Ustaše, a dreaded corps of Croat thugs organized on similar lines to the German SS. There was therefore a most complex situation throughout the whole of Yugoslavia.

It is a small wonder that Tito and his friends were not only looking over their shoulders but under the table as well. Tito had a clear idea of what he wanted after the war; he was determined not to get involved more than necessary with the Allies and was fearful of Russian influence; and he wanted a clear field to deal with his internal situation.

On arrival on Vis I wondered how it was that the German command did not attack the island, which lay so close to the mainland. Certainly, they could have done so successfully, but at the cost of heavy losses because we had command of the sea and the air and also the means of receiving an early warning. Tito and his small staff would have been evacuated by air within half an hour, and the entire garrison could have got away within a very short space of time by sea. The Balkan Air Force would have bombed the attacking force mercilessly from their close Italian bases near Bari, and an occupation of the island would have been untenable unless the Germans were prepared to turn it rapidly into a fortress. They had not the means to do so at this stage of the war, so we were left in peace.

Life at the villa was totally unreal. The sun shone down on our beautiful private bay with its white sandy beach. We ate, drank, slept, sunbathed and swam. Our communist servants were professional in their attendance. Trooper Brash had a holiday in the sun and even got someone to clean his boots. He had been a postman at Aldershot after years spent wandering about Australia. He was forty at this time and had a fine set of false teeth. He had volunteered to come with me, and when I had told him we might have to parachute somewhere he had merely shrugged his shoulders.

After a week or two of this uneasy holiday it became clear to me that I had lost my out-of-date tanks. I borrowed a grey pony from the partisan headquarters. The island was rocky, but cultivated with vineyards. It was hot, and inland the horseflies were a pest, clustering about the pony's head and ears. The roads, few as they were, were dusty, and the vineyards walled in by grey stone. One day, I came upon an overgrown cemetery wherein were buried some of Nelson's sailors from the Battle of the Nile. Some fresh mounds covered several of our troops and airmen killed recently in the abortive attack on the nearby island of Brac. One hundred and forty years separated the burials. In the early part of the nineteenth century we had occupied the island for a number of years for purposes of transit trade to Central Europe, and now again it was occupied by British troops, with ships of the Royal Navy resting once more at anchor in the port.

I made myself known to the partisan formation commanders. The General commanding the 26th Dalmatian Division was a Montenegrin, Bozo Bozovic. He was still in his thirties, tall and thin, with a perpetual stoop, a sallow, unhealthy complexion, and looking as if he was weighed down with sorrow and anxiety. I soon found out his appearance was very deceptive.

The 26th Division was at this time the crack formation of the Yugoslav Partisan Army. Apart from a few mortars, their armament consisted entirely of infantry weapons, the most prized being the German Schmeisser, a beautifully effective automatic with a range of 300yds at a very high velocity and considered a much better and handier weapon than anything we had given them. They had at this time no artillery.

All formation commanders, down to platoon level, had political commissars at their elbow to see that they did not stray from the narrow path of communist doctrine by word or deed. I was introduced to the Commissar of the 26th Division. He was a heavy man of middle age with black hair and a black moustache, a caricature of Stalin, whom I think he knew he resembled. A copy of Karl Marx was always on the trestle table which served as his desk. To an Englishman the whole set-up was intensely strange. A strict moral code was in force which prohibited the sexes from behaving naturally, and there were few smiles and no jollity whatever. To some extent this sort of discipline was justified, as there were quite a lot of young women in the formations and during the periods of guerrilla fighting the sexes slept side by side in the woods, among the rocks or in the villages.

I had been nearly three weeks on the island by this time, during which time no one appeared to be doing anything and no orders came from Italy. We had a few visits from Tito's headquarters on matters of parachute supply drops to the formations on the mainland and the islands. A typical request was received from a partisan commander called Nandi, operating a group on the island of Krk, not far from Pola; in his own words, which he sent in English, this read as follows:

Flour 600 kilos

Meat 250 kilos

Rice 150 kilos

Dehydrated Potatoes 80 kilos

Grease 25 kilos

Salt 25 kilos

Sugar 15 kilos

Coffee 3 kilos

Underclothes for 60 men

Shoes with rubber soles 20

Trousers 20

Jackets 20

To amuse ourselves we tried out the latest underwater equipment in the bay and practised with the Schmeisser, but this curious state of affairs was not to last for much longer.

Chapter 15

The Battle for Brac

One sunny morning, as we were taking our leisurely aperitif on the stone-flagged balcony of the villa, a messenger arrived from General Bozovic. He wanted to see me. I had a good lunch and set out on foot for his headquarters. His tent was crowded with partisan officers and their commissars. Bozovic spoke no English, but we had exchanged words previously in bad German. An interpreter introduced himself, telling me they intended to attack Brac within two days and asking what we could do to help.

Brac is one of the larger islands off the coast of Dalmatia, lying only a few miles off the mainland and dominating the approaches to the town of Split, the most important harbour on the Yugoslav Adriatic seaboard. It had been heavily garrisoned by the Germans since their occupation of the country and, indeed, it had to be, as even medium artillery could find the range on to the mainland. It is true that this could, of course, work both ways. A concerted attack on the island in June by partisans and our No. 2 Commando had been disastrous and was repulsed by the Germans with heavy casualties on both sides. (I was informed by Admiral Morgan Giles twenty-six years later that this disastrous attack on Brac was designed to mislead the Germans into thinking that a major Allied attack on the coastline was imminent.)

The island is about 15 miles long by 8 miles wide and contains four small fishing ports, the largest of which is Supetar, facing Split to the north. Sumartin lies at the eastern extremity, with Selca close by and Bol to the west. In the centre of the island is the town of Nerezisce, on high ground, which was the main German position, heavily protected by anti-personnel minefields which had caused such havoc amongst the commandos in the June attack before they were finally driven off.

I asked Bozovic for his operation order. He looked at me with a puzzled and offended expression. It was clear he had nothing in writing and had no intention of putting anything on paper, but he outlined his intentions.

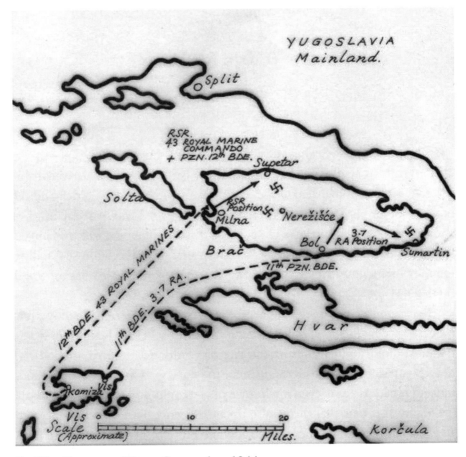

5. The Capture of Brac, September 1944

He was to land his 12th Brigade on a sandy beach in the channel between Solta and Brac; the 1st Brigade would land near to Bol and advance as quickly as possible during the night to cut the road between the garrisons at Nerezisce and deploy in an attempt to isolate the enemy's forces [The author's map incorrectly labels 1st Partisan Brigade's route as '11 Bde']. The 12th Brigade were to march during the night on to the hills above Supetar and were to attack and take the port as soon as possible. He asked if we could send in the Commando Regiment to take the beachhead in front of the landing of the 12th Brigade. He did not think there would be any opposition but wanted to be sure of a quiet reception to take in his men and land six of his Stuart tanks.

My heart sank. I wished the wretched things at the bottom of the sea, as the terrain of the islands, with their fierce rocky outcrops and few roads, made tanks less effective in my opinion than a dozen good riflemen. However, as they had been a gift from his generous allies, I felt I could hardly point out that the tracks would be torn off by the rocks, that the 37mm guns could not penetrate more than a few inches of concrete and that the telescopic gunsights had long ago become opaque with age. However, his plan was at least wonderfully uncomplicated. He estimated the enemy's strength at not more than 3,000 men, concentrated at Nerezisce, Sumartin and Supetar, and said their morale was low.

I left, wondering how on earth I could present this sketchy plan to Headquarters Land Forces Adriatic. Brigadier George Davey, a distinguished 3rd Hussar officer, commanded this formation, which had authority over all the ground forces in the northern Adriatic. He had no headquarters on Vis but was established on the Italian mainland. He in turn was subject to the overall command of the Balkan Air Force, under Air Vice-Marshal Mills and his Chief of Staff, Air Commodore Laurence Sinclair.

I returned to the villa to compose a signal of our intention, to which I expected later that night an emphatic 'No'. Much to my surprise I was told to go ahead provided there was a reasonable chance of success.

I suddenly realized that my appointment as advisor on armoured warfare to the Yugoslav Army of National Liberation had ceased and that I had now become the self-appointed Liaison Officer to the 26th Dalmatian Division. As I had taken it upon myself, I was stuck with it.

Early the next morning, I set out to try to sell my operation, as I had mentally called it, to the prospective participants. My first call was on the Commanding Officer of the 43rd Royal Marine Commando. He had overnight received orders to cooperate, but I had a rather cool and critical reception. However, he agreed in the end to embark his troops for Brac and to attempt a safe beachhead for the partisan landing at the appointed zero hour.

My next sale was much more easily effected. Captain Dizzy Ross of the Raiding Support Regiment had four beautiful little American 75mm Pack Howitzers, which could be taken apart, carried piecemeal by hand anywhere, put on mules or in jeeps and reassembled within minutes. He was very enthusiastic, falling in with the plan without question.

The Royal Artillery willingly agreed to hold themselves in readiness with a troop of 3.7 converted AA guns, which had a long range with high explosive shells. The Royal Navy would cover the sea voyage, with four MLs (Fairmile Motor Launch of 114ft) with Oerlikon guns mounted in the bows and Marlin machine guns on the bridge. They also agreed to land me with the headquarters of the Partisan 12th Brigade as well as the whole 43rd Marine Commando in LCTs (Landing Craft Tank).

It proved extremely difficult to get any firm timetable for the operation from General Bozovic. The whole proposal was so amateur that it frightened me to death. However, I wrote out an operation order as best I could.

The opposing forces were orthodox divisions of the German Army. The Devil's Division occupied Split and elements were on garrison duty on Brac. The 369th and 118th were north and south of the Devil's Division along the coastline, with garrisons on the islands. This was not quite as ominous as it sounds, as the rank and file were not all first class troops. A considerable number of Russian ex-PoWs were included, who were hated and feared by the partisans and were all volunteers, preferring life in the army of their enemies to imprisonment. When off duty they had perpetrated many crimes of violence, rape and murder. These divisions were staffed by SS officers and NCOs. Information about the enemy was precise, and the names of the enemy commanders even down to company level could be obtained.

I considered that the danger to the success of the operation lay in the enemy's ability to reinforce their Brac garrison during darkness; or that they would make our position untenable by shellfire, as it was known they had 210mm artillery in the coastal batteries. However, the latter threat would be hampered, in the event of our initial success, because they would be firing blind unless they had some means of observation, which we had to deny. The rocky outcrops on the island were so marked as to make cover against random shellfire very effective.

At last light the following evening I got aboard the LCT with my two signallers, their heavy radio set, the Partisan Brigade Commander and a company of depressing looking communists with their red stars, Schmeissers and Bren guns. There was a heavy swell, and within the hour my two signallers were badly seasick. During the night the partisans started cooking fish on a primus stove in the well of the LCT which made matters worse, and I myself began to feel squeamish.

As the hours went by I prayed that the 43rd Commando had got ahead of us and had established a beachhead. The troops were singing quietly, with that very high quality I got to know so well. The singing was nearly always led by a tenor voice. There was a Moorish strain in the songs, and I think the lead singers were Serbs or Montenegrins. This community singing was very much a part of the partisan psychology. Later on, in the north, I was to find it highly developed but more Slav in character.

The night was very black and we could see little, but the navigator knew well his own coastline and the islands. In the small hours we landed without a sound. No opposition, no lights, not a shot fired. The LCT ran gently on to the beach and the ramp was let down. No word was spoken. There was only the sound of metal as weapon touched weapon and boots hit the ramp. We were quietly and quickly ashore.

There was no sign of the Marine Commando, and the Brigade Commander turned to me with an unspoken question. A moment later, I almost collided with a blackened face under a familiar 'cap comforter' (a woollen cap worn by British commandos). A sergeant of the Commandos whispered that they were ashore without incident and his Colonel wanted to see me. McAlpine had his men spread out to cover the partisan landing.

The 12th Brigade intended to march overnight to attack Supetar, and I had asked the Commandos to march on a given centre line to take Nerezisce. This centre line was precise to avoid any clash with the partisan forces during the night, but McAlpine was not at all happy with the situation. He told me that, shortly after landing, local inhabitants had said that the fortress had been heavily reinforced from the mainland, and he feared a worse fate than No. 2 Commando had experienced in June.

I hastily conferred with the Brigade Commander, who assured me that Nerezisce could easily be taken, insisting that the locals' information was false. However, McAlpine was not convinced. This conference was held in the dark, and there was not time to sit round a table or to verify any information. Much to my surprise and relief, the Partisan Commander eventually shrugged his shoulders, telling me that in any event he would march overnight on Supetar. So we set off.

In the darkness I could see here and there, as I walked forward, the prone figures of the commandos, their faces blackened, their feet in rubber soled shoes, their weapons at the ready. Suddenly I felt a hand in mine. I looked down and saw a little girl with long hair. She had taken my hand in hers and was leading me, in the wake of the partisans, through the blackness of the night by a scarcely perceptible path. The situation seemed utterly unreal. Following us were my two signallers, whose morale had been sapped by sea sickness, their bulky radio carried by partisans on an improvised stretcher. Presently my delightful little guide slipped away into the dark, like a will-o'-the-wisp.

We travelled through the night over a rocky and rough terrain, sometimes by paths, more often over rock-strewn scrub, until at last, still in the darkness, a halt was called. By this time one of my signallers was nearly in tears through seasickness, fatigue and fear. I told them both to set up the radio and get into contact at once with the Commandos and, essentially, the Raiding Support Regiment, which I hoped had landed safely. An hour later, just before dawn, I was told the set would not work at all; my communications had therefore completely broken down. I sent off two runners to find the guns at all costs, giving my position by a map reference which I prayed was correct, because I was not able to work it out with any great certainty after our cross-country march in the dark.

Dawn broke and the sun rose over the horizon. I felt a passenger in the forthcoming conflict. As the light increased, there below us, at not more than 1,000yds distance, lay the enemy, entrenched in the garrison of Supetar. I would at that moment have given anything for one Sherman tank with its low velocity 75mm gun. My total armament was one regulation Webley revolver. I felt shamed by failure. There was little I could do but sit on a rock hoping that the two runners I had sent off would find Dizzy Ross and his little guns.

The infantry had deployed for the attack shortly before dawn. At first light firing broke out. There was no sign of movement from the garrison, the stone buildings affording good cover for the defenders. We stood behind a stone wall on high ground overlooking the scene of battle.

When I was at the point of despair, one of the runners I had sent arrived with a hastily written message from Lieutenant Phillips, the Raiding Support Regiment's second-in-command. It read:

'I am in position and ready to fire on anyone's direction or off the map if necessary.'

I have the original message still. It was dramatic under those circumstances, but it was of little avail without communications. As Phillips had signed the message, I thought his commanding officer had probably set out to try to find us; therefore I sent off two more runners to search for him.

Below our vantage point, increased firing broke out. Shellfire began to bracket our position and mortars splattered the forward slope. I began to fear that the infantry would not take the port unaided.

I turned in the sunshine to see the tall, thin figure of Major Ross, his hand on the bridle of a mule laden with his radio and accompanied by the runners I had sent. He was a languid young man. His unhurried speech and deliberate movements gave an impression of great self-confidence. He wore a Victorian military moustache.

'Well', he said, 'What do you want me to do?'

Before him was a gunner's dream. His able second-in-command had his guns ready to fire, well positioned and protected by the Commandos. I asked him if he had the range, as I feared the distance was too much for the short-barrelled howitzers. He reassured me with a nod. We waited for the sighting shot, which landed well out to sea beyond the port, and very soon the town was bracketed.

The Brigade Commander could scarcely conceal his excitement as he stood beside Ross, pointing out the targets one by one as his men advanced; we could see the infantry darting from cover to cover, closing in.

The enemy shore batteries inexplicably fell silent, and only spasmodic mortar and machine gun fire came from the garrison. The howitzers were doing deadly work with pinpoint accuracy and, as the sun rose higher, it became plain that the garrison could not stand the accurate shellfire for much longer. Sure enough, at midday we could see scraps of white cloth stuck out of the windows of some of the buildings. In a moment, it seemed, the firing ceased and the partisans were inside the town. The garrison, or what was left of it, surrendered. Columns of sad grey figures emerged, their hands on their heads, escorted by the jubilant partisans.

Suddenly we saw, in the valley behind us, a column of the 1st Brigade moving up the road to attack Sumartin. The familiar sound of aircraft cannon made me look up. There were four Spitfires diving down the road firing on our own troops, who were scattering to right and left for cover in the scrub. Shouting for a Verey pistol I ran down the hill firing cartridge after cartridge into the air in a hopeless protest. I do not think much damage was done by the aircraft, and they were gone in a moment. I later learnt, after my furious report to Balkan Air Force, that the Spitfires were piloted by Yugoslavs, who had mistaken their own 1st Brigade for German troops of the Nerezisce garrison evacuating their positions.

Everyone was elated at the success of the attack. The Partisan Commander asked us to go down to the port to inspect the results of the action, but we declined because at this time I was not at all sure that the Geneva Convention would be observed as regards the treatment of prisoners. Both sides were capable of anything in this theatre of war, and my fears were later confirmed. This was not the gentlemanly war of the Western Desert. Many of the combatants were known to each other personally by name and were marked men before the battle commenced. The Germans and Italians had occupied Yugoslavia for nearly four years, and the partisans had many scores to settle.

We were tired and hungry after 24 hours with no food or sleep. The partisans carried their rations in their pockets and could exist for days under these conditions on dried figs and raisins. We held a council as to what next to do. The 12th Brigade was to leave a garrison in Supetar, moving the remainder of its force to attack Sumartin. I asked Ross to get ready to support the next operation, sending a signal by runner to McAlpine and his Commandos that we proposed to move and asking him to transmit my news on his radio to headquarters in Bari and Vis. The Commandos had been right out of the action, but at least they provided a reserve force and a sense of security at the beachhead. McAlpine's reply came back by runner and read as follows:

> Your signal for air support on Sumartin passed Vis immediately on receipt. Information Supetar clear of enemy also passed and enemy strength Sumartin. It is imperative that I contact Partisan Commander. Understand you are moving up to Sumartin. Urgently request that you contact us at your present headquarters. I am leaving immediately upon assumption that is possible. Inform partisans that I consider counter attack still possible and in this matter consider protection from the west imperative. Will not move until contact with you or responsible partisan officer has been made and preferably both so that mutual understanding is established. Partisans refuse mules for our supplies and long carry over hard country. Our boots are in a sad state. I have no information of any

partisan reinforcements at Bol or south of Brac and do not know total partisan forces in Brac at present moment, or if it is their intention to reinforce, and if so in what strength.

Signed

Ian McAlpine Lt. Col.

This uneasy signal meant that I had to return to the beachhead to reassure the commandos that all was well. Ross had also to go back to find out the state of his troop, what ammunition he had left and how to carry it across the island to new positions for the attack on Sumartin.

Ross and I set off back down the way I had come the previous night. We were accompanied by the mule and his escort and my two signallers, whom I had determined to get rid of at the first opportunity. I doubt if we looked like an efficient military party.

The date was 14 September 1944. The day was fine, the sun shone, and as we marched back we could enjoy the island scenery for the first time without the anxiety of the night. I determined to have a swim as soon as we got back to the beachhead. Our hunger became painful, saliva gathering in our mouths at the prospect of food. As we passed through the village of Sutivan, which I had not seen during the night march, we were almost pulled into a cottage and invited to a meal and wine. There was a white cloth spread upon the table, and the whole household waited upon us until we were well and truly fed. The lavish hospitality was almost embarrassing. During the next eight months I was always sure of the same treatment. If the communists were suspicious of the British, the civilian population were certainly not. Our reception by these simple peasant people was touching, and I wondered what the future would bring for them.

We arrived at the beachhead of the previous night. The Commandos were mostly stripped to the waist, enjoying the sunshine and the scenery, the tensions of the night having vanished. Behind the battery there was a pile of spent shell cases, and the crews were draped about the gunsite in relaxed satisfaction at their success. Ian McAlpine himself was somewhat mollified and less tense, but I shared his reasonable anxiety that there might be a counter-attack, either from the mainland or from Solta, so very near across the sparkling water. The 12th Brigade Commander had agreed that the Commandos should remain in reserve against such an eventuality. Ross busied himself with his guns, and I agreed to join him within the hour for our journey overland towards Sumartin.

Feeling tired and dirty I set off to find a secluded place to relax and have a swim. The island scenery is as beautiful as any to be found in the world. Brac is famous for its white stone, which is so fine that it has been used since Roman times for the sculpture of monuments. The natural rocks jutting out into the clear waters had a beauty of their own. I found a small cove hidden away by an orchard of olive trees. The swell from the night had subsided into a flat calm. The cove was deserted, and the war might have been a thousand miles away. As I plunged into the inviting clear water, the splash seemed to resound over the stillness, and I wondered if a far-ranging bullet from Solta might join me. But nothing moved. It was a great temptation to stay there indefinitely.

By dusk I was passing the infamous Nerezisce in Ross's jeep loaded with 75mm ammunition. The town was sited on a rounded hill, forming a natural defensive position, and it would have been impossible to approach it except by climbing the gently sloping sides. The perimeter was a mass of barbed wire, and the slopes had been sown with anti-personnel mines. Now it was empty, for the garrison had evacuated immediately upon our landing, having got away to Sumartin before the arrival of the 1st Brigade astride the road.

Not many months before, a young British Commando officer had by some means got ashore on Brac from Vis. Sheltered by the villagers, he had gained entry in civilian clothes into the garrison and eventually into the very house occupied by the Garrison Commander, whom he had shot as the wretched man had sat at his desk, late into the night. The young officer escaped and was awarded the MC. I could not approve of this action, which in my opinion was not justifiable warfare. Twenty men of the village had been taken out the next day and executed as a reprisal. It was a bad bargain, having no effect on the course of the war.

By dusk we approached the hills overlooking Sumartin. The 12th Brigade were marching up the road from Supetar. The 1st Brigade had already deployed for the attack, their rear echelons bivouacked on each side of the road. Many young women were in the Signal Corps, which manned the few dozen telephone sets and lines, most of which had been captured from the enemy. They were dressed in drab blouses and skirts and wore the inevitable forage cap with the red star on their heads. They were mostly Dalmatians of Italian origin and were extremely good looking, being careful of their appearance even under these circumstances. I had not seen uniformed women anywhere near the front line in all the years of the war and I was disconcerted that they should be so employed. This may sound odd today, but events proved that when there were casualties amongst the women, the demoralizing effect on the troops was so marked as to make their employment in this role at any rate a liability.

In the gathering dusk we came upon the four long barrels of the Royal Artillery's 3.7s. Here they were, all according to the hasty operation order I had concocted two days previously, protected by a company of the Highland Light Infantry. I had hardly dared hope that it would work out so precisely according to plan. They had just arrived, having followed up the 1st Brigade along the road from Bol. The gun trails had just been put down and the men were busily engaged about the gunsite. The Raiding Support Regiment came up the road right behind us, and Ross dispersed them amongst the scrub.

The Artillery Commander was anxious to have his targets, so I set off to partisan headquarters to find out what plans were now afoot. Bozovic had established himself in a cottage not far away. His disconcerting appearance was even worse in the light of the fire which burned upon the raised hearth. Upon seeing me he put his head on one side, rolling his eyes and saying in German, 'Ich bin krank.' He held his stomach with both hands in an appealing gesture. The cottage was full of woodsmoke from the fire and was crowded with partisans; the night had become chill, and everyone pressed round for warmth and comfort.

I told him that we now had eight guns in position and the Commandos were still available if required against a counter-attack. He introduced me to a tall young officer of about my own age who spoke French, assigning to him the task of coordinating artillery fire with the infantry.

The Nerezisce garrison were by now joined by the defenders of Sumartin. It was clear that the Germans wanted to evacuate Brac in the face of the attack, but the paranoiac in Berchtesgaden had decreed that all should stand fast, and our intention was to seek and destroy the enemy wherever he was to be found. Bozovic meant to attack with the 1st Brigade during the night. We had no sight of the defences during the closing light of dusk, and I could not foresee that the guns would be effective before dawn. I left to establish myself with the artillery and to find a safe place for a few hours sleep, siting my headquarters behind a wall with good solid stones as an overhang. The partisans ran a telephone line to this position with the instrument to my hand, and soon I fell sound asleep, enjoying a delightful dream totally unconnected with war.

I was rudely awoken by Ross standing above me in the dark. He said the partisans were nervous, telling him that the Germans had reinforced Sumartin and were counter-attacking. He asked what he should do. It was a dark night and we could not see more than a hundred yards. I told him to get his battery ready for a quick getaway, back down the road to the 43rd Commando position. The heavy artillery was much more of a problem, but I decided to put them into a state of alert. These were big guns designed for anti-aircraft defence and were cumbersome and unwieldy on the rough dirt roads. Meanwhile, Ross got his men out to vantage points to give us warning of any hostile action which might threaten our position.

Sporadic firing went on during the remaining hours of darkness, but my telephone was silent as we waited tensely for the dawn. As soon as there was enough light I went over to Bozovic's headquarters. He looked even worse than before. There was a sorry tale to tell. Two companies of the 1st Brigade, believing the Germans were counter-attacking, had mistaken each other for the enemy and had fought it out with considerable casualties. He gave me a roughly drawn map of Sumartin with enemy positions marked by a cross. The Germans had three pieces of artillery in the town. He wanted our guns to shell all the positions marked and asked if I could get bombing support from the Balkan Air Force.

I hurried back to the gunsite, where Ross and I conferred, calling in the Royal Artillery Commander. I told them the partisans wanted the enemy shelled to pieces and that there was to be no attack by infantry during the day after the fearful fiasco of the night, so they would have a clear field of fire.

The bombardier of the 3.7s, a little rotund warrant officer, set up his plotting board. He marked the targets from my map, and soon the long barrels were recoiling, their trails jumping, and morale soared at the reassuring sound of our gunfire. My headquarters on Vis had sent me another signaller, who had come over with the Highland Light Infantry company. He had with him a small radio transmitter in what looked like a suitcase which worked only on key (Morse code) and could reach Balkan Air Force in Italy. I decided to go forward to get a better view of Sumartin and work out some accurate map references for our bombers. My signaller and I set off down the hill road and, seeing a pinewood to the left, we moved over to it, creeping through the trees to its edge. Down below lay the town and the port. It was very beautiful. It was heartbreaking to think that our task was to destroy it, and I wondered what the wretched civilians were doing and what cover they had for the women and children. I got out my map and began to mark out the town. Suddenly the crack of mortars was all about us. Shells were hitting the pine trees above our heads, and I realized suddenly I had committed an unforgiveable sin. We were on a forward slope and had been seen. My signaller was hit in the chest by a mortar fragment. We struggled back to the gunsite, and I got the wounded man behind my wall under the rock overhang. The mortar fragment had cut away the nipple from the left side of his chest but had not penetrated his body, and he said he could continue to man his radio.

By this time Ross had got two of his Pack Howitzers in action and the gunfire was deafening.

An hour later, there was a tremendous explosion as a heavy shell from the German batteries in the mainland landed behind us. It seemed to me that we were now really in for trouble. I waited for the bracket to fall, but nothing happened. It was like waiting for the man upstairs to throw down his other boot on the floor. As the day grew older, we realized that this was a random shot. I could not see how the mainland batteries could find us without observation. The range was eight miles, and inaccurate fire might have fallen into their own positions; nor did they want to waste scarce shells simply at random. Unfortunately, a few shells the following day killed some of our men at the gunsite, but at no time during the operation were the shore batteries a real hazard to our success.

Bozovic determined to attack that night, 15/16 September, with a concerted effort by both the 1st and 12th Brigades.

The little town withstood our shellfire with great fortitude. The buildings were solidly constructed of stone, and the relatively small calibre guns made little impression on the thick walls. Not a single fire was started, or if it was, it was quickly extinguished. A German garrison under pressure proved hard to dislodge. I wondered what the poor devils were thinking, besieged so far from their homeland in such a desperate situation. The myth of German invincibility had been broken, first by our victories in the Western Desert, then at Stalingrad and now in Normandy; and even here in the small, remote island of Brac, death and destruction faced them. I knew nothing of the powerful counter-attack by Von Rundstedt or of the V2s which were so soon to be directed against England, but the outposts of the German Army were under pressure that proved impossible to counter.

As dusk fell, the firing ceased. The barrels of the guns were wearing out, and mounds of spent shell cases were behind the gunsites. In the small hours of the morning the partisan infantry attacked. My telephone started buzzing. The young officer at Bozovic's headquarters was shouting into his mouthpiece, 'Tirez! Tirez!' He explained that boats were coming into the harbour either to evacuate the garrison or to reinforce it. In any event, he wanted the approaches to the harbour to be shelled at random. The 3.7s opened up, the flashes from their barrels lighting the scene to such an extent that I feared the mainland batteries would see our position.

All night the battle went on, but towards dawn the rate of fire dwindled to an occasional shell. Bozovic sent an officer to tell us that Sumartin had fallen. Ross and I got into the jeep and started down the steep winding road to the town, but as we reached the harbour, heavy shells plastered the port. Now it was the turn of the enemy's mainland guns, which at last had a fixed target. Ross whipped the jeep round and tore back up the road. We reached the comparative safety of the gunsite with much relief.

Meanwhile, the colonels at the villa on Vis had swallowed their martinis and with a reluctant sigh had set off in a naval motor launch for the sound of battle, the smell of cordite and the sight of blood. There they stood, side by side, surveying the scene. It was all over. Brac was now in our hands.

During the night a company of the 43rd Commandos accompanied by partisans had attacked the neighbouring island of Solta, but the garrison after a running fight had been taken off by the Germans, though not without casualties.

Columns of German prisoners were being escorted up the roads past our position, their faces grey with fatigue and fear. Such a different sight from the bronzed and fit soldiers of Rommel's army who were lucky enough to fall into British hands. Partisan wounded were making their way back to Bol, some women amongst them. There was a good deal of wailing and weeping, and I shuddered to think how many casualties there had been amongst the civilian population of Sumartin. I did not wait to find out.

By the afternoon I was sitting in the comfortable cabin of a Fairmile ML, drinking whisky and water and reading an old copy of the *Tatler*. The powerful engines were driving us across the sunlit sea at high speed towards Vis. I looked forward to the civilized comforts of the villa.

An aircraft cannon shell smashed the skylight over my head; once again, the familiar sounds of a Messerschmitt's cannon pounded in my ears. There were shouts on deck, a splatter of belated fire from the Marlin guns on the bridge. Broken glass was all over the cabin, on the pages of the *Tatler*. My whisky was ruined. I ran on deck to see two specks disappearing into the distance, skimming low over the sea. We were a sitting duck, and I wondered if they were going to turn for a second run in. There were only two minor casualties on the deck, which seemed miraculous. The MEs had flown across our line, but if they had come up on our stern there would have been a different story to tell, or perhaps a story that would never have been told.

Chapter 16

A Strange Affair

Trooper Brash welcomed me back to Vis. He took away my filthy clothes, and I went for a swim, afterwards retiring to the balcony of the villa to reflect on another job done without disaster.

After a few days respite, I was soundly asleep in my comfortable room when I was suddenly woken by the two Colonels. John Clark and Andrew Maxwell were in their dressing gowns, and it was still long before dawn. As I have related, I have always been a heavy sleeper, and my brain does not function properly for at least half an hour after waking. This was a great disadvantage in a war, having something to do with metabolism, but there is nothing one can do about it. I struggled for consciousness.

Gradually their words became sentences. Headquarters of Land Forces Adriatic had received a report from a two-man patrol of the Long Range Desert Group that the garrison of Uljan, an island 80 miles to the north-west and only a few miles from the port of Zadar, wanted to surrender. I was to be taken there by the Royal Navy with a detachment of the Royal Marine Commandos to ask the German garrison commander if he would kindly step aboard with his men to become prisoners of war. It sounded remarkably simple.

As my brain began to function and full consciousness returned, I began to think that it was the most crackpot plan I had ever heard. However, I was no more than a field officer, and there before me stood my two seniors, and they too had their orders. 'Yours is not to reason why . . .' I had no intention whatever of submitting to the second part of the quotation.

I dragged on my battledress and boots, and Brash kitted me up with the essentials. We set off on foot for the port of Komiza, where lay the Royal Navy with three Fairmile Motor Launches and a Landing Craft, which was to carry the commandos.

I got aboard a Motor Launch, and in the cabin I met the Senior Naval Officer, a Lieutenant Webb, inevitably 'Spider' Webb. He was a very experienced officer and had been sunk twice on destroyers in the Mediterranean. He told me that on the last occasion his hand was on the rim of the funnel as the ship went beneath the waves, but he never could explain how he was not sucked down with the sea rushing into the vacuum. He was a delightful companion. There was a great deal of tension in these little ships as they were very lightweight, badly armed and no match for the German 'E' boats in the area, which were much faster and had a more practical armament. Moreover, navigation was hazardous on account of the rocky outcrops from the seabed about the islands. The Luftwaffe was still sending out occasional patrols of Messerschmitts, against which they had practically no defence. The Oerlikons on the bow could not be raised to a sufficient elevation and the Marlins were known to be unreliable and unhandy. I had already had one experience of such an attack and I did not want to go through another. However, it was not quite so bad on this occasion as there were now four ships together supporting each other. The waters of the Adriatic were still warm from the summer, and a good swimmer stood a fair chance if the worst should happen.

So we set off in the dark for our voyage to the north-west. Webb and I conferred in the comfortable cabin. The sound of the sea along the hull and the throb of the powerful engines were exhilarating. The Navy have an advantage over the Army as long as they stay afloat, because they always have storage space for the comforts of life, dry, warm clothes, food and drink. The cabin was arranged to sleep the officers by night, and by day the bunks were folded away to provide a most civilized saloon.

I told Webb that I considered the plan was based on faulty information. The Long Range Desert Group had done good work in the Western Desert, venturing miles behind the enemy lines in jeep patrols for information and occasionally disrupting German communications. They had not been entirely disbanded after the victory of the Eighth Army, but I had not known that any of their patrols were in the Adriatic.

It seemed very unlikely that the Preko Garrison, which had been left in peace for so long and never under pressure, would want to surrender, since Zadar was but a few miles away. The entire garrison could have been taken off within hours if any alarm arose. The German guns at Zadar had the whole range of the island of Uljan, of which Preko was the principal town.

I had no information on the strength of the enemy on the island. Even if all went according to plan, could we embark several hundred men in our four little vessels? Webb declared that it could be done, but as we studied the chart in the cabin he was as sceptical as I as to the outcome of the adventure.

There were 50 miles of open sea until we came upon the large group of islands between Zadar and the Istrian Peninsula. The Germans had a naval force at Pola, 100 miles to the north-west, but apart from sorties by 'E' boats, the Royal Navy had blocked the port. We decided to make for Dugi Otok, an island to the west of Uljan. We could keep to the east of Kornat and navigate up the Shrednji channel to avoid being seen from Uljan. There were several small fishing villages on the north side of Dugi Otok, and we thought we could feel our way into one of them and should be able to contact the local partisans in that area.

At dawn I went on deck. Our four little ships were travelling at high speed over the calm sea, their sharp bows throwing up spumes of spray, their sterns well down in the water, the wakes trailing miles behind. I hoped we could reach Kornat before the sun shone down to expose our flotilla to any prowling aircraft.

Under different circumstances I could have been enjoying a millionaire's holiday. I had a fine yacht, a competent captain, superb scenery, the Adriatic Sea, a highly disciplined crew, a good cook, plenty of food and even an armed escort. We could have cruised about the Adriatic for the rest of the war if we had not, unfortunately, had our doubtful orders.

As the sun broke over the horizon and Kornat came into view, Webb slowed his flotilla to a few knots. I was glad to see our streaming wakes die down as we nosed gently through the shallow waters between Dugi Otok and Kornat. The sun rose, and we felt very exposed. The gun crews were at their stations. I knew Webb was anxious lest the bottoms of his ships might be torn out by the rocky outcrops not far below the surface. Wild duck rose into the air, disturbed by our approach. Through our binoculars we could not see a sign of life on the shores as we turned north-west following the shoreline of Dugi Otok (which translated means 'Long Island'). It was indented with creeks and inlets, many of which would have provided a good hideout. About ten miles up the coast we saw what we thought was probably Sestring, a small fishing village [probably modern Sali]. We lay off about a mile, and as there was no hostile action or sign of it, we decided to approach.

As we got nearer we could see fishing boats moored beam to beam in the small harbour. There was little movement in the village. The gun crews were tense, their Oerlikons and Marlins trained on the shore. We strained our eyes for any sign of the enemy as Webb led his flotilla in, but to our great relief we saw the villagers coming down to the quay. There were no uniforms and no red stars.

I cannot tell what effect our arrival had upon the local people. They were quiet and reserved, and I supposed that after all the years of occupation, first by the Italians and then the Germans, they could not believe that we were truly British. The partisans were also under suspicion by the ordinary people, for no peasant or fisherman, by his very independence, takes kindly to authority, and communist authority is very demanding, especially under conditions of warfare.

We were led through the village up the hill to a house commanding a view of the harbour where, sitting on a wall polishing his glasses, was the elderly Captain Vulin. He never even bothered to get up to greet us. Webb and I, falling in with his mood, sat beside him on the wall. This was a much better atmosphere than I had hitherto encountered. Vulin laughed dryly when I explained our intentions, telling me that he could see no reason why the Preko garrison should surrender and that he thought it highly unlikely, as a number of the garrison, including several Russians, were wanted for murder. He even showed us a list of those men who were marked to be executed if the partisans or the local inhabitants could get their hands on them. He wanted to know from whom we had got our information. Vulin declared that if we could get rid of the enemy then he personally would like to help, but so far he had no instructions and without authority he could not act. This was one of the few partisan officers I had met who had a sense of humour. He was not excitable or pompous like most of his uniformed compatriots.

Our naval force had meanwhile moored gunwale to gunwale in the small harbour. The guns were pointing out to sea, fully manned, and the commandos were ashore, taking up defensive positions at strategic points.

There, across a few miles of water, lay the long island of Uljan, on the other side of which was my objective. If we acted directly, that meant landing at night with the commandos, approaching the perimeter of the defences, calling on the commander to surrender. When I considered this direct approach to the problem, it seemed out of the question. Was I to advance with a white flag for a parley? If our information was faulty, as I was nearly sure it was, especially after Vulin's amused incredulity, then I would either be shot on sight or taken prisoner. I must confess I had absolutely no intention of exposing myself to such a risk, even though at the time I had no knowledge of Adolf Hitler's top level order, paragraph 3 of which, dated 18 October 1942, read:

> From now on all enemies of so called Commando missions in Europe or Africa challenged by German troops, even if they are to all appearances soldiers in uniform or demolition troops, whether armed or unarmed, in battle or in flight, are to be slaughtered to the last man. It does not make any difference whether they are landed from ships or aeroplanes for their actions, or whether they are dropped by parachutes. Even if these individuals when found should apparently be prepared to give themselves up, no pardon is to be granted to them on principle.
>
> This order does not apply to the treatment of any enemy soldier who in the course of normal hostilities (large scale offensive actions, landing operations and airborne operations), is captured in open battle or give themselves up.
>
> I will hold responsible under Military Law, for failure to carry out this order, all commanders and officers who either have neglected their duty of instructing the troops about this order or acted against this order where it is to be executed.

In any event, I could not hazard the commandos or the naval force unless I was first sure that the surrender would take place. If there was opposition, then we had to take into account the probability of German reinforcements from Zadar, only a few miles away, and the threat of heavy artillery, to say nothing of a possible attack by 'E' boats. The more I thought about it, the more unpleasant and difficult the problem became. One thing was clear, we had to have full cooperation from the partisans.

Webb sent a message over his naval wireless to the headquarters on Vis:

> Liaison effected with partisan commander name Vulin. All here eager to take garrison simply as British Prisoners. Authority not

given to Vulin. He is referring Cerni. If answer is NO, then Macmis must ask Arso as it is useless to expect any authority from local commander on alternative condition.

The alternative condition was, of course, that the garrison would be handed over to the partisans. In that event, presumably we were bound to see some bloody events, and I do not think that any of us wanted to be witness to any hangings. Cerni was a General on Tito's headquarters, and 'Arso' was Arso Jovanovic, his Chief of Staff. Macmis was headquarters '37' Military Mission.

Now we had to wait. I was not at all happy with our present position. If we waited too long the news would spread that we were here, and I feared an attack. We were not more than 12 miles as the crow flies from a formidable German force, and I could not believe that the enemy would remain inactive if they knew that four vulnerable craft of the Royal Navy and a detachment of British troops lay so close.

So we waited two anxious days, during which I developed a bad headache and wished either we could get on with it or get out of it. On the third day Vulin got his orders to cooperate. He suddenly became businesslike, and at last we could make a reasonably sensible plan. I was to leave in a small boat under cover of darkness that night for the island of Pasman. An Able Seaman with a radio telephone set, which could be carried on his back, was to come with me. The boat was to be manned by a civilian fisherman, and I was to be escorted by a partisan officer. We were to wait in a bay on the south side of Pasman for a fishing boat, which would pick us up the following evening and take us to Kukijica, a village on the southern extremity of Uljan. Vulin said he would lay on a reception party at Kukijica, advising me to discuss with the locals there the best way to deliver our ultimatum.

I conferred with Webb, and we got out an operation order in case the surrender came off. Upon my signal he was to land the commandos in a bay on the southern side of Uljan. In the event of any enemy surrender, the evacuation would have to be effected with the utmost speed in darkness before the mainland guns were alerted. I marked another rendezvous in case I had to make a getaway.

Only Vulin amongst us could speak German properly. We composed a demand for surrender to the Garrison Commander which read as follows:

To Lieutenant Frommer

Preko Garrison Commander 4 Company, 1 Battalion, 891 Regiment, 264 Division

The British Adriatic Command has had information according to which you are prepared to surrender to the British troops. British land forces and ships of the Royal Navy are closing and will be prepared to take the entire garrison as British prisoners of war.

In case you agree to this you should send an answer with a messenger by return on Wednesday at 9.00 a.m. You should send an officer to represent you to make an agreement on your behalf and he should be unarmed and without a helmet and should march on the road towards Karli.

The representative mentioned would come across with a white flag and at this point he should halt and stay there until two English officers approach him and start negotiations.

We assure you that the German officer who comes as negotiator will not be handed over to the partisans.

Peter Crichton, Major 4th Hussars. K. Webb Lieut. RN.

Note: there was no second British officer.

Vulin had three copies of this formidable ultimatum typed out. I put one in the breast pocket of my battledress. As the light began to fail we went down to the harbour to board our small craft. She was a 20ft open boat with a single-cylinder petrol engine. A fisherman was already sitting in the stern. Vulin introduced me to a very tough-looking partisan officer who was waiting to receive us. The volunteer Able Seaman was equipped in what I suppose was naval boarding party rig, a tommy gun slung over his shoulder, the walkie-talkie set strapped to his back. He looked very young and fresh-faced. Webb wished me luck, and the motor started up.

It was a brilliant night and the sea was flat calm. The noise from the wide exhaust of the single-cylinder engine made a fearful echo across the water. It was bitterly cold. I was travelling light, taking nothing except a bag of gold napoleons for small change and a .45 automatic, which I had drawn from the mission stores before my departure. If anything went badly wrong, the Able Seaman and I could make a run for it. The going across country on the Dalmatian islands was very hard because of the sharp rocky outcrops everywhere, but the rocks made excellent cover and rendered pursuit difficult. I had got through a pair of boots during the few days in Brac and I now had a fine pair of Finnish make, which proved much tougher and more practical than the British Army issue. I have them to this day.

Within a few hours the shoreline of Pasman showed up. We entered a little cove, a small promontory hiding us from the open sea. The bow ran on to a sandy beach, and to my great relief the engine stopped and its fearful exhaust note died. The silence of the brilliant night was wonderful.

I got ashore to explore the vicinity and to get warm. On my return I found the fisherman engaged upon an extraordinary sport. He was throwing into the sea a rounded stone tied securely to a long line, hauling it gently and slowly on to the beach. Every so often a squid would be pulled in, tenaciously clinging to the stone, which the wretched creature had evidently mistaken for its prey. With deft movements of his sharp knife the fisherman cut off the tentacles, putting them in a frying pan. The revolting mess did not look appetizing, but when he started to cook his harvest on an oil stove he produced from the well of the boat, the resulting smell, rather like fried prawns, excited our appetites, and although rather leathery the taste was excellent.

At the appointed hour before dawn the Able Seaman set up his walkie-talkie set. Webb had agreed to sail out in his flagship off the Pasman shore to pick up our signals simply to maintain contact. I waited tensely whilst the Able Seaman gave out his call sign, and sure enough, to the exact time, we had a reassuring answer. The risks of this operation were out of all proportion to the possible gain, and there was indeed nothing to report, but at least our communications functioned properly.

As the light of dawn rose over the sea and the landscape, we heard the unmistakable sounds of a marine engine. The exhaust note came loudly across the water. It was clearly no more powerful than a small four-cylinder engine, having a more sophisticated rhythm than our own single cylinder. The partisan officer was listening attentively, his head on one side. He gave a nod of satisfaction. In the cold light there came into the cove a rather smart cutter, more a yacht than a fishing vessel, not over 26ft and flush-decked except for a cockpit in the stern with a bare pole amidships. There were several figures on the deck. She lay off not more than 50ft away in deep water. This was our escort to Uljan.

I was welcomed aboard with curiosity, and the sole representative of the Royal Navy, in all his traditional gear, was examined in detail. We set off at once for Uljan. I do not think we were making more than five knots. The light was growing fast as the sun rose and lit up the flat calm sea. Soon we were cruising along in brilliant sunshine, totally exposed to aircraft or naval attack. The half dozen crew, heavily armed with Brens and Schmeissers, were constantly on the lookout. No one spoke. There was nothing I could do but await further events. The whole scene was bathed in sunshine, and the view of the islands on all sides was very beautiful, but I must confess my aesthetic feelings were much subordinate to my instinct for survival. With our present armament we could give an 'E' boat a hot reception, but the outcome of any clash would be inevitable.

In broad daylight we put into a little fishing village on the south-eastern extremity of Uljan. Almost at once the narrow streets became deserted, doors were shut and a silence fell upon the little place. Clearly, the inhabitants were terrified of reprisals. Our party, now about a dozen, tramped through the narrow streets to a house on the outskirts near to the shore. The partisan officer, who had accompanied us on Vulin's orders, told me that the Germans had raided Pasman, off which we had laid the previous night. There had been a battle between the raiding party and the partisans at Tkon during the hours of darkness. The local partisan commander had not returned to Uljan, and we had to wait for him. There was nothing to do but sit tight during the day. Vulin was evidently not in touch with the situation on Uljan and Pasman, and the plan was going wrong. I became very anxious to establish my contact again with the Royal Navy, as I had no intention of spending the rest of the war hiding in the Dalmatian islands. I went out on a personal reconnaissance to find a vantage point from where I could post my faithful Able Seaman to pick up the ML as soon as light went. I hoped Lieutenant Webb would be able once again to get out of port to cruise about. It was of course highly dangerous for a single small naval vessel to sail in these waters without any protection except its speed and very light armament.

On returning to the house in the village I found my partisan officer in a state of obvious satisfaction. His local commander had returned from Pasman and wanted us to go at once overland to the nearby village of Kukijica. He apologized for the lack of organization but said that the enemy raid on Pasman had been responsible. At any rate, he declared, the garrison would almost certainly withdraw into the perimeter of Preko after the encounter at

Tkon, making it easier for us to approach without so much likelihood of an enemy sortie.

The Royal Navy was on time, and I sent the following signal to Lieutenant Webb:

> 04.1615 hours. We are spending the night at Kukijica. I hope to see the local Commander there. So far he cannot be found and I consider it essential to find him before we can make any progress. There has been a battle at Tkon. Most of the troops who would normally be in this part of the world were occupied there and this is the reason put forward for the disorganization.
>
> It is probable that I shall not get you by RT whilst you are in port, therefore will you please cruise about again tomorrow morning starting at 0800 hrs. Listen hourly for 10 minutes.
>
> If I succeed in meeting local Commander tonight, there is no reason why surrender note could not be delivered tomorrow morning and in case of surrender coming off we should be able to complete the job by late evening. I hope you give them hell up the hill for this nonsense!

My request was a tall order; I was again exposing the Navy to great risk on my account. On the other hand, I had to have communications the following day. In the event of surrender I had to be able to call in the commandos, and my own security depended on the Navy. The walkie-talkie set could not reach Dugi Otok, and there was nothing for it except to establish communications by closing the range.

We set off at dusk for Kukijica. The route lay over broken ground. The partisans always seemed to have a man well out in front as we marched steadily without a halt. I was at any rate entirely in their hands, and I ceased to think about the next move. It was rather like being in an aeroplane seat; if you are not at the controls you have to accept what comes. My Able Seaman trudged behind me with his heavy pack. At Kukijica we found the same sort of reception, but by this time it was dark. The doors were closed, there was no one in the streets and even the windows were shuttered. We halted outside a house on the outskirts of the village and were silently invited inside. As usual, it was solidly constructed of stone. The wooden floors were scrubbed almost white and there was little furniture, except for heavy, solid tables and chairs and here and there a chest or cupboard against the wall. There were no carpets or ornaments, but the house had a wholesome atmosphere of severe orderliness and space. The heavy boots of our party upon the clean floors seemed offensive. Our host was an elderly man, plainly of some substance and authority, as he was treated with respect by the partisans, but it was impossible not to detect the tensions that existed. Doubtless he was frequently subjected to the indignity of visits from the Preko garrison, and I wondered what questions he had to answer, and how many lies he had to tell under the circumstances. For four long years he had put over a pretence of neutrality in the conflict, at least sufficiently well to prevent his execution. It could not have been very easy to keep this up over such a long period. I doubted very much if he was sympathetic to his communist compatriots; indeed, many responsible, hard working people in Yugoslavia found themselves in a terrible predicament at this time, since all over occupied territory the most effective militant organizations were communist-dominated.

Our host provided a meal of soup and bread, and a bottle of *rakija* was produced. This was the local hard drink, tasting rather like Bols. At first I thought it unpleasant, but the sensation of comfort as soon as the liquid reached the stomach was wonderfully reassuring. I was shown to a bedroom on the first floor, which was as clean and as bare as the rest of the house. The windows were thrown open, and I was told that if there was a raid in the village during the night I must jump out and make off towards some trees 100yds away, where I would be covered by our armed lookout.

I arranged for my faithful Able Seaman to be escorted to the bay, which I had designated as a rendezvous in case we had to make a getaway. He was to hide up there with his escort and signal his ship at 0800 hours, keeping in touch during the following day in accordance with my message to Lieutenant Webb.

The party broke up downstairs. I flung myself on the bed fully clothed after a last look through the windows to make sure I could get out in my usual early morning state of semi-consciousness. I slept soundly, with the relaxing effects of several glasses of *rakija*. A knock on the door woke me before dawn, and the ghastly reality of the ridiculous situation hit me like a cold shower as I struggled for consciousness.

We set off from the silent village again across country. The only sounds were our boots on the rock and scrub. First light broke to find us on a woodland pathway with the seashore on our right hand. To the north-east, across only a few miles of water, was Zadar, with its heavy guns and the German divisional headquarters. Here and there along our path we passed a silent partisan; they had been out all night to watch for a possible sortie by the Preko garrison, and we should therefore have had good warning back at the village. The tactics of the German command as an occupying power seemed to me to be all wrong; by staying in heavily defended positions with only occasional sorties in force they lost the initiative. The partisans could take advantage of the situation to wander about almost at will. If the enemy had well run patrols just as mobile, then the partisans would have found it far more difficult to organize their resistance. As it was, here we were, a lightly armed party, approaching a powerfully defended enemy position with apparent immunity.

Just before sunrise we came upon a house close to the shore. The terrified householder did his best to welcome us. We sat round a table, the woman of the house spreading upon it a snow-white table cloth. The wire perimeter of the Preko garrison was only a few hundred yards from the house. Several of the local inhabitants came in furtively, and somewhat desperate conversations in Serbo–Croat followed. The Partisan Commander was trying to make up his mind who to select to carry our surrender ultimatum into the garrison. I could not follow what was happening. Eventually, a middle-aged woman was brought into the room. She was clearly not a peasant, and the company showed her some deference. It turned out that she was the local schoolteacher. It was she who had the luck to be chosen to deliver the ultimatum to Leutnant Frommer.

I produced the letter from my battledress pocket and handed it over. The poor woman attempted to hide her agitation with a joke of some sort, at which the company laughed dryly. It was a dreadful experience to expose her to such a risk. She was accompanied to the door, and we watched her as she walked swiftly along the path on her hazardous mission.

The door was shut upon us and we were served a meal of small fried fish like whitebait, with brown bread. My companions seemed quite relaxed and were joking and laughing together, not at all concerned at the possible fate of the schoolmistress. I hoped Leutnant Frommer was not an SS officer.

Regular officers of the Wehrmacht could generally be relied on to behave decently. I looked out of the window and there, behind the trunk of a tree, with his Schmeisser under his arm, was one of our scouts.

Hours seemed to drag by, and it was nearly noon before the agitated woman burst into the house, shaking and laughing in a state of near-hysteria. She was told severely to sit down and was given a glass of water before she managed with a great effort to compose herself. Fortunately, she spoke English and gave me an account of what had happened within the garrison.

She had gone directly to Frommer's house. He had been on the point of shaving and had come into the room with his razor in his hand and soap on his face. She had handed him the letter, at which he had burst out laughing and then questioned her severely. She said she had told him that she had seen the British officer herself. He had dismissed her without reply. I asked the partisans if they were satisfied she had delivered the letter. They assured me they were quite certain of it. Her detailed account of her meeting with Frommer hardly left much doubt. They considered whether to send her in a second time, asking me what I thought. The poor woman was in such a state, and the issue such a foregone conclusion, that I thought no useful purpose would be served. We could expect a sortie at any moment, and we had little time now to make a getaway, having so exposed our position. I thought of Webb hazarding his ship in the Srednji Channel in broad daylight and my Able Seaman patiently waiting in the bay for my appearance.

I concluded that if, after one hour, Frommer had failed to conform to our ultimatum, we would vanish from the scene with all possible speed. That hour seemed like ten. There was no movement, no shots were fired. At last, time was up. We left the house and were quickly amongst the trees on our way to the bay. There, to my great relief, I found my Able Seaman in company with a partisan, entirely composed and relaxed as if he was on a seaside holiday. He was in touch with his ship and had got a glimpse of her once as she cruised at high speed up the channel. Lieutenant Webb was listening at the hour, and I called him up and asked him if he could sail to the bay as soon as the light went, to pick us up. It was a great relief to hear his confident voice over the radio.

We waited impatiently during the remaining daylight. A small rowing boat was moored between the rocks out of sight in which we intended to put out as soon as the ML came into the bay. At the pre-arranged hour, almost to the minute, close in shore we saw the ship steam at high speed right across the shoreline and away out of sight. Thinking Webb had mistaken the rendezvous I pulled out my automatic to fire a shot to attract him, but the wretched thing jammed as I pulled the breech back to put a shell into the chamber.

For some horrible minutes we waited whilst I thought out the next move if the worst should happen. Suddenly the ML came dashing into the bay, her bow wave cutting the still water. We tumbled into the rowing boat, and our partisan oarsman pulled hard as the ship cut her engines to lie in the centre of the bay waiting for us. I listened for the sound of heavy shells overhead. Nothing happened. We came alongside the ship and climbed on board in a hurry. Our partisan oarsman pulled away for the shore with a wave of his hand. The ship put about, and we were away on the open sea. Webb was on the bridge, tensely on the lookout, and I joined him without a word, as together we watched the shore of Uljan receding.

There had been a disproportionate risk to the whole operation, but the orders had to be carried out. It was a great relief to have done with it. When we were clear of the Shrednji Channel, Webb and I returned to the saloon for a strong drink. He had signalled his ships to put out for Vis, and the little flotilla was now on its way back to its home port.

I regret I gave no thought at the time to the wretched schoolmistress of Preko, or to our hosts who had received us into their houses. The partisans could look after themselves. They had the whole archipelago to hide in, supported by the civilian population, but what of those poor people who had to suffer from so many years of oppression and fear?

Chapter 17

The Capture of Ston

After a few days respite on Vis, Bozovic decided to attack the Peljesac Peninsula. He wanted our guns, and this time he said that bombing support was essential. The peninsula is about 30 miles north-west of Dubrovnik, narrowing as it joins the mainland at the small and beautiful fortified town of Ston. The General said that if he could take and hold the peninsula he could then threaten the main coastal road, upon which the enemy garrisons of Dubrovnik and Cetinje depended.

Webb and I agreed to provide artillery and naval support, and I asked the Balkan Air Force to hold medium bombers available.

Whilst we made preparations and plans for the landing we received the important news that the Germans were withdrawing from Greece and southern Yugoslavia. If we could take the Peljesac Peninsula and the town of Ston we should be in a position to cut off the enemy's retreat to the north. It was evident that the small force available would hardly be sufficient to do it effectively, but at the least we could make their withdrawal hazardous.

Further information reached us that the Peljesac garrison had withdrawn to Ston, and if this was true, then we could land on the peninsula unopposed. The neighbouring island of Mljet was also reported clear. The whole situation provided a marvellous opportunity to attack the enemy.

With hindsight, I should have done everything I could to get a substantial British force to come with me. There is no doubt whatever that if this had come about we could have cut the road at Neum and taken Sarajevo. However, even now, I do not know if we had such a force available. We were still at a point of stalemate in Italy, where the going was extremely tough. Nevertheless, Churchill envisaged and planned a few months later to land at Zadar and push through to Vienna via Istria. I was to be recalled to be briefed for this possibility, but the plan was later abandoned. Tito was very averse to any landing by British troops, which he thought might undermine his authority, and every major move we made was subject to long drawn out

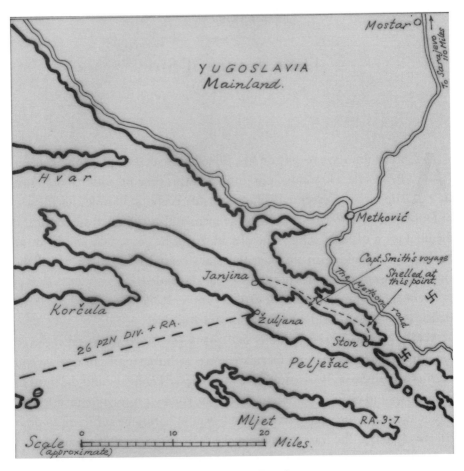

6. The Attack on Ston and the Metkovic Road

negotiation. Communist ideology came before the proper prosecution of the war. I was myself to be put under guard before long.

However, I sent out the following signal across the Adriatic:

Pzns intention: to capture and to cut enemy communications DUBROVNIK METKOVIC. This operation co-ordinated 29 Division attack on Dubrovnik from South-East.

Method: 1st Brigade to attack SLIVNO RAVNO 8989 NEUM 9588 DUZI 9985 OSLJE 0683 DUNTADOLI 0974. Groups on mainland under command 11th Brigade will harass enemy OSLJE and attack bridge between SLANO 1871 and TRNOVE 1674.

11th Brigade task one attack STON clear cove PRATRATNA and channel MALI VRATNIK 0969 of mines. Task Two. After capture STON advance inland to area main road and attack SIPAN.

Paragraph 2: Request bombing as in my last signal Serial Two.

Paragraph 3: Naval requirements. One unit as covering force operating in NERETVA channel as far east as 17 degrees 28 mins. My serial one refers. Partisan craft here will be informed our movements.

Paragraph 4: Anticipate this major operation with great possibilities.

Little did I realize that General Headquarters in Italy were considering just such a possibility, but my signal did not spark off any major initiative in this direction and the opportunity was lost.

Bozovic assured me that his 'swimmers' could clear the Pratratna cove and the Mali Channel of mines. The partisans had among them a considerable number of highly technically competent and adventurous young men who were well able to defuse a mine where it lay, or raise a wreck in record time or change a tank engine in pouring rain in the middle of a forest, as I was later to see when the last of my original charges came under repair.

In fact, all I could get were eight guns, a company of the Highland Light Infantry and the strength of the Balkan Air Force. Bozovic was well pleased with this promise of support. He had yet another opportunity to distinguish himself and the 26th Division.

The troop of heavy artillery was to be landed on Mljet, covered by the Highland Light Infantry and a detachment of partisans. Captain Smith of the Royal Artillery was to come with Webb and myself with his troops of 75mm Pack Howitzers and a detachment of mules to carry the guns over the difficult rocky terrain. This time I made sure I had a first class signaller and radio equipment to reach out to Balkan Air Force Headquarters in Italy. Bozovic assigned to me an interpreter, a sophisticated lawyer from Zagreb, who looked upon our military antics with amused tolerance. Although he had a red star on his forage cap he was about as far removed from a communist as could be imagined. It tickled his sense of humour that the rank and file still addressed him with the prefix '*Gospodin*', which is a title of respect for the bourgeoisie.

Trooper Brash, who had got bored with his holiday on Vis, decided to keep me company, and I was to be very glad he did so. He was very powerfully built, and although of middle age he had greater stamina than I possessed. He carried his Enfield service rifle everywhere and mistrusted automatic weapons.

I went to inspect the mules, which were so essential to our success. They had only just been brought over the Adriatic by sea to Vis. I expected to see a dishevelled lot of animals, but there they were, drawn up as if about to go into a county show ring. Although it was October, their summer coats were still shining like silk, their shoulders rippling with muscle, their indestructible feet beautifully shod, their hooves oiled, their tails twitching with energy. They were as level a lot as one could wish for, and one could have searched the Mediterranean to match them. They were far too good for this sort of work. I had seen the terrible destruction of the mule contingent which had been taken to Greece in 1941, and I hoped fervently that the fine animals which were to do us service in the coming operation would not meet the same fate. I am glad to say every one survived, but not without hazard.

The pack harness was nearly new. I had never seen such equipment before. It was, I believe, standard British design, developed over decades of practical application, no doubt in India. The Cypriot muleteers were plainly proud of their charges. This was possibly the last occasion on which guns were transported by mules by the British Army in any operation.

Zero hour was 1000 hours on 15 October 1944. It was wonderful autumn weather as our little expedition set sail for the invasion of the Peljesac. The sky was brilliant with stars and the sea calm. The heavy guns with their support troops sailed away from us for Mljet. We headed south of Korcula eastwards through the Lastovki Channel towards the small village of Zuljana, about 100 miles from our base.

Webb was determined to reach our destination with a few hours of darkness in hand. The Luftwaffe were still occasionally patrolling with fighters, and if we were caught on the open sea we should have been in real trouble. The Balkan Air Force were to cover our landing and the subsequent operation with Spitfires and Hurricanes from Italy, but we could not expect anything like safe cover at sea. Once ashore, enemy air attack was unlikely to be a serious hazard because the nature of the terrain provided such excellent protection.

The Peninsula is a beautiful place. There is a hill range running along the whole length of it, rising to a height of 3,000ft. We had to get the guns across the hills to a position on the northern shore, where they had the range of the main coastal road.

A few hours before dawn, we reached our destination. The MLs and the LCTs slowed down, the bow waves cut to silence as we lay off the coast for a signal to come in. A single torch light shone out. Webb gave his orders, and we steamed into the little harbour.

The advance party of partisans were in control of the port. As the ML's gunwale came alongside the wooden jetty, a partisan jumped down on to the deck. He called out to an Able Seaman, '*Sdravo, Druge*', which means 'Hello, Comrade'.

The Able Seaman replied tersely and without good humour, having picked up the essentials of the language on Vis, 'Don't you bloody *Druge* me mate.' It was not very civil, but there was a clear-cut implication.

Webb and I, accompanied by Trooper Brash and our interpreter, got ashore and moved off to our rendezvous with the headquarters of the 26th Division in a village near to the one and only roadway. Captain Smith, with his guns and mules, was left to disembark under cover of the last remaining hours of darkness.

We arrived after a hard march just as dawn was breaking and were welcomed into a house in a remote village high up in the hills. As usual, the hospitality of the poor people was wonderful. We were taken in as honoured guests and given a splendid meal. Webb and I, by this stage in the war, were seasoned enough to accept gratefully any respite from our endeavours and were not too struck by conscience to refuse comfort when we could get it. We therefore settled down to await poor Captain Smith and the approach of the headquarters staff of the Division.

I hoped to get the 75mm howitzers in position to fire on the main road by the evening and to move up to Ston with the 11th Brigade for the attack on the following morning. By daylight the guns and mules had arrived. Smith went off with a strong detachment of partisans across country to the northern shore of the Peninsula. Webb was to remain at the village to keep in contact with his ships, whilst I took six mules and my signal equipment, setting off with an escort up the rocky road to the position of attack on Ston.

The lawyer from Zagreb was by this time getting footsore and weary. He had struck up a curious relationship with Trooper Brash, who had taken him into protective custody, setting him upon one of the mules and driving the animal and its cargo in front of him. In fact, my clever interpreter was vital to me. He was an extremely intelligent and pleasant companion and had a very good idea of the worth of his compatriots in a given situation. He was to be with me for several months, and we still exchange Christmas cards, more than a quarter of a century later.

Towards evening, the sky became heavily overcast, black clouds rolling up from the south-east. A thunderstorm broke, and we were drenched to the skin. The flanks of the mules steamed, and I was much relieved when at last our bedraggled party reached the shelter of Cespinica before the defences of Ston.

My signallers set up their radio set and established contact with Balkan Air Force Headquarters. My interpreter and I, after a good meal in a cottage, went to bed in a double room provided for us. After a few minutes' glorious relaxation I was awakened by the most fearful itching. I had slept rough in many places, but never before had I been assailed so remorselessly by bedbugs. My companion knew at once what to do. He was similarly in trouble and said he would light candles and the bugs would stop biting. This he did, and he was as good as his word. I cannot understand how the dim light of a candle can have any effect on microscopic insects under several layers of blanket, but it certainly does.

We were up before dawn. The 11th Brigade Commander came to see me. He wanted a bombing attack on Ston as soon after first light as possible and before he committed his infantry.

My request to Balkan Air Force was immediately confirmed: medium bombers were to come in over Ston at 0630 hours. I also had a comforting signal of support as follows:

Eight Spit bombers will be standing by from 0800 hrs to support attack on Ston. Spits will sweep Dubrovnik/Mostar road.

I moved up to the heights overlooking Ston. There it lay in all its beauty, and I could hardly bear to think what was to follow during the next few days. So far, all the initiative had been ours. Not a shot had been fired by either side since our landing the previous night. I hoped that Captain Smith was in a secure position with the 1st Brigade on the northern shore. My signallers had failed to maintain contact with him, and my only communications with his position were through the 11th Brigade Commander, who assured me all was well. At this time I learned that elements of the 1st Brigade were to cross the Neretva Channel in local boats to attack the Metkovic road, and I hoped that Webb's MLs would have cleared away from their night patrol by first light. The difficulties of liaison with partisan forces, who never issued concise operation orders, was somewhat nerve-wracking at times.

The familiar whistle of shells from the German shore batteries of the 390th Division opened hostilities. Shells were bursting at random over a wide area. The enemy had no observation post and were firing on speculation, but we could stand any amount of random shellfire, the rocks as usual, affording such secure cover, and only a lucky shot could inflict casualties. I did not think the enemy would waste valuable heavy shells for long in such a manner, but the initial bombardment lasted for more than an hour or so. I went to see how the mules were standing up to it. The muleteers had sheltered them in a gulley, where there was a sparkling stream. One mule had a minor swelling on its flank, and its groom was busy swabbing it with cold poultices. The picture of this man tending his animal under fire has remained with me ever since.

The shellfire ceased abruptly and all was silent. I strained my ears for the sound of our bombers. The partisans were watching me, and I was acutely aware of it. This was the first occasion in the war when I had the ability to call in such a powerful destructive force. Our troops were close in to the German defences, and I hoped that the bombing attack would be accurate.

Dead on time, we heard the sound of aircraft. Twelve medium bombers came over, very high up. There were tremendous explosions in Ston, and clouds of smoke rose from the town. For half a minute or so there was silence, followed by intense small arms and machine gun fire. We were now properly engaged.

During the day the Brigade Commander gave me targets for our guns on Mljet, and the shells from our 3.7s joined in the attack. Counter-shelling from the mainland started up again, and by midday it became clear that we were in for a prolonged battle. The enemy had to protect the coastal road at all cost. Meanwhile, news reached us that the 1st Brigade had got ashore on the mainland and were attacking Neum and Rudine. The partisans asked me for air support, and I sent the following signal to Balkan Air Force:

> Situation report 0900 hrs. Heavy fighting in Neum area position not yet clear. Enemy headquarters 370 regiment and garrison of 280 men in OSLJE. Headquarters first house western outskirts of village and near church E 048827. Four 105 mm guns RUDINE E 044810 and four 105 mm guns USTRIKOVA E 080770 in action against partisans NEUM area. Enemy position ZAMASLINA E 050760. Information received that enemy are sending reinforcement from Dubrovnik to Neum area.

By nightfall, in front of the defences of Ston, we had got nowhere, and partisan casualties started filtering back to headquarters. The enemy were not to give up their natural strongpoint easily. This was probably the first occasion on which the Yugoslav Army of National Liberation had been engaged in a full scale orthodox military attack on a strongly defended German garrison. The attack on Brac was, in comparison, a guerrilla action against evacuating forces. As the number of casualties mounted, I wondered how our allies would cope with the situation, as there were no base hospitals. The casualties suffered in inland hit and run operations were patched up and hidden in the villages, but these were very light compared to the present scale of operations, and very soon the area about our headquarters became littered with wounded.

The following day saw the same pattern of attack. Medium bombers came over to drop their loads of high explosive on Ston. Spitfires and Hurricanes continued to strike the Metkovic road, which was by now thick with enemy troops and transport withdrawing northwards. The Balkan Air Force were responding to my every signal, and my communications with a 22 w/t set and first class signallers were so far faultless.

I had an uneasy feeling about Captain Smith and his battery, as he had not enough ammunition for any sustained operation. I had thought him to be in a safe gun position six miles in my rear firing across the channel on the Metkovic road, but I was quite wrong.

The pattern of attack of the first day was repeated, and the infantry of the 11ᵗʰ Brigade were making little impression on the defences. Meanwhile, casualties were mounting, and ammunition was getting low. We moved our headquarters forward, and I took over a wooden hut in a gulley which I hoped would be tolerably safe from shellfire.

On the 17th Captain Smith suddenly turned up, having marched the six miles overland. He had run out of ammunition and had an astonishing tale to tell. After his initial shoot, the partisans of the 1st Brigade transported him across the Neretva Channel under cover of night, in fishing boats. He had disembarked his battery on to the mainland and shot up the Metkovic road the following day, using up all the ammunition he had shipped with him. This was a very dangerous adventure, since if the Germans had suspected and located his gun position they would certainly have sent a strong force of infantry from the road to take his guns, and he could not have got away by sea in daylight across the channel without being sunk by the shore batteries. As it was, the next night, the 1st Brigade had got him back to the Peljesac. Smith was awarded the Military Cross for this effort. Nothing succeeds like success. Webb was promoted Lieutenant Commander, and I myself narrowly avoided a court martial, having been ordered not to employ the guns in any hazardous undertaking without British Infantry protection.

Meanwhile, I had a signal from the battery on Mljet that their barrels were wearing out and asking if they could get them changed. Smith badly wanted more employment for his howitzers. The action was drawing out much longer than we had anticipated. There was a shortage of ammunition all round, and the mules had long ago eaten up all the scant fodder we had been able to bring with us.

It became clear that our whole effort was running down. The little town of Ston, with its solid stone buildings and professional garrison, was standing up to our attacks with astonishing fortitude. One way or another, the battle for possession would be resolved within the next 48 hours. Either we should take the town or we should be forced to withdraw and disperse into the hills and rocky crags of the peninsula. There was no time to change the barrels of the guns on Mljet or to get up further ammunition for the seventy-fives. Our base was still on Vis, and it was many miles from the Peljesac port of Zuljana to our present position.

I reluctantly told Smith to get his guns back to the port for re-embarkation to our base.

By 19 October we had taken Mali Ston, the outlying harbour. The 11th Brigade were at last in possession. German prisoners started filing through our headquarters camp, their faces as grey as their dust-covered uniforms. A German officer was sent to me for interrogation, but my interpreter, who was a brilliant linguist as well as a lawyer, could get no information from him which we did not already have. I was embarrassed to be face to face with a professional soldier under these circumstances as I could not guarantee his safety and, indeed, I had no troops to do so; he was a prisoner of the Yugoslav Army of National Liberation [JANL]. He behaved with impeccable fortitude, and his clear-cut German voice was a relief from the Serbo–Croat language, which I regret to say is rather ugly to English ears. His answers to questions were delivered in a precise and curt manner. Needless to say, we got nothing out of him.

Shortly afterwards, a single pistol shot rang out close to the hut. I sent a guard to investigate. He returned in a moment with a youth, who was brandishing an automatic. My interpreter took it from him and passed it to me. On one side of the butt the composition material of the grip had been removed and replaced by a piece of fashioned Perspex, under which had been pasted the cut out picture of a nude. I learnt to my disgust that the wretched creature had shot to death a wounded German officer who was considered a hopeless liability.

That evening, the Commander of 11th Brigade was apprehensive about a counter-attack, because during the day, and in spite of the bombardment, the enemy were seen to reinforce the Ston Garrison from the road. I was glad I had sent Smith off with his battery. Nevertheless, there was no great anxiety as the whole peninsula was behind us, and our rear was unlikely to be threatened. Most of the wounded who had littered our headquarters area had been got away somehow. Much to my surprise, on the 20th, after the Balkan Air Force bombing at dawn, the Germans evacuated Ston itself, and the partisans were now in command of the town. Just when we thought we had exhausted our effort, we had achieved our objective. The Metkovic road was still thick with traffic, as the RAF attacks were not too frequent or in great strength, and we did not have a sufficiently powerful force to halt the enemy's movements northwards.

With my two supporting batteries now out of action and Ston in the hands of the JANL, I considered my useful part in the battle was finished. My concern now was to get my small party all the way back to Vis.

The capture of the harbour surprisingly revealed several craft which were still afloat. Sooner than trek overland with the remainder of the wounded, the Brigade Commander decided to load them into the hold of a large wooden auxiliary ketch and sail down the channel to Janjina. I was offered a passage.

As light was fading we arrived at the quayside with our mules and equipment. The animals refused to board, but the muleteers were very competent. They took off their battledress tops, covering the animals' heads and eyes and coaxing them onto the wooden deck. The hold seemed to be full of wounded, the hatches being left off. We sat on the deck, and as the light faded the crew started the auxiliary and the vessel got under way out of the harbour north-west up the channel.

Ten minutes later, we came under shellfire from the German mainland batteries. I cursed myself for being so foolhardy. We could have been bivouacked safely by now on the peninsula on the way overland to Zuljana. This was no way to take a short cut. The helmsman panicked and put the huge tiller hard down away from the spumes of spray thrown up by the shells. The shore gunners soon bracketed the vessel, and the helm was put hard over the other way. The wretched mules were slithering from side to side on their haunches, and I was fearful they would go overboard as the deck tilted to alarming angles, first one way and then the other. The wounded in the hold were crying out as they were crushed against each other. To make matters worse, I developed a splitting headache, and I became quite determined that, if I got out of this alive, I should never go to war again.

The failing light and finally the dark saved us. The helmsman straightened his course as near to the Peljesac shore as he dared steer, and we safely reached our harbour. I could scarcely believe our good fortune.

Chapter 18

An Italian Holiday

I was given a week's leave and boarded a battered Dakota on the runway on Vis for the take-off to Italy. This type of aircraft was the taxi of the war, but the runway was too short for safety. As the engines roared for lift-off, and with only a few hundred yards to go, the pilot changed his mind, considering no doubt he had insufficient velocity to take to the air, and instead applied his brakes. A tyre blew out and we slewed round at right angles. A new wheel was quickly fitted and, at the second attempt, we were airborne.

On the outskirts of Bari, '37' Military Mission had a comfortable villa as headquarters. On my arrival I found the sole resident was Evelyn Waugh, the novelist. He was a curious figure. Short and rotund, he was got up in an ill-fitting service dress, with the badge of the Household Cavalry. He had been in Glina in the interior of Yugoslavia with Randolph Churchill and Lord Birkenhead. He was an avowed Catholic, and I thought it incongruous that he should be employed in any connection with the communists. I never did discover what he was doing there, and I never shall know, as only one of the trio is still alive [he later used his experience of Yugoslavia in the wartime trilogy *Sword of Honour*]. Waugh was a highly successful novelist and had been taken up by the London society of the 1930s as a wit and satirist. I had read his books, *Put Out More Flags* and *Black Mischief*, neither of which amused me. Nevertheless, I was intrigued to be closeted with a well known writer, and I questioned him about his works and beliefs. He told me he absolutely hated writing. That exploded the myth that you cannot succeed at anything unless you like doing it. He also loathed music of any sort. These two remarks have stuck in my mind. The world must be bleak indeed for anyone who cannot appreciate music.

Bari was shabby and war-torn, and the population, who had suffered the indignities imposed upon them by their arrogant allies, had not taken kindly to the British soldiery. There was a scarcely concealed undertone of hostility. The fine opera house was in full swing. An enthusiastic company were playing to packed houses, and they had a beautiful soprano. She was very young, and I understand made a great name for herself after the war. This was the only light relief in the town, which was otherwise drab and depressing.

Fortunately, I met an old friend from Cairo. Bill McLean, now a Colonel in the Royal Scots Greys, had been in Albania, next door to me, and had gathered around him a private army with the aid of gold napoleons supplied by the War Office. He, too, was taking a respite from the hazards of war and we decided to get away from it all, borrowed a jeep and set off southwards, to the rear of all the military paraphernalia. We motored as fast as the jeep could go, and as fast as Bill could drive, until dusk found us entering the beautiful town of Lecce.

We drove into the large open square. Dilapidated classical buildings of small proportions flanked it on either side. There was an atmosphere of stillness and few signs of life. My first impressions were that dust and cobwebs had taken over, but it suited our mood. A shout might have echoed over the whole town. It was late evening, and the light was fading. My impressions were an illusion. Bill started up the jeep and drove over to a building with the sign *Albergo* in fading letters on a board over the ancient portico. He shut off the engine, and we entered through the heavy, elaborate doorway into a large paved hall. I shouted out in English, and the host appeared with a shuffling uncertain step, unshaven, in his shirt sleeves and wearing old carpet slippers. When we asked for rooms for the night he showed us without enthusiasm into a large room with a high ceiling which was as sparsely furnished as the rest of the building. There were several old fashioned iron bedsteads covered in doubtful looking blankets. With an apologetic shrug he indicated that this was all he could offer. Bill and I were so charmed by the extraordinary appearance of the town, and the total absence of any sign of the military, that we agreed to stay, asking for a meal to be prepared. It was now quite late, and darkness fell.

Our room was on the ground floor, and its windows overlooked the square. As we were shaking the dust from our battledress and washing in the large china bowls provided, we became conscious of faces peering in through the window from the street. There were no curtains, even had we wished for privacy. There were the musical sounds of an Italian crowd gathering;

talking and laughing together, and presently the great double doors of the room were gently pushed open and heads appeared peeping into the room at us. The hallway of the hotel began to fill with voices, and in time the cautious sorties through the door gave way to a bolder approach. Soon our room was full of the townspeople, mostly very young and predominantly women and children. Neither Bill nor I spoke more than a few words of Italian. Nevertheless, we were greatly amused and delighted at this intrusion. Who wanted any privacy in this company? Southern Italian women are usually extremely good looking.

I do not remember much of what took place through the rest of that night. I woke in my bed with a dry mouth. The sun was pouring into the room through the dirty window, shining on the dust and cobwebs. Above everything else, I wanted a hot bath and coffee. I pulled on my clothes, dashed water on to my face and went out into the hallway. My shouts for service echoed through the building to no avail, so I went out into the square, leaving Bill still soundly asleep. He was the sort of man who can breakfast on brandy, go to bed at midday and be up all night.

But the square was again deserted. I searched without success for a café, and on my return, completely unsatisfied and with my stomach groaning for comfort, I found Bill sitting up in bed happily sipping coffee from a large mug.

On our return from Lecce, Bill McLean had to go back to his private army in Albania and, as I had another week left, Brash and I decided to visit the eternal city, which had just been liberated. Moreover, my fiancée had an aged aunt living in Rome who was the widow of the Norwegian Consul, long since dead, and I thought it my duty to see how she had fared.

We drove across Italy by way of Melfi and Avellino to Amalfi, from the Adriatic to the Tyrrhenian Sea. As we pulled up on the corniche road at Amalfi to gaze upon the wonder of the Gulf of Salerno, a middle-aged woman approached us to ask if we wanted a guide to the sights. She spoke with the unmistakable accent of the East End of London and was clearly longing for the conversation of her countrymen. For twenty-five years, since she was a young woman, she had been making a precarious living, so far from the foggy streets of her home environment, as a tourist guide on this beautiful coast, having somehow weathered the dangers of the conflict which had outraged the country of her adoption. I wondered how she had managed during the years of war as an alien, but when I asked her she answered me merely with a shrug. It was a strange encounter in the middle of a war.

We scarcely stopped in Naples, which was packed with American and British troops from the countless installations in the area and from General Wilson's elaborate headquarters at Caserta.

We had not seen United States troops before at any time during the war, and the sight was something of a novelty. Truckloads of men, many of them negroes, were seemingly dashing at high speed in all directions, miraculously directed in some sort of order by imperious-looking steel-helmeted military police. The western half of this theatre of operations was predominantly under the command of the controversial American General Mark Clark. The Allied advance from the toe of Italy had met with determined resistance, resulting in the most bitter fighting, with appalling casualties to both sides, which have never been properly recorded in history.

We passed the vast ruins of the Monastery at Cassino, high on its hill dominating the Liri Valley and the highway known as Route Six, where the 1st German Parachute Division had bravely withstood for week after week the most devastating bombardment by guns and bombs ever launched against a single position in the history of warfare. They held the key to the gates of Rome and they died before it was seized.

We entered the most beautiful city in the world by the Via Appia. I found Brita's aunt, Madame Brunchorst, who had managed to get through the years of occupation a good deal thinner but otherwise with an unimpaired zest for life, at home in her flat in the Palazzo del Grillo. This little palace was so near to the Forum that when I leant out of the window I could look down on the white marble ruins to the place where Mark Antony delivered his oration on the death of Caesar.

We dined on the pavement outside a restaurant in the Piazza Navone, the most beautiful square I have ever known. Children played about the fountain designed by Bernini, and I made a vow to return, which I am glad to say I have kept in more tranquil times.

I had a happy time during my few days in Rome, and it was with reluctance that Brash and I set off once more for Yugoslavia, where I found an important letter waiting for me which had come all the way from Lisbon by the impeccable Army postal service addressed c/o '37' Military Mission, British Army.

Chapter 19

The Liberation of Split

On my return, I found the 26th Division licking its wounds from the Peljesac attack. They had increased their strength with recruits from the mainland, and there was a lot of activity. I learned that the Germans had halted their withdrawal northwards and were still in possession of Split. The Division was to take the port at the first opportunity.

Marshal Tito was apparently adamantly against the use of British troops on the mainland, and I thought the 1st Brigade Commander must have kept very quiet about Captain Smith's exploit. It was clearly important that I should get into Split if I could. We wanted the excellent port facilities for the Royal Navy and a good shore base from which to harass the enemy. I told Bozovic of my intention. He looked even sadder than usual, referring me to his Political Commissar, who had been perfecting his imitation of Stalin; as I could get no answer from him, I put my interpreter to work. He told me that Bozovic was furious at the official line. At a conference to decide whether I should accompany the division in the coming attack on Split, he strode up and down waving his arms and declaring that it was not right to put politics before action. He had his way, and the Political Commissar sent me a message that I was to accompany him with the headquarters staff; I supposed that this was a compromise arrangement and that he had every intention of keeping a strict watch on me to make sure I did not spread capitalist propaganda amongst the inhabitants of the mainland. Subsequent events confirmed that there were some grounds for his uneasiness.

It was now mid-November and the weather was getting cold. Brash and I kitted ourselves out with warmer clothing, and I made sure my signallers were also ready at short notice with their equipment. Towards the end of the month, we had news that the 29th Division, which had occupied Dubrovnik, was in a position to join in an attack on Split. I sailed for Brac with the divisional headquarters. We again landed at Bol and marched overland to Supetar, the scene of our first battle on the island. The local partisans had gathered a number of fishing vessels in the harbour which were to be the assault craft to land us on the mainland. Politics had denied them the use of our own fast, efficient landing craft.

One dark cold night, in pouring rain, we embarked for the invasion of Split. The vessel carrying my party with the Political Commissar on board was a heavy 40ft wooden launch with a cargo hold. One hatch was left off as we huddled below decks in the gloom of an oil lamp, and the smell of previous cargoes and our damp bodies produced a fearful stench. There was a choppy sea running.

We knew that Split harbour had been sown with mines, but Bozovic had said that his swimmers had been clearing them for several nights previously and had marked out a channel. They had devised a technique for defusing mines and even for extracting the explosive for use in their own destructive devices. Their information, due to the observations of the civilian inhabitants, was usually very accurate. I certainly hoped it was on this occasion, as we began to approach the harbour.

The sound of battle brought me up on deck. To my astonishment, the whole town of Split appeared less than a mile away, brilliantly lit by street lamps. I could make out the tall lamp standards along the sea front as our boat now lay still and silent in the quieter water of the harbour. I could see men running along the quays, and there was the staccato sound of machine gun and small arms fire. The cold and damp was penetrating, but the rain had ceased. We lay off, rocking in a gentle swell for hour after hour, listening to the street fighting in the town. Several fires broke out, adding to the light from the street lamps. The total absence of shellfire in the harbour puzzled me, and I expected at any moment the crash of shells, but none came. As the firing ashore gradually diminished, the Commissar ordered the helmsman to put into the town. The engine started, and we shortly came right under the lights along the sea front up to the quay, where we leapt ashore and struggled with our equipment along the roadway, following our guides.

In the face of the attack by two partisan divisions, the enemy had decided to evacuate Split. It was not a good defensive position for an army on the retreat, and they were to consolidate their defences farther north. Having knowledge of the partisans' intentions, they had left only a rearguard, which explained the absence of artillery in the battle.

I was escorted through the empty streets to the principal hotel on the sea front which was already littered with troops lying exhausted in the smartly carpeted corridors. The atmosphere steamed with wet uniforms. Ammunition boxes and arms were carelessly stacked against the walls. Wounded were being attended to by civilian women. I took possession of three rooms on the second floor, giving me a view of the harbour.

The luxury of the hotel was incongruous under the circumstances. There was, however, no heating or hot water. Trooper Brash tried the taps in the fine tiled bathroom, but only a trickle of rusty-looking water came out. I told him to leave the plug in the bath and keep the tap running. It later became apparent that the Germans had blown up the town's water supply, and my precaution was justified. It was now bitterly cold in the building, and I started to shiver badly.

Trooper Brash and my senior signaller, Corporal Knowles, organized themselves in the room next door, putting up their radio equipment. I sent a signal to Italy that we were in the town and were well established, and then got into bed under the sheets, pulling the eiderdown over my head.

With the dawn, firing had ceased. I looked out from the balcony of my room at the deserted appearance of the town. The civilian population had shut themselves in their houses, evidently as afraid of the partisans as they were of the enemy. Doubtless there had been collaboration, but even the innocent did not want to witness reprisals.

A luxury hotel without water or heating in winter was extremely uncomfortable. Moreover, food was short. My shivering continued. Either I had influenza or a recurrence of the sand fly fever which I had contracted in the Western Desert. I signalled the Balkan Air Force to ask if they could send a token force of Spitfires to fly low over the town, to show the flag and restore my morale. Air Vice-Marshal Mills agreed at once. The following morning, in brilliant sunshine, a flight came over, performing a victory roll. I believe it had some effect, because I began to receive visitors. Nearly all of them wanted to know when the British Army would arrive, but sadly I had to tell them that such an event was unlikely. Some, risking the displeasure of their communist countrymen, openly said they wanted to get away. It was a difficult position to be in, and I longed to move out of the town as I was sure the Commissar was taking note of all my visitors.

Most of the population remained in their houses throughout the day. There were no victory celebrations and, in spite of the brilliant sunshine, the atmosphere was heavy with fear. There were rumours that execution squads were at their work in the town. Later, I learnt that twenty-five so-called collaborators were executed around 29 November, including such prominent citizens as Lukas, Ljubic and Carie. Many Domobran, the militia recruited by the Ustaše, deserted to the partisans, but most were treated as prisoners. The local Domobran Commander at Drniz was reprieved, as it was believed he had prevented the enemy from damaging the power station beyond repair.

Some of my visitors declared that the Germans had behaved very correctly in the town throughout the occupation. There was a curious implication in what they said: they were patriots; they were not pro-German or pro-Italian but were simply anti-communists and feared yet another tyranny.

My headquarters on Vis sent the rest of our personal kit by partisan vessel which consisted of blankets, my old scarred bedroll, several cases of regulation rations and, to my great joy, a few bottles of whisky with a good store of cigarettes. The golden liquid soon finished off my fever. The rations, to our dismay, consisted solely of tins of sausages and Maconochie stew, which I hated. Sores began to develop on my ankles, the delayed effect of the lack of vitamins we had suffered in the Western Desert.

The number of my visitors increased to embarrassing proportions, but I could not reassure them. It was obvious what form the post-war regime would take, and that the Western Allies would have little influence hereafter, but the news that a British officer was billeted in the principal hotel had got around. Whether this was the reason for an abrupt visit from the Commissar I could only guess but, much to my relief, we were moved out of the town to a large private house on the coastal road. The hotel had been like an icebox. The water had not been restored, and our supply of rusty looking liquid in the bath was nearly exhausted.

A jeep arrived from Vis, and now I was mobile. We loaded up and transferred our headquarters. We were received by a charming family. My host was an elderly, educated man, and he and his wife and very attractive daughter put themselves to great trouble to make us comfortable. This was civilization, which I had not enjoyed since leaving Egypt ten months previously. My bedroom was old fashioned, well furnished with solid furniture and good carpets. I was told by my host that we should have dinner at eight. I strode about the room revelling in the luxury, had a hot bath, putting on my one and only service dress. Brash had shone up the buttons and badges, and my morale was fully restored as I looked forward with pleasure to the company.

Then I heard a sudden commotion in the house. Loud voices were raised and heavy boots approached my door, which was thrust rudely open. Framed in the doorway were half a dozen aggressive faces as the partisans burst in. I saw a hand go to a pistol holster. I reassured them in English, but they withdrew still puzzled and with hardly an apology for their intrusion. Evidently they had thought my host was harbouring a reactionary.

It was wonderful to be once again in sophisticated civilian company. The daughter of the house was gorgeous; tall and well built with very blonde hair and a beautiful smile, and breathless with excitement. It was a delightful dinner party, and I went happily to bed at long past midnight.

Corporal Knowles brought me a signal the following morning. I was ordered to proceed at once to Zadar, 70 miles north of Split, as fast as I could. The British intention was to establish a forward raiding base to accommodate a squadron of fighters on the airstrip and to negotiate the use of the harbour for the Royal Navy and the Commandos.

The Germans had halted their withdrawal to the north, having consolidated their positions. The Devil's Division held the coastal area north of Zadar at Jesenica, the 369th and 370th division were east and west of Drvar and the SS Prince Eugen divisions still held the left flank at Sarajevo.

I had to take my leave of the 26th Dalmatian Division and get authority to move so far north in face of the suspicion in which we were held. With my beautiful Dalmatian in the passenger seat of the jeep, I drove into Split in the morning. In the grim atmosphere of the town we created quite a stir. Her blonde hair streamed in the wind as we sped through the streets, and I pulled up ostentatiously in front of the hotel, where the Divisional Headquarters had established some order. Armed guards were at the entrance. I went at once to seek out the Commissar. He was seated behind a table, and his heavy-lidded eyes looked at me without humour, his black drooping moustache hiding his expression. The copy of Karl Marx was close to his right hand, and I wondered if he would turn the pages to find out if he had authority to give me a pass to proceed with. He was now the personification of autocracy, and Marx would never have approved of him. The state had become paramount, and to this day it has never withered away, either in Russia or in any other country where the militant minority hold power [this was written in 1970/71]. The interview was entirely unsatisfactory, and my request was to be referred to higher authority. My companion had a flat in Split, to which we repaired for refreshment.

I was still in my twenties, and it was a temptation to stay put and to accept the confinement to Split and my comfortable billet. But I decided to leave before light the following morning to avoid any further consideration of my request, and to escape any measure which might follow to restrict my movements. I told Trooper Brash to pack up the party as quietly as he could to leave before dawn and told my host of my intention only after dinner, to avoid any embarrassment he might find confronting him after my departure.

We left in the dark. I drove as fast as I could along the coast road. It was bitterly cold and now midwinter. We encountered no roadblocks. As dawn broke we had reached Marina. The few armed partisans simply stared as the jeep sped through the village. The only town on our route of any importance was Sibenik, 50 miles to the north. I told Brash and Knowles to see that the magazines of their rifles were full and to put a round up the breech. It had only been a few days since the enemy withdrawal, and there might be parties of Ustaše in the hills who would dearly like to have our jeep and supplies. Ice lay in patches on the road surface.

Sure enough, at Sibenik there was a roadblock. The sentries were curious at our appearance, but we wore battledress. Trooper Brash's black beret, my service dress cap and perhaps our well-shone regimental badges were the only oddities. Corporal Knowles and his fellow signaller were hardly distinguishable from partisans, but obviously we were British, and the broad grins of the partisans gave us incredulous recognition.

Upon the German withdrawal from Greece and the southern part of Yugoslavia, Tito had to organize his guerrilla forces rapidly into regular formations. He was now faced with orthodox warfare and, before leaving Split, I had learnt that this transition was in full swing.

Ten miles north of Sibenik, where snow lay over the ground and the ice increased, we came upon an astonishing sight. Our way lay across a causeway straddling a large lake, and the tarmac was black with wild duck. The lake on either side was frozen solid, and the duck sat on the road to get relief from the ice. They had no fear of the approaching vehicle, and I had to hoot the horn to get them out of the way. None of us had any thought of killing them for the pot. With all the killing we had witnessed, I think we were comforted by the sight of these homely-looking mallard and teal, with which we were so familiar. Surely, if they could speak, they could only speak English. They got off the road just in front of the wheels, only to settle down again behind us. Evidently there had been few wildfowlers about for the last five years.

The country over which we travelled was bleak and barren. The rocky hillside rose steeply on our right hand, and to our left we caught glimpses of grey sea. There was a light covering of snow over the scrub and rocks. In that frozen landscape all my defensive instincts were alerted. Only a few days previously, the road must have been stiff with enemy transport. I turned off into a gulley, stopped the engine and listened. Not a sound from any direction. Since leaving Split we had not encountered a single transport in sixty miles.

There were a fair number of Ustaše in the Devil's Division. They would know the country, and it must have been apparent to them that, in the event of a German defeat, their position would be desperate. Bozovic had told me that they would be hunted down and shot as traitors, since they had copied the ruthless habits of the German SS troops. It was probable that they would desert the Germans if a total withdrawal was imminent and go in for brigandage in order to survive. The remaining Četniks were still banded together into small defensive groups. I did not want an encounter with either of these factions.

We sped toward Zadar. Sure enough there was a roadblock, heavily manned by partisans, just outside the town. We were surrounded in a moment, and it was clear that news of my unauthorized journey had got ahead of me, an event I had anticipated. Four of the partisans climbed into a small captured German staff car and signed to me to follow them. The town seemed almost deserted. My guides pulled up outside a small villa fronting the northern side of the wide harbour, and I was directed to drive the jeep through a gateway into a walled yard at the rear. We were nearly frozen stiff by this time. My one thought was to get inside for warmth and comfort, and my small party were all of the same mind. No questions were asked whilst we unloaded the jeep. The villa was sparsely furnished, but in such good order that it was evident that the owners had only just been told to leave; wood fires were still alight in the stoves. The town's electricity supply was working, and clear water came from the taps. In no time Trooper Brash had us organized and got busy cooking up a meal from our rations. I did not know it, but this was to be our home and headquarters for the next three months.

With the food and warmth, my brain started to function again more or less normally, and I decided to take a look at our surroundings. I had smartened myself up for an encounter with communist authority but I got no farther than the entrance gate to the courtyard when a sentry held up his Schmeisser against my path. We were under house arrest. I decided to wait until morning before I began our battle for freedom. It was a black, cold night.

Dawn broke over a lovely scene. The villa was almost on the water's edge, separated from it only by a narrow road running round the harbour. My room had a balcony beyond the French windows. The still sea soon lay shimmering in the morning sunlight. To the west lay the snow-covered island of Uljan and the town of Preko. I looked across to it and wondered what had become of Leutnant Frommer. If I was to be confined, this was not a bad prison.

I called my small party together. We were only four: Brash, Corporal Knowles, Signalman Stark and I. I told them I thought we might be confined to the house for some time and that I was bent on a strategy of reprisal for the insult. First, we would smarten ourselves up as far as possible to parade standard. We would demand food and service. Meals were to be provided strictly at appointed hours: lunch at one and dinner at eight. We would eat formally together. Our conversation with our guards was to be polite but firm. Until we were allowed our freedom we would not fraternize. I determined to insist that the airstrip should be ready for the Royal Air Force. We were here to prosecute the war and nothing else. What was the Yugoslav Army of National Liberation doing about it? Why were we under arrest? I intended to prick our captors into shame. Fearing our radio would be taken, I warned Knowles that one of us would be on guard over it day and night. We would overhaul our weapons, three Lee Enfield rifles, my own .45 automatic and my regimental Colt revolver. Hardly a formidable armament.

My aggressive indignation was almost at once dampened by the arrival of three strapping-looking young women in khaki skirts and green cotton blouses buttoned over ample bosoms. The day was young, and we were refreshed after our comfortable night. This was our household staff in force. The troops stood around gaping whilst the young women started work, making up the beds and cooking our breakfast. We were in all truth much disarmed, and the wind was taken out of my sails; nevertheless, I was sticking to my predetermined policy.

During the course of the morning I had a visit from a young partisan officer. He informed me that orders had arrived from a certain General Drapsin, of whom I had never heard, that we were to be confined to the house until such time as Marshal Tito had agreed to the terms of cooperation against the common enemy. I told him that I wished to see the local Commander immediately and that my intention could not be delayed except to the advantage of the Germans. To his credit, he was much embarrassed but he could give me no information.

I sent a signal of my situation to Italy. At least we had established ourselves in Zadar, and I was glad I had decided to set out from Split without waiting. It was at any rate a journey in the right direction; I was not more than ten miles as the crow flies from the Devil's Division.

During the next few days we settled down to our extraordinary routine. My signals to Italy received acknowledgements, but they offered no solution to my predicament. The weather was fine, our household staff arrived daily to make the beds, clean the house and get our meals. We were treated with such consideration in our confinement that it became increasingly apparent that our guards and staff were desperately trying to make up to us for orders of which they were thoroughly ashamed. It was quite touching, but I could not let up on my outward show of indignation. The three young women not only swept the house but daily scrubbed the wooden floors so that they were white with cleanliness. Sweet-smelling wood was brought in to keep the fires going day and night. There were three stoves in the house. They were tall and rectangular, with decorative tiled panels and stood in the corners of the rooms with a flue pipe into the concealed chimneys. Similar stoves are still in use in most of the Scandinavian countries, and they are wonderfully effective. Outside the temperature was below zero during the night.

One morning, a few days after our arrival, the lawyer of Zagreb arrived from Split. I had kept from him our intention to leave. I knew he was already suspected of being anti-communist and I do not think he really tried to conceal it, but I had not wanted to get him into trouble by taking him into my confidence. At any rate, he had proved his worth to the cause by risking his neck in a pretence at cooperation with the Italians during their initial invasion of Yugoslavia. He had saved the life of a wounded partisan by a lawyer's guile, something for which he would have been shot if detected.

His arrival was a great relief to me. He was not confined to the house and could go where he pleased, so I relied on him for a situation report at the earliest opportunity. He went off at once and returned towards evening to give me news at which I was delighted. Captain Vulin, whom I had met not long before on the island of Dugi Otok, had been promoted Major and commanded the partisan garrison of Zadar which now had been given the designation of Second Sector. He had not known the identity of the British officer who had arrived by an unauthorized journey and he was furious that we had been arrested. Second Sector was apparently under command of a new Corps which had been formed to contain the enemy on the line at which they now stood. This was the Eleventh Corps, commanded by General Drapsin, by whose orders we had been incarcerated. Drapsin began to take on the appearance of an ogre, and I suspected from his subsequent behaviour that he was a member of the secret police. This organization went by the pompous title, *Organizacija Za Zastitu Naroda* (Organization for the Protection of the People), and its representatives were of all ranks in any formation. It was comparable to the Russian OGPU or the German Gestapo. At the head of this sinister force was a man called Marko, who was at the time Secretary to the Communist Party in Yugoslavia and Tito's political adviser. All the essentials of a totalitarian regime were already in existence.

The following day, Vulin and his Commissar arrived; no commander was ever free from his political shadow. However, the Commissar turned out to be a handsome, dark-haired young man called Branko Mamula, who spoke excellent English and had very disarming manners. I told them both that we had been ordered to get on with the war, that a squadron of fighters was waiting to come in as soon as they could make the airstrip serviceable and that the Royal Navy wanted the port in order to be in a better position to blockade Pola in Istria and to use as a harbour.

Vulin said he would see if he could start work on the airstrip as soon as possible but that it was in a terrible condition, and there was a shortage of labour to clear it. I asked him when we were to be given our freedom. But, of course, this was a matter for higher authority. No one was allowed personal initiative under this regime.

However, on 17 January I received a perfectly astonishing signal. Our headquarters in Italy had arrived at an agreement with Tito for the use of Zadar as a base of operations. No fewer than eight fighter-bomber squadrons were to come in; three thousand Air Force personnel were to be accommodated; Allied naval vessels were to use the port; British and Allied army personnel were to be shipped in for airfield construction and maintenance of the base; the whole operation was to go under the code name Baffle. The agreement had been signed on 6 January, and it was now the 17th, but apart from receiving a copy of the agreement, I had received no instructions from Balkan Air Force.

I read the signal through several times in disbelief. Before a build-up of this nature could take place, it was obviously necessary for a fighting force to precede it. The enemy were in good order in the positions they had occupied now for more than a month. The Devil's Division were still holding the coastal area only ten miles to the north. The partisans had nothing like enough troops or armament to withstand a German assault on Zadar.

If we truly had the ability at this stage to mount such a substantial build-up in Yugoslavia, then we should make the most of our resources for a British attack, with Istria at least as our objective. Although I knew that our front-line troops were hard pressed, particularly on the Western Italian front, it had always seemed that we were never at full stretch. Perhaps there was a reserve for just such a purpose as this. After all, Vienna was only 280 miles to the north of Zadar.

The Colonel of my regiment at No. 10 Downing Street had his own ideas on the matter, as I was shortly to find out. Churchill's active mind, constantly ranging over far-flung military strategy, and impatient over the slow progress of the Allies against the determined German resistance in Italy, conceived a plan to outflank the enemy by landing a mobile striking force on the Yugoslav coastline for a drive to Vienna. The text of the agreement was as follows:

PRIORITY: DEFERRED DATE & TO 161220A FROM: REAR MACMIS

TO: FISHER   GO/933...16 JAN 45 TOPSECRET (.)

FOLS TEXT OF MILITARY AGREEMENT FOR OPERATION BAFFLE SIGNED BY TITO

6th rpt 6th JANUARY 1945 (.) QUOTE (.)

1. IT IS AGREED FOR THE PURPOSE OF SUPPORTING THE JANL IN THEIR FIGHT AGAINST THE GERMANS IN NORTHERN JUGOSLAVIA AN AIR BASE WILL BE ESTABLISHED IN THE ZADAR AREA WHICH WILL BE USED BY UNITS OF THE RAF AND USAAF (.) THE ESTABLISHMENT AND MAINTENANCE OF THIS BASE WILL NECESSITATE THE USE OF THE PORT OF ZADAR BY ALLIED NAVAL AND MERCANTILE VESSELS (.) THE OBJECT OF THE AIR BASE IS TO FACILITATE OUR COMMON OPERATIONS FOR THE DESTRUCTION OF THE ENEMY AND THE AIR FORCES AND OTHER AUXILLIARY UNITS WILL BE WITHDRAWN WHEN NO RPT NO LONGER REQUIRED FOR THIS PURPOSE (.)

2. IN ORDER TO TAKE THE FULLEST ADVANTAGE OF THE OPPORTUNITIES OFFERED BY THE ENEMY'S WITHDRAWAL IN NORTHERN YUGOSLAVIA IT IS AGREED THAT CONSTRUCTIONAL WORK ON THE AIRFIELD AT ZEMUNIK AND ITS SATELLITE PRKOS SHALL BEGIN FORTHWITH (.) AIRFIELD CONSTRUCTION ENGINEERS AND THE NECESSARY MAINTENANCE UNITS WILL ACCORDINGLY BE SENT TO ZADAR AT ONCE (.) AS WELL AS A PARTY OF AIRMEN TO BE USED FOR REFUELING AND REARMING AIRCRAFT(.) A PARTY OF AMERICAN AIRFORCE WILL ALSO BE SENT (.) TO BE EMPLOYED ON SERVICING AIRCRAFT WHICH LAND IN A DAMAGED CONDTION ON RETURN FROM RAIDS INTO GERMANY (.)

3. IT IS AGREED THAT THE AIRFORCES EVENTUALLY
   ESTABLISHED IN THE ZADAR AREA SHALL CONSIST
   OF (,) SIX FIGHTER BOMBER SQNS INCLUDING THE
   TWO JANL SQNS(,) ONE DEFENSIVE FIGHTER SQN
   (,) AND ONE NIGHT FIGHTER INTRUDER SQN (,)
   ANCILLIARY UNITS INCLUDING RADAR UNITS (,)
   THE TOTAL ALLIED AIR FORCES WILL BE APPROX.
   3700 OFFRS AND MEN (.) THE COMMANDER OF THE
   AIR BASE WILL BE A MEMBER OF THE JUGOSLAV AIR
   FORCE (,) BUT THE FORCES OPERATING FROM THE
   BASE WILL BE UNDER THE OPERATIONAL CONTROL
   OF AN RAF OFFR (.)

4. IN ADDITION TO THE RAF PERSONNEL SOME ARMY
   PERONNEL WILL BE EMPLOYED IN THE ZADAR AREA
   FOR MAINTENANCE PURPOSE AND FOR THE AIRFIELD
   CONSTRUCTION WORK REFERRED TO IN PARA TWO
   (.) THERE WILL ALSO BE A SMALL ARMY DET FOR
   THE AA DEFENCE OF THE PORT (.) THE TOTAL ARMY
   PERSONNEL WILL BE APPROX 3000 ALL RANKS.

The day following the receipt of this agreement, Vulin called for me with the news that I was to be released from my comfortable incarceration, and we set out at once to inspect Zemunik in my jeep. The airstrip was in a terrible mess. It had been bombed repeatedly by the RAF and was pitted with craters and littered with debris. Snow covered the landscape, and ice lay thick on the tarmac.

For some reason or other, I instinctively felt that the terms of the agreement would not be carried out. It was drafted and approved by negotiators who had no idea of the realities of the situation. The very wording was amateur in a military context.

At any rate, it was clear that we had to get the airfield serviceable as fast as we could. The town still appeared almost deserted, and I wondered where the labour would come from; but it came, little by little. In place of the army of constructional engineers and maintenance units envisaged in Paragraph 2 of the agreement, local men, women and even children arrived in the bitter cold with shovels, brooms, pickaxes and improvised tools. Every day, I went out to inspect progress, walking up and down the airstrip in the hope that my presence would encourage the workers. The buildings were completely unserviceable, and I signalled a situation report daily. At the end of a week I thought that a Spitfire might land without coming to grief.

Meanwhile, from the balcony of my room at the villa I could see the local inhabitants clearing the harbour of sunken wrecks and obstructions. There never seemed to be many men at work, but the ingenuity with which they raised wrecks with the absolute minimum of manpower and equipment was remarkable. The absence of any considerable number of partisan troops in the town and local environment was curious. Tito was now in Belgrade, and I do not think that he was greatly interested in anything else at this point in the war except political power. The outcome for Britain was far from being a foregone conclusion. Two weeks previously, Von Rundstedt had threatened the entire Allied effort with his offensive in the Ardennes. The German armies in Italy were still holding their line, and the Eighth Army was fighting hard for supremacy.

By 20 January the 19th Dalmatian Division had turned up. I went to see General Drapsin, who failed to apologize for my imprisonment. However, he had his orders, and I had a copy of the agreement. I told him I intended to signal that the airstrip was ready to receive the Royal Air Force and the harbour was clear of obstructions. He raised no objections. With the arrival of the 19th Division I considered there were sufficient ground forces available to provide at least some protection to the Royal Air Force installations. If there was an enemy attack, the aircraft would have enough time to get off the ground.

On the 22nd a squadron of Spitfires and Hurricanes flew in, commanded by Squadron Leader Bartlett. It was a wonderful sight to see these beautiful aeroplanes landing one after the other. They were followed by Dakotas carrying their back-up supplies and tents. I told Bartlett he would have to be constantly on the alert to evacuate in view of the proximity of the enemy and the doubtful protection the partisans could afford.

A squadron of MLs and four gunboats arrived in the afternoon and established themselves in the harbour. To my delight, they brought with them, carried by LCTs, a troop of the Raiding Support Regiment with Major Bethell in command.

During the succeeding few days Lieutenant Colonel Sutherland disembarked with a company of the SAS. The RAF, in response to my caution about protection of the airfield at Zemunik, sent in two companies of the Royal Air Force Regiment; we now had a small striking force which, however, was very far short of that required by the grandiose design set forth in the agreement.

I suddenly received orders to report to the Eighth Army Headquarters in Italy for instruction in the latest methods of close air support for ground troops. Leaving Corporal Knowles in charge of our establishment, Brash and I got into a Dakota at Zemunik for Bari, where we were provided with a jeep, setting off at once to drive 100 miles to the north. The weather was foul, alternately raining and snowing. The roads had been carved up by army transport, bomb craters had been hastily filled in and wrecked vehicles lay on each side of the road as we bounced and skidded through the slush. It was not until dusk that we reached General McCreery's headquarters.

There we found a maze of armoured command vehicles and caravans. Dimmed lights lit up the mud and the duckboards. It was now pouring with heavy, cold rain. To my surprise, the Military Police were expecting me. This was most unusual. I had little experience of high commands, but more often than not they had never heard of you, whatever your orders had been.

I was led by a military policeman through the muddy lanes between the vehicles to a large caravan, where I was greeted by Christopher Smuts, a nephew of the renowned General. I had known him before the war as a barrister, but he was now a senior staff officer. He told me to turn around and go back to Zadar at once. I tried to pump him for an explanation, but he was non-committal. When I asked him if we intended to outflank the Germans in Italy by an invasion of the Yugoslav mainland at Zadar, he remained silent. He simply repeated that I was to get back as fast as I could to await instructions. His silence on the subject simply confirmed my interpretation of this sudden order.

The German armies in Italy had fought a most stubborn retreat and were now holding a line north of Foggia. From the Adriatic to the Tyrrhenian Sea was only 80 miles at this point, and the ground favoured defence. We had suffered heavy casualties, particularly on the left flank. A colonel of the Queen's Regiment told me they had suffered 100 per cent officer casualties in six months' hard fighting. A flanking movement on the other side of the Adriatic with a drive towards Vienna would be sensational.

Smuts gave me welcome refreshment before I trudged back through the mud to the jeep. When I told Trooper Brash we had to turn back the way we had come, he cursed under his breath. We reached Andria shortly before midnight and with difficulty found a small hotel. Our bedrolls were soaked. Brash tugged at the sodden ropes to unload, really letting off steam in a flow of invective. He was usually good tempered and wonderful company, but we had only that morning left Zadar. It had been a long journey for nothing, and I could not for security reasons tell him the truth. The following day, we flew into Zemunik.

As I went happily to bed that night in my room at the villa, I must confess I was highly excited. I had visions of leading a victorious British army into Vienna to the resounding applause of the population. Alas, it was not to be. Churchill was overruled by the Allied command.

Meanwhile, Major Vulin had decided on a less ambitious plan, to attack and take the island of Pag from the Devil's Division. He asked me if I could produce naval and air support, so I called in Squadron Leader Bartlett and the senior naval officer. The latter soon arrived at the villa. Christopher Stocken looked as if he had just left school; however, he was a regular naval officer, and his appearance was extremely deceptive, for he soon revealed an air of absolute confidence. It took but a few seconds of his acquaintance to know that you could rely on him, and his judgement proved to be thoroughly professional. Most of the ML captains were Royal Naval Volunteer Reserves. They were all very high class people and wonderfully good company.

Our small-scale war, seemingly so remote from the main theatre of operations, was in fact directed at the extreme left flank of the whole German war effort, which accounted for the determined resistance of the Devil's Division and their firm stand north of Zadar. My companions and I did not appreciate this at the time, but doubtless the fact had been brought home in no uncertain terms to the small German garrisons of islands such as Brac, Pag and Uljan, who were not merely defending the territory of their occupation, but the very flank of all their armies fighting now desperately from the shores of the Baltic Sea to the Adriatic.

Chapter 20

Nothing Ventured, Nothing Gained

The Vidovac battery dominated the whole island of Pag. It was manned by the artillery of the Devil's Division and was sited north of Karlobag on the mainland.

I asked Vulin what he proposed to do about it, as I could not see how an infantry attack on the island could succeed unless the battery was silenced, at least during the initial landing. It was true that if the partisans could take the town, the cover the island afforded would subsequently give considerable protection, since the town itself was more or less a fortress, lying between two hills in a valley running northwards to the sea. It was stone-built and, as I had witnessed at Ston, Supetar and Sumartin, the buildings could withstand a terrific amount of shellfire without much damage to the defenders.

In reply to my question, Vulin said that the 20th Dalmatian Division, which was arriving shortly at Zadar, was to attack along the coast road, and he thought the Vidovac battery would be therefore so heavily engaged against it that it would be distracted from the defence of Pag. He asked if the Royal Air Force could attempt to knock it out. But Bartlett only had one squadron of Spitfires and Hurricanes, and they could not be expected to fly continual sorties on a single position at a low level, because the enemy had anti-aircraft guns. Even a full squadron attack would not guarantee the permanent disablement of a single heavy gun.

Nevertheless, if the partisans could take the high points on Pag, where the observation posts were sited, the battery would be left to fire in defence of the town at random. These higher points were situated to the north and south, at Gradac and Juraj. An assault as quickly as possible after the initial landing on these positions was therefore the first task.

Vulin and Branko Mamula declared they had taken this into consideration. But neither of them had any previous experience whatever of orthodox warfare, and although their intention was just what we wanted, I was sceptical about the outcome. Vulin had been given a battalion of the 20th

Division to supplement his own Second Sector. As far as I could make out, the total front-line troops would number fewer than 1,000 men, armed only with automatics, rifles, grenades and a few mortars and captured Breda light machine guns. They still had no artillery, but there had been no request for our howitzers, and I was determined not to hazard them in this operation unless far more force was committed. In any event, I was ordered never to employ our guns without British ground forces to protect them.

Lieutenant Stocken was longing for some action. He was willing to provide LCTs to carry the assault troops from Jasenovo to Pag to land at Vlasivi, and agreed to support the operation with five 'D' class MLs and one gunboat.

Bartlett committed the Royal Air Force to strafe and bomb the observation posts on Gradac and Juraj as far as his force would allow. I intended to sail with Vulin's headquarters to land at Povljana, and I had to be sure of reliable radio communication with the airfield. Our radios, even at this stage in the war, were still far from reliable, and the radio telephone had a short range. From Povljana to Zemunik was sixteen miles, and as I could only be sure of maintaining contact over half that distance, I had to establish a radio link at Nin, eight miles north of Zadar and Zemunik. With this arrangement there was always the risk of garbled signals, but unless we were prepared to use Morse code, this was the best we could do.

Vulin and his Second Sector were to sail from the coast near Nin in partisan vessels, and I was to go with them together with my signallers. I was continually surprised at the number of small craft which were available to the partisans. If I had been a ruthless commander of the German forces I would have sunk every vessel which could float. But there were nearly a hundred islands in the Archipelago, and this would have meant starvation for a large population in a matter of months, since the island people depended on their fishing industry and the importation of grain. The German command was never noted for its humanity, and I can only suppose that their ultimate defeat in Yugoslavia was not seriously contemplated, even at this late hour, because a force of 'E' boats from Pola could have made a raid on the islands, sinking everything on sight without much risk in a relatively short time.

On 21 February we called a conference with all the partisan commanders on Stocken's flagship – an ML fixed up as a Headquarters Ship. One of the difficulties of the operation was to get the LCTs from Zadar to Jasenovo undetected. The Lutwaffe were still flying reconnaissance Messerschmitts at odd times of the day and night, and if the vessels were seen lying off Jasenovo before 'D' Day, our intention would have been suspected. On the other hand, the voyage itself was hazardous. The narrow strait between the island of Vir and the mainland had to be negotiated, and the Povljana channel itself was only two miles wide. Stocken decided that the ships would have to make the voyage the night before 'D' Day and enter the bay at Jasenovo in the dark. If they got close in to shore they would be hidden by the promontory enclosing the bay from the north. We hoped they would not be spotted from Pag at night. They were to cruise at slow speed to cut down the noise. If the ships were detected, the whole operation was to be called off, and they were to return to Zadar.

The partisan commanders were evidently greatly impressed by the Royal Navy and particularly by the youthful Senior Naval Officer. Stocken was in fact only a few years my junior, but he had been trained in naval warfare since the age of fourteen, and Britannia still ruled the waves, as far as I was concerned. The MLs under his command were manufactured by an ex-artillery officer, Sir Noel Macklin, whom I knew well; I had often visited his house at Fairmile in Cobham, Surrey. I cannot say they were nearly as good as the German 'E' boats, however. They were fast, very light craft, but could not take much of a sea. After our conference with the partisan commanders, Stocken got out a naval operation order. It would not have got a first prize at Staff College, but it was practical. We called the operation COZA TWO. 'D' Day was set for 24 February. 'H' Hour was 0700:

TOP SECRET FROM: L.C.H. 97

TO: G/C SELBY.   W/C BARTLETT.   MAJ. CRICHTON.

S.O.O. R.N.

FEB.   22   1945

OPERATION COZA TWO

'D' DAY FEB. 24. 'H' HOUR 0700 A

INFORMATION. (One) Partisan Eleven Corps intend to commence an offensive to disrupt enemy lines of communication BIHAC-OTOCAC. OTOCAC-GOSPIC. If successful the Gospic Garrison will be forced to rely upon Karlobag for line of communication. Duration of offensive may be three days.

(Two) In conjunction with the attack by Eleven Corps three battalions of partisan troops intend to attack Pag Island and enemy defences and garrison in area of Pag Town. If successful it is intended to capture and hold these positions. Duration of attack possibly three days.

INTENTION   (a) To support the mainland attack by air attacks on the following roads – OTOCAC-SENJ. Coastal road SEMJ-KARLOBAG. KARLOBAG-GOSPIC. These roads will be clear of partisans. Other specific targets to be attacked if called for by Eleven Corps.

(b) To deliver a preliminary air attack on all known enemy defences (including O.P.'s) on Pag at H hour on D day. Thereafter aircraft to be on call for further attacks on specific targets at the request of the assault force commander who will be in direct W/T contact with O.C. Parkhos. These attacks to be made for a period of three days if necessary.

EXECUTION   (one) On D Day at 0700 hours Spitfires and Hurricanes will attack enemy gun positions, bunkers and other targets as detailed on the plan handed to the force commander. In addition to these targets attacks are to be made on the following O.P.'s

(O.O.) Gradac Position 200. Reference 0.828389

(O.O.) Sv. Juraj Position 204. Reference 0.844409

(O.O.) Position 263 reference 0.850404

These O.P.'s are known to contain machine guns

(Two) In support of Eleven Corps regular sweeps will be carried out on the following roads:

(a) OTOCAC SENJ.

(b) Coastal road SENJ-KARLOBAG.

(c) KARLOBAG GOSPIC.

All these roads will be clear of partisans. Sweeps to be repeated as necessary up to a period of three days.

(Three) Royal Navy: Three M.T.B.'s will patrol Podgorski Channel during daylight to prevent enemy reinforcements landing on the south end of Pag and thus outflanking partisans.

If available one L.C.G. will bombard Karlobag (or other targets that may be specified by the assault force commander) from the west coast of Pag during daylight. No naval forces will operate after sunset.

(Four) By night: Rocket Hurricanes will carry out sweeps during moonlight with the same intention as in Para Three above.

NOTE (one)   Known enemy armament is as follows:

2 x 105 mm near cemetery wall in Pag. 2 x 105 mm position unknown.

(Enemy defences) – 2 small anti-tank guns (sometimes moved from Pag to Levada or as far as Poljana) 2 x 81mm mortars. M/G's in O.P.'s and bunker defences as illustrated on plan.

NOTE (two) It is of paramount importance that aircraft sweeping the mainland endeavour to spot the Vidovac Battery. This consists of four mobile 210 mm guns which are known to move from Karlobag along the Karlobag Gospic road up to a distance of 5 kms. Aircraft should search this road and report position immediately if sighted.

RECOGNITION 1) To denote capture of enemy strongpoint – Red Verey pistol

2) Position of our own troops indicated by a white arrow – base 1½ metres length 3 metres.

SIGNALS   M.T.B.'s patrolling Planinski Channel will listen out on channel 'C' 6450 kcs. When aircraft in vicinity (.)

Fighters should establish contact and co-operate if required (.) Aircraft call sign 'Fighters'. M.T.B. call sign 'Navy'.

The German Command had entrusted the defence of Pag to the 283 Regiment of the Devil's Division and the 999 Festungs Battalion. Included in the garrison were a number of Ustaše and some Domobran. The latter, the Croat militia recruited by the Ustaše, were unreliable and at this time deserting to the partisans. The four 105mm guns in Pag, and the ever present Vidovac battery, which we now learnt was mobile, gave the enemy a total of eight guns. Against this armament we had our one naval gun and Bartlett's squadron of fighter-bombers. There was always the possibility that the enemy would use some of their Messerschmitts against our Hurricanes, but we knew they were getting very short of aircraft as the Luftwaffe was heavily engaged in the Italian campaign.

I must admit I thought we had a hard nut to crack, but the plan was made. On the evening of 23 February all was ready. I told Corporal Knowles and Signalman Stark to go to bed. Brash was to drive us to the point of embarkation at Nin at midnight. Our radio equipment was stowed in the jeep and had been checked and rechecked. Communication with the Navy and Air Force depended entirely on the efficiency of the two radio sets, and my previous experience of military radio had been terrible. Techniques in this field lagged far behind, and there was always the nightmare that the wretched apparatus would go wrong.

I lay on my bed trying to sleep, but without success. I kept thinking of the Vidovac battery. In my imagination I could visualize the mobile guns motoring up and down the coastal road and firing on us without hindrance. Hitherto, except for my recent experiences, I had gone to war in a tank. An armoured vehicle could stand a great deal of high explosive and gave its crew a sense of security. At Alamein the plight of the infantry under shellfire on the open desert seemed to me almost intolerable, yet, oddly enough, few infantrymen would have changed places with a tank commander.

At eleven o'clock we got ourselves ready. Brash was to be left behind to look after the headquarters after he had driven us to the rendezvous with the partisans near Nin. I suffered more than usual from butterflies, but at Nin we met Vulin and Branko Mamula, who were taking copious draughts of *rakija* with goat's milk. I could not imagine a more disgusting combination, but we were unlikely to have time to take on fuel for the next 12 hours at least, so I joined in. As I had previously discovered, if you could get the mixture past your throat, it had a wonderfully warming effect.

The night was bitterly cold, but there was no wind. Some of the Second Sector had already embarked, and we heard the exhaust notes of the oil engines as they set off ahead of us. The loud plonk of these old serviceable marine engines always seemed to echo over still water, and I could hardly believe we should land at Povljana without being detected.

We got aboard a wide-beamed fishing boat. Vulin, Mamula and I stood in the wheelhouse, which was close to the stern. Our radios and ammunition was stowed in the hold. Second Sector troops stood or crouched on the decks forward, their weapons at the ready.

It was only a 12-mile voyage to the bay below Povljana, and in two hours we were in the channel. There was no indication that we had been detected, and by now surely our advance party would have landed. We could not see the shores of Pag or Vir. There were shallows to the north and south of our course, but the helmsman knew the waters intimately.

I could not understand the evident lack of vigilance of the enemy. It seemed all wrong. But the Germans had been far too long on the defensive, and if you lose the initiative you are at a disadvantage. They should have had reconnaissance patrols along the coastline. One determined machine gun, or even a patrol armed with automatics, would have created havoc amongst our wooden flotilla and, with the channel being only two miles wide, the maximum range to the middle was only 1,700yds. Even a Schmeisser had a killing range of 300yds, but the voyage was uninterrupted. The deafening roar from the exhausts reverberating, or so it seemed, over the still water in the dark night telegraphed that an attack was imminent, but we were allowed to land at the jetty leading to Povljana without a shot being fired.

In the dark I was very concerned that our radios and equipment should get ashore intact. Vulin had assigned some of his men to carry it up the rocky path to Povljana on improvised stretchers, but it was nearly a mile up the steep hill. The only sounds were our boots kicking against the gravel and rock, and the whispered conversations of the partisans.

Povljana is a very small village on a hill overlooking the sea. Its buildings, as always in this part of the world, are of stone. It is a beautiful place, but the villagers are poor and rely on marginal agriculture. I could see little of it as we arrived, since there was a cloud over the moon. Small groups of partisans were silently awaiting our arrival, their backs against the walls of the buildings. Vulin was suddenly approached by a diminutive figure clad in peasant dress and in a highly excitable state, his voice rising high above the murmurs of our party as he welcomed us.

His house was to be our headquarters, and Knowles and Stark got busy setting up our radios in the farmyard. I was glad to find that the back of the house faced towards the enemy and would afford some protection from shellfire. The front looked south over the channel and the bay, and was a good vantage point. Knowles soon reported contact with the Royal Navy and the Royal Air Force. The house had one large room, with a huge wooden bunk against one wall which could have accommodated a whole family. Upon it were a collection of blankets and clothes, and I had a fair bet it was full of bed bugs.

Shortly before first light I was joined by Captain Smith of the Royal Artillery who had been landed by his gunboat and escorted up the hill with his equipment by the troops Vulin had left at the jetty. He was no relation to my companion of the Peljesac, but I was to be just as much in his debt. He had with him an Aldis lamp, with which to signal his position to Stocken, who was now in the Povljana Channel.

The scene was now set for the battle. As the cold light began slowly to steal over the island, Smith and I set out to a vantage point from where we should be able to observe the two enemy observation posts at Gradac and Juraj. The Royal Air Force were due to bomb both points at 0700 hours but, to our consternation, we found ourselves shrouded in mist.

Smith stood facing south and told me he would risk using his signal lamp. I held my breath. His signal snapped out and, at once, from the gunboat somewhere down in the channel the answer came flashing through the mist. Sometimes things work out according to plan, but more often in warfare they do not.

Vulin set off for his forward headquarters to make contact with the battalion of the 20th Division, which we learnt had landed without incident at Vlasivi. Now we waited for full light, which I prayed would bring the opening attack by Bartlett's Spitfires and Hurricanes. As my watch showed one minute to seven we heard the unmistakable sound of aircraft. They appeared very high up in two flights, peeling off over their targets and diving into the attack. The flash of explosives lit up the rocky hills and the crash of bombs echoed over the island. We could hear the staccato sound of aircraft cannon. The enemy had been taken completely by surprise. There was no answering fire from the ground and no telltale flak bursts.

It seemed to be ages before the defenders woke up to reality. An unexpected attack at dawn is indeed a horrible thing. This was the first occasion since the island was occupied that any serious attack had been made upon it, which no doubt accounted for our unopposed landing and unhindered deployment. I could imagine the garrison pulling on their trousers and jackboots, reaching for their weapons and rushing to the gunsites, their eyes bleary with sleep, their limbs shocked by the cold.

Soon, however, the splintering crash of shells about our position told us in no uncertain terms that the Devil's Division was now awake.

Vulin ran a telephone line from his headquarters to Povljana by which he was able to pass targets for our naval gun. This was run out by a couple of partisans, each holding one end of a spindle through a large wooden drum. They literally ran with it, doing a steeplechase over the walls and dodging the shell bursts. The boom of our gunboat in the channel was a reassuring answer.

The sun now rose on the battle, and it became a brilliant day. Knowles and Stark were busy with the radios in the farmyard. Suddenly, two Messerschmitts dived on our position. I rushed out to cover the equipment with any camouflage that came readily to hand. We heaped coats, blankets and bits of straw on it. We were well within range of the 105mm guns from Pag town, and the Vidovac battery had not started up as yet.

My telephone line was busy as Vulin gave me targets for the Royal Air Force. His first priority was still the observation posts of Gradac and Juraj, but the 105mm guns in the cemetery were next on the list.

By midday Second Sector had captured Gradac, and I was glad to be able to call off the air attack, as flak bursts were now seen in the sky. The pilots were coming in on the target in much too regular a pattern. After the initial attack Bartlett was sending out four aircraft at a time, and in my opinion this was not sufficient force to keep the defenders' heads down. Juraj still held out in the face of the attack by the 20th Division battalion.

It was not until mid-afternoon that a tremendous shell burst made me look up. The Vidovac battery had now joined in the battle. The shell had fallen short of our position by about 500yds, and I told Knowles to get our radio inside the house backed up against the thick north-facing wall. The 105mm guns from the cemetery were now firing on the Povljana Channel, but having lost their observation post, the shellfire seemed at random. Nonetheless, it forced the gunboat to keep changing her position, which made Smith's task more difficult.

As the light began to fail and darkness quickly descended, the Germans were still in possession of all their strong points and bunkers, with the exception of Gradac. Firing died down, only sporadic sounds of small arms fire disturbed the night. Wounded partisans started coming back through our position to be evacuated under cover of darkness.

We spent an uneasy night. The peasant farmer refused to leave his house. He was a weather-beaten, leathery-looking little man, who never seemed to be still. In spite of the risks to his life and property, he was frequently joking and laughing with his countrymen, but there was a note of hysteria in his behaviour.

At first light the battle started up again with renewed efforts to take Juraj. At eight in the morning the Devil's Division on the mainland sent off two vessels loaded with reinforcements for their garrison. They were attacked by Hurricanes but succeeded in getting into the harbour. This was bad news. Nevertheless, by midday Juraj had fallen to the partisans.

Our gunboat was now left to fire on the defences of the town itself. I had a signal from Bartlett that one of his Hurricanes had failed to return. It had been hit by flak, but the pilot had bailed out not far from Vlasivi. Vulin sent a patrol to search for him, and we got him back unhurt that evening.

By nightfall of this second day the Vidovac battery was firing with deadly effect on the two key strong points the partisans had taken. The Devil's Division now began a counter-attack. The RAF had sent a signal that they had located the battery on the mainland and had bombed it, but alas without much effect on its power to decide the battle. Fighting went on all night, and by dawn the partisans were driven out of all the strong points they had fought for.

There was an air of great despondency. I could sense the troops were getting jittery. In spite of our air attacks, the Devil's Division succeeded in landing further reinforcements in some strength. Vulin told me they had landed 500 men, and he decided to withdraw and evacuate his main force from Vlasivi.

We could not get there ourselves except by a strenuous overland march, dodging the shellfire which was now plastering the island. I sent a signal to Stocken asking if he could take off a small party by ML in the Povljana Channel and gave the RAF a definitive bomb line. My final message to Christopher read as follows:

> Things are getting warmer. If you come my way this morning, I suggest you plaster Cradac and the forward slope down to Kosljun with any gun of any calibre. Enemy line 873334 to 903362. Enemy land 500 men. I regret things are getting out of hand. We shall withdraw.

Stocken and Smith sailed their gunboat away during the night to avoid meeting with a chance shell. I had a reassuring signal that he was coming back up the channel with his gun and his flagship to give our retreat covering fire and to take us off.

I told Corporal Knowles to pack up his radio on the stretcher and detailed a carrying party of partisans to set off for Vlasivi, with instructions that if they could not make it with their load they were to destroy the equipment and save themselves.

I sent Vulin a message that the Royal Navy was coming in to take him off as soon as he could disengage. The handful of partisans about our headquarters were grey-faced and nervous, standing at the corners of the farm buildings fingering their weapons. The poor little peasant started to lay waste to his own home. First he broke his crockery by hurling it on the floor and against the walls, then, seizing an axe, he set about smashing his furniture. I could not bear to watch any more. I set off with Knowles and Stark down the path across country to the rendezvous with the ML. A valley and a further hill range lay between us and the channel. As we reached the bottom of the valley there was a strange silence. I disliked the sensation of being temporarily blind to events, which were now so completely out of hand. As we gained the crest of the hill, there in the channel lay the gunboat and the ML. My inclination was to run down to the shore, but I knew that naval field glasses would be focused on our retreat, which I was determined should be as dignified as possible.

Pulled up on the shingle was a tiny ship's dinghy, the painter tied to a rock. Knowles and Stark got aboard, and I shoved off. The ML lay 200yds offshore in deep water. I took the oars and pulled towards her. We must have appeared an odd sight to the crew of the ship, three soldiers in a small dinghy rowing for safety. We climbed up the ship's side and I went to the bridge with a wonderful sense of relief.

But Stocken and Smith were still ashore directing the fire of the gunboat. My legs felt like lead. I did not know their position, but there was nothing for it but to go back. I dropped into the dinghy and rowed for the island, pulling the boat well up on the shingle. Halfway up the hill, pausing for breath, I saw three figures standing in silhouette against the skyline – perfect targets for any infantryman. It was lucky for me that Stocken was so foolhardy, since if he had taken cover according to the book I should have had a job to find him.

Now I was in a position to direct our covering fire off my map. Shells whistled overhead to drop on the approaches to Povljana. If any heads appeared across the valley we were in a splendid position to fend off the infantry. Minutes later, two solitary figures climbed the hill to join us – Major Vulin and his Commissar Branko Mamula. He greeted me with the words 'Dobra Majoru', which is hard to translate but is a mildly complimentary term of friendship. Anyway, he was now in the hands of his allies. The Royal Navy took him off in style and, as we sailed back to Nin, he began to murmur apologies for his failure, but I stopped him with the old proverb 'nothing ventured, nothing gained'. This rather lame remark seemed to cheer him up tremendously.

The failure to take Pag was primarily due to the power of the Vidovac battery, which drove the partisans off the two high points which they had gained. The attack by the 20th Division along the coastal road had been cancelled, for reasons I never discovered, leaving the battery to concentrate on the defence of the garrison. Bartlett's single squadron of fighter-bombers was no substitute for artillery. We had nothing like enough firepower.

The Devil's Division was left in peace until 4 April, when we were to return, this time with British artillery. The little peasant was to welcome us again to his devastated house. A few days later I had a very nice letter from Major Vulin and Captain Mamula. It was an extravagant and undeserved compliment, but one which I treasure. It was written in Serbo-Croat, and the following is a translation:

STAR 11.POMORSKOG OBALASKOG SEKTORA

28.FEBRUARY 1945.

CC.BRITISH   MILITARY   MISSION   ZADAR   MAJOR CRICHTON

Dear Major,

We feel we should like to express our thanks to you, on the occasion of our combined military action, which you undertook on the island of Pag from 23 to 26 February 1945, for the military assistance which we obtained in the carrying out of the task due to your help.

The cooperation of the British Navy and Air Force gave us the chance to confirm our opinion of the high efficiency, skill and courage with which your soldiers carry out their tasks in battle against our common enemy. In addition to that, this cooperation in connection with our ground forces was an outstanding example of a combined operation of all branches of arms, both allied and of our own forces.

We should like on this occasion also to thank you personally for the help which you extended to us in coordinating, with complete success, the work of the individual branches of the allied arms, and also for giving, by your presence in the front line during the encounter, a magnificent example of your own personal courage and determination, leaving on our soldiers a fine impression of a true representative of our great ally.

With sincere greetings,

Political Commissar   Commandant Major/Branko Mamula/ Major/Ivan Vulin

Chapter 21

Zadar

After the discomforts and anxieties of the last two days it was wonderful to be back at my own headquarters. Our household ran like clockwork. The daily scrubbing of the floors continued, our buxom staff were jolly and efficient. We ate well from fresh provisions provided by our allies, and the hospitality we now received was touching. Food was scarce for the troops, but I cannot say in honesty that our consciences were much troubled. I had a present from the Second Sector of a case of rather sticky liqueurs, for which the country is famous. The Royal Air Force at Zemunik provided beer and cigarettes. The sun began to shine, and life took on a rosier hue.

My report on the battle for Pag brought a rather swift reaction. Air Commodore Laurence Sinclair flew in to see the form for himself, and I went out to Zemunik to receive him. He had been a distinguished fighter pilot in the early stages of the war and was now second-in-command to Air Vice-Marshal Mills of the Balkan Air Force, under whose command I now served. He flew in with the latest Spitfire, making such a perfect landing that I heard murmurs of admiration from the pilots watching. At my headquarters I gave him a full account of the Pag operation, and he took my view that sorties by four aircraft on heavily defended positions were ineffective and disproportionately dangerous. He said that if there was to be another offensive, he would lay on a petrol bomb attack on Gradac and would supervise it himself. In due course, this is exactly what he did.

At his invitation I flew back to the Balkan Air Force Headquarters in Italy, where I was lodged in Air Vice-Marshal Mills' house. At dinner that night I gave him a situation report as I saw it. The Germans showed no sign of any withdrawal from their present positions, which they had now occupied for more than a month. They were in good order in their present line from Karlobag in an arc southwards to Sarajevo, where the Prinz Eugen Division was still entrenched. I understood that there was still a possibility that we should land a substantial force at Zadar to outflank the German resistance in Italy, even if Vienna was not to be the objective. There were serious political considerations about Istria. If Allied forces could take the Peninsula from the south, there would be less likelihood of a dispute over the territory between the Italians and the Yugoslavs after it had been liberated. (In fact, as events unfolded and as Churchill's plan was overruled by the Allied Command, the Yugoslavs got to Istria first, following up the eventual enemy retreat. This resulted in the inevitable dispute, which created yet another world crisis in 1947, the Russians taking one side and the Western Allies, the other.)

Mills asked me if I thought Zadar was sufficiently secure for its use by larger ships of the Royal Navy. I replied that the harbour had been cleared of mines and a chain boom strung across the approaches, but the proximity of the enemy only ten miles away was a hazard. If the German Command seriously wanted to retake the port, I did not think the partisan build-up in the area could stop it, but we should have some hours warning of an impending attack. The Navy were blockading Pola, but 'E' boats were still able to get in and out at night, more or less at will.

I flew back to Zadar the following day with the knowledge that I had the full support of the Balkan Air Force. The Dakota skimmed over the Adriatic in brilliant sunshine, and we had an escort of two Spitfires somewhere high up above us. Group Captain John Selby, who had been one of the original members of '37' Military Mission, was piloting one of them. He was to be my guest at the villa on many occasions during the succeeding weeks, proving a very good companion. A large, cheerful person, he confessed to me that he absolutely hated flying over the sea in a single-engine plane. At breakfast one morning in the villa, having received orders to fly to Belgrade, to Tito's headquarters, he worked out his route with a map on the table, drawing a straight line from Zadar and laying a schoolboy's protractor upon it to give him his bearing. To a soldier used to studying his route with such painstaking considerations as geography, it seemed wonderfully simple.

In the early days of March the cruiser *Delhi* arrived in the port. The captain was anxious that his crew should not land, in case he had to make a quick getaway to sea, and General Drapsin of the partisan Eleven Corps made sure they would not, by placing armed guards on the quayside. Quite suddenly, the Yugoslavs produced an admiral on their Adriatic seaboard, in the person of Admiral Manola. He was a tall, handsome man with gold teeth and side whiskers, the personification of authority. His uniform was very grand. He wore a long grey coat decorated with gold braid over his tunic and breeches, and affected soft, black leather knee boots. All this finery contrasted strangely with the run of the mill uniforms of the rank and file, which were modest in the extreme.

Major Vulin called a conference to consider the general administration and protection of the port in the light of the arrival of such a powerful ship as the *Delhi*. I was invited to attend. Sinclair had gone back to England to get married and had sent me his dog, a crossbreed German police dog, which he had picked up in the Western Desert. It was extremely docile and affectionate but would attack anyone on even a whisper of command, according to its training. It was much admired by the partisans, and I took the dog with me to the conference. Brash fixed me up with a well brushed service dress and shiny Sam Browne belt. I was now fit to represent the British Army and to confront the authority of the new regime.

The conference was held in the town hall. When I arrived, a large company was already assembled, many of whom I now knew personally. My arrival with the dog amused Vulin and Mamula. There was a friendly atmosphere as the minutes ticked away and there was no sign of the arrival of the Grand Admiral. Friendly conversation and ease gave way to a nervous tension of expectancy. There was the sound of marching steps outside the conference room, the door was flung open, and Admiral Manola stood on the threshold in all his finery. The whole company stood up in respectful obedience. I followed suit, stirring the dog with my foot and whispering a command. There was dead silence, except for a bloodcurdling snarl from under the table. I bent down to reassure the dog, the tension was broken and my companions hid their smiles. Perhaps I was not the best of ambassadors, but I knew the majority was still with me.

At any rate, the crew of the *Delhi* were now to be allowed ashore at their Captain's discretion. I went aboard the cruiser, into a totally different world. To appreciate your fellow countrymen you must be absent for a while.

Our concern was rapid communication between the ship and my shore-based headquarters. There was no difficulty during daylight hours, but an enemy attack by night being more probable, we had to come to an arrangement whereby the ship would receive good warning, at least to give her time to get to sea. I borrowed an Aldis lamp, which Corporal Knowles knew how to operate. If the cruiser wanted me, the Captain said he would turn his searchlight on my bedroom window to get me up. We had occasion to see how it worked only a few nights later.

I was sound asleep in my room when I was woken by a blinding light. I leapt out of bed. The cruiser's searchlight was full on. I pulled on my battledress trousers over my pyjamas and got more or less dressed, before Brash burst in. He wore only a shirt and had a rifle in his hand. The warning searchlight was followed by the urgent 'whoop, whoop, whoop' of the cruiser's sirens. The sound over the harbour in the dead of night echoed and re-echoed with piercing urgency.

Brash got out the jeep. The searchlight was switched off, and by the waterside there was silence. Out of the stillness and the dark a German voice was heard crying out across the water, '*Hilfe! Hilfe!*' There was no sound of marine engines, or indeed of anything else, not even of running footsteps. I drove the jeep flat out to the other side of the harbour, where the cruiser lay.

The Germans had sent out an 'E' boat with two small torpedo craft from Pola. These small boats had a torpedo in the bow, and their pilots would go into the attack at full speed, directing their craft at the enemy and jumping from the cutaway stern at the last moment before impact to save their own lives. But the chain boom across the approaches to the harbour had foiled the attack, the two boats having failed to jump it. The cries for help from one brave man had sickened me, as he was never recovered. The second pilot was found exhausted the next day on Uljan. I asked to interrogate him but I was never allowed to do so, and I do not know to this day how his fate was determined.

It was evident that we had still to be very alert.

I was now receiving daily intelligence reports from the partisans. Some were written in English, but most had to be interpreted. They were always stamped with the star in a circle, the insignia of the Yugoslav Army of National Liberation, and finished with the overdramatic words, 'Death to Fascism – Freedom to the People'.

We still had our partisan guards at the villa during the night for our own protection. Late one evening, whilst I was sitting comfortably by the stove in my room, after the troops had turned in, I heard the door downstairs shut quietly. The dog growled, got up and pricked his ears. I went out on to the landing overlooking the hallway below. A powerfully built man was standing there, looking about him in a furtive manner. In the dim light of the single bulb which was left burning it appeared he was dressed as a partisan, but I felt something was wrong. I peered over the balcony and could see he had on a German tunic. I called out to him and he answered in German. Brash, whose room was a few yards from mine, came out to see what was going on, carrying his rifle in his hand.

My interpreter, the lawyer from Zagreb, also slept in the house. I sent Brash to get him, and an extraordinary interview followed. The man said he was a deserter from 999 Festungs Battalion and had been given a document of identity by the partisans, which he produced from his tunic. He asked if I could get him by any means to Italy, where he wanted to continue with his studies, which the war had interrupted. This story seemed so ridiculous that I almost believed it.

There was no significant bulge in his pockets to denote a grenade, and he was otherwise unarmed. When I asked if he was challenged by the guard at the gate to the villa, he told me he had simply held out his pass. He was perfectly cool, not at all agitated; an upright and powerful figure. In any event, we were not here to aid and abet German deserters, and I was pretty certain this was a trick by LSNA, the Secret Police, to discover what my reactions would be under the circumstances.

I told him I could do nothing for him, that he should put his request to the partisan command. Accordingly he left, not at all put out, simply asking that I should not report his visit. But of course, it would in any event have been reported by the guard. In future I kept my pistol handy by my bedside.

About the middle of March, a Russian Military Mission arrived in Zadar, travelling overland from Belgrade and commanded by a full Colonel with a numerous entourage. This grand arrival contrasted in pomp with my establishment of four. Nevertheless, the Yugoslavs did not take the Russians into their confidence, and they were accommodated rather shabbily outside the town. Tito was extremely suspicious of the post-war intentions of the USSR, and his fears were shared by most of the officers with whom I came into contact, so that the mission was treated coldly. Moreover, the Russians could not at this time contribute any practical military assistance, and for this reason also they were ignored by the Formation Commanders.

One day, two officers of the Second Sector invited me to go with them to Split. Zadar offered no light relief; there was a constant state of alert due to the proximity of the enemy. The total ban on any form of ordinary relaxation was still very much in force. This must have been quite a strain, as the Dalmatians in particular are a gay, handsome and delightful people. I was beginning to feel the strain myself and readily accepted the invitation, although there were rumours of terrible retribution on anyone breaking the rules.

On a fine morning the three of us set out in my jeep to the south. It had been two months since the liberation of Split. There is a very early spring on the Dalmatian Coast. The sunshine was exhilarating as we drove through the beautiful countryside, with constant views of the Adriatic and the islands, and we shook off the grey oppressions of war.

My companions were returning to their home town. My experience during its liberation had been so grim that I could scarcely understand their enthusiasm for the port which, they declared, was the gayest and most beautiful in the world. I simply remembered the desolate streets, the grey, fearful faces and my attack of fever in the freezing cold hotel. I had not had the time or inclination to explore the great palace of Diocletian or the splendid creations of Greek and Roman culture which are everywhere to be seen.

It was a wonderful evening as we arrived. I dropped off my companions, who made a rendezvous to meet me by the Silver Gate in two hours' time. The streets were still rather empty, but for a few civilians who looked at me curiously and a little band of children who followed me as I wandered about the town. The only marked distinction in my uniform was my service cap and the bright regimental badges on the collar of my battledress. I carried my Webley pistol in a webbing holster, as tank crews used to, which contrasted with the heavy leather holsters and strappings carrying Luger automatics which were favoured by nearly all the partisan officers. My interpreter had told me that my modest military gear was a constant source of surprise to the partisans. They expected a British cavalry officer to be booted and spurred at least, and in fact the senior officers of the JANL did affect a grand appearance. Many wore soft, black leather, knee-high boots with breeches which, in truth, were very practical and smart.

It was nearly dark by the time one of my companions turned up at the Silver Gate. He directed me, by a devious route, through the narrow streets to the rear of a modern block of flats to the south of the harbour, where I parked the jeep in a blind alley out of sight of the road. We entered through the service doors, climbing numerous flights of concrete steps to a flat high up in the building which must have had a splendid view of the sea and the town.

The party was already in full swing. Half a dozen officers and as many young women were laughing and drinking together, standing around a great rectangular table set out for dinner, laden with shining cutlery, china and candlesticks. The blinds on the windows of the spacious flat were carefully pulled down. There was a lull in the festivities whilst I was formally introduced to everyone present, then someone produced an accordion. It was warm, bright and friendly, and never had I seen such a collection of pretty young women at any one party. Most of the company spoke some English, and I found myself quickly at ease. The *rakija* and the wine began to have its effect.

The party was suddenly summoned to sit down, but to my astonishment, the young women did not join us at the table; had I noticed it, places had been set only for the men, and we were waited on by this bevy of beauty, one behind every chair, more or less.

Once or twice during dinner an officer left the flat to spy out the land. I understood they had faithful lookouts posted about to prevent a sudden intrusion by the Organization for the Protection of the People. During these expeditions we kept quiet. The window blinds were furtively lifted and the lights dimmed. The risks they ran only seemed to heighten the enjoyment as the party became hilarious.

The Yugoslavs are wonderful singers with an acute musical sense, and an accordion accompanied many voices. It was all great fun. There was much dancing and drinking. In the small hours of the morning several of the party left the flat. The remainder slept where they lay. The morning after is always a heavy price to pay, and we left Split in the grey light of dawn in silence with hangovers and happy memories.

Immediately on my return to Zadar I learnt that plans were afoot for a second attack on Pag.

Chapter 22

The Capture of Pag

We now had the advantage of fighting over the same ground, against the same enemy, in the positions they had occupied in February. The nature of the ground made it nearly impossible for them to change their gun sites or observation posts, and the fortified bunkers around the perimeter of the town remained. They had reinforced their armament with a considerable number of machine guns and mortars, including four big ones of 81mm.

Partisan Second Sector were to be given another chance to take the island, but my friend Major Vulin was succeeded by Major Grubelic, a much younger and tougher individual. He was short and stocky, with black hair and a black moustache, and was a dedicated communist.

The Partisan 9th Division was ordered to attack the mainland enemy garrison of Karlobag and to silence the guns of Vidovac. I was called to Eleven Corps Headquarters to confer with General Drapsin, by whose orders I had been imprisoned on my arrival in Zadar. He was a heavy, pompous individual, over-conscious of his new authority. I had the impression that he terrorized his subordinates and gathered from my interpreter that he had made curious enquiries about me. How was it, he asked, that this imperialist officer sat down to meals at the same table as his troops? In any event, he was now on the spot and he could not hope to succeed in his objective without our help.

Our build-up in Zadar had increased. Lieutenant Stocken now had four gunboats, and the Royal Air Force had two fighter-bomber squadrons at Zemunik, with two field squadrons of the RAF Regiment. Major Bethell had succeeded Dizzy Ross as Commander of the 75mm howitzers. We also had a considerable number of LCTs to land our forces.

I had several conferences with the General, who was even more put out than his predecessors by Stocken's schoolboy appearance and easy manner. Evidently, we were not at all his idea of what British officers ought to look

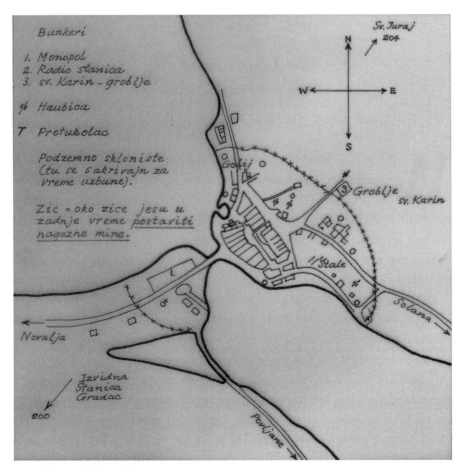

8. The Fortified Town of Pag – the most extreme right flank of the German defence in April 1945. Reproduced form the original partisan map.

like, and our casual behaviour clearly irritated him to distraction. The modest double gold rings of a Lieutenant of the Royal Navy on a rather crumpled blue jacket did not indicate authority. In a little while we were to be seriously at loggerheads.

We reached a broad agreement with Drapsin that the Royal Navy would land elements of the 9th Division at Lukovo, a small fishing town on the coast, during the night of 3 April. One gunboat would be allocated to their support. The RAF would use their fighter-bombers in close support of the main body of troops moving up the coast towards Karlobag. Three gunboats would support the Second Sector attack against Pag from the Povljana

Channel, and the four guns of the Raiding Support Regiment would be landed at Vlasivi on the island itself, protected by a company of the RAF Regiment. British Forward Observation Officers would accompany the 9ᵗʰ Division. I was to go myself with Second Sector as before. The details were to be drawn up with the respective formation commanders. 'D' Day was 4 April; H Hour was first light, 0700 hours.

When our plans became known at the Balkan Air Force Headquarters, Air Commodore Sinclair soon flew in with his Spitfire. As good as his word, he laid plans for the all-important first light attack by petrol bombs on the key enemy observation posts of Gradac and Juraj, which had caused us such trouble in February. Land Forces Adriatic sent me an officer with experience of close air support to accompany the headquarters of the 9ᵗʰ Division and to keep me in touch with the mainland operation. The scene was now set.

However, about the last day of March, an unfortunate incident took place. I learnt that the crew of an American Flying Fortress, which had crashed after a bombing attack on Klagenfurt and had subsequently been rescued by the partisans, were now imprisoned by General Drapsin for making anti-communist speeches to their rescuers. This was incredibly stupid. As soon as it became known in Italy, I had orders to secure their release. Drapsin was adamant; he said he could not do so without instructions from Belgrade. I was sure he had acted on his own initiative, a privilege only assumed by the OSNA or top party members.

Finally, I paid him an official visit, Sam Browne belt and all. I asked if he was more interested in politics than warfare. American aircrew were highly trained combat troops. By their detention he was aiding the common enemy, and in the last resort I would call off our support for the attack on Pag and Karlobag. He glowered at me, muttering a question to my interpreter. I insisted on a literal interpretation. Embarrassed, the poor fellow, who was by now thoroughly intimidated, replied, 'The General says, how is it that the Major is allowed to talk to me like this!'

That same afternoon, the Americans arrived at my headquarters. In spite of the fact that they had certainly not been ill treated and owed their rescue to the partisans, they were unshaven, dirty and truculent. Trooper Brash was not impressed, and we sent them off to Zemunik forthwith for transhipment to Italy. Meanwhile, far across the Adriatic, a staff officer drafted an operation order. It was so inaccurate that it amounted to no more than a letter of authority. Even my name was spelled incorrectly. The signature of the officer at the bottom fortunately remains indecipherable. To their credit, the Headquarters of Land Forces Adriatic never interfered with what we were doing on the other side of the sea. In eight months I did not receive more than half a dozen orders. Brigadier Davey backed us up as long as we got on with it. It was the sort of loose command that suited me, as I always hated having anyone breathing down my neck.

Lord Nelson, as I had privately called Christopher Stocken, now became wildly enthusiastic. He fairly bustled about the port, conferring with his captains, breezily calling on me at the villa. He, too, got out an operation order with the unpronounceable code name 'SMRT'.

We called a conference at the villa for the evening of 2 April. Bethell asked if I could arrange an escort for his second-in-command to reconnoitre the landing place for the guns at night. Major Grubelic readily agreed, and this small party set off during the evening before the final conference in a fishing boat, returning safely after a satisfactory reconnaissance, not only of the landing place, but also of a selected gunsite. It looked horribly close to the defences of the town, even on the map, but they had encountered no enemy patrols.

There was another interruption on the morning of 2 April. I was ordered to fetch Randolph Churchill from a village some 80 miles away in the hinterland. He had been in territory now clear of the enemy but had got stuck for lack of transport. I could not drop everything just before 'D' Day, so I sent Corporal Knowles in my jeep with a partisan escort to fetch him.

The villa was packed with officers for the final conference. They arrived after dark for security reasons. It would have been a simple matter for an Ustaše or Četnik spy to travel the 12 miles to the enemy's lines with news of our preparations. Major Grubelic brought half a dozen officers with his second-in-command, Captain Hrnjak. Stocken arrived with Lieutenant Lloyd Hirst and his forward observation officers. The RAF was represented by the Squadron Commander who had taken over from Bartlett.

The air was soon thick with tobacco smoke and the fumes of alcohol as we pored over the maps spread out on the dining room table. The atmosphere was more that of a party than a combined operation conference. The Victor of Alamein would surely have disapproved, but the nearest General Staff Officer was more than a hundred miles away across the sea.

Who should arrive in the middle of all this but poor Randolph, looking defiant as usual, but rather tired and dust-covered. I gave him a drink, lent him my razor and sent him off to the cruiser, where I assured him he would be more comfortable. His famous father wanted him back. The party broke up well after midnight with toasts to our success.

The next day, 3 April, was a holiday. The warm spring sunshine sparkled on the sea, and the morning mist rose over the island of Uljan. I went swimming with Laurence Sinclair's dog, my constant companion. He loved the water and was so powerful he could pull me along in his wake if I held on to his tail. He was to go with me back to England to live happily ever after.

Towards nightfall, Brash drove me with my two signallers to the rendezvous with Second Sector Headquarters at Nin, a small fishing village at the southern end of Ninski Bay. Grubelic was already installed in the priest's house. It was a solid stone building, scrubbed clean and as bare of unnecessary furniture as my host's of Kukijica.

The partisans were about to sit down to supper. The priest sat at the head of the table, dressed in a black cassock, a Catholic entertaining atheists. He looked upon the company with a wry smile, at their pistols, map cases, leather strappings and Schmeissers propped against the walls of the room. He asked a question of Grubelic, at which there were roars of laughter, and when I insisted on being included in the joke, Grubelic turned to me and said, 'He wants to know what we are going to do, and I replied, "Wouldn't you like to know?"'

I did not think this funny. It was a foretaste of conflict between Catholic and Communist. After the priest had left the room, Grubelic asked me, in a more serious tone, if I thought we should succeed in taking Pag. I told him I thought we should, but only if the mainland batteries were silenced.

The partisans were amused at my personal preparations for war. They were very keen on my map cases, chinagraph pencils and professional-looking equipment. As I stood, I had only my Webley pistol in its webbing holster, my binoculars around my neck and my maps in the leg pocket of my battledress trousers. I used to cut out the maps carefully, stick them together and fold them conveniently before a battle. I had long ago discarded map cases, which are doubtless useful for a staff officer, but infuriatingly impractical inside a tank or in the front line.

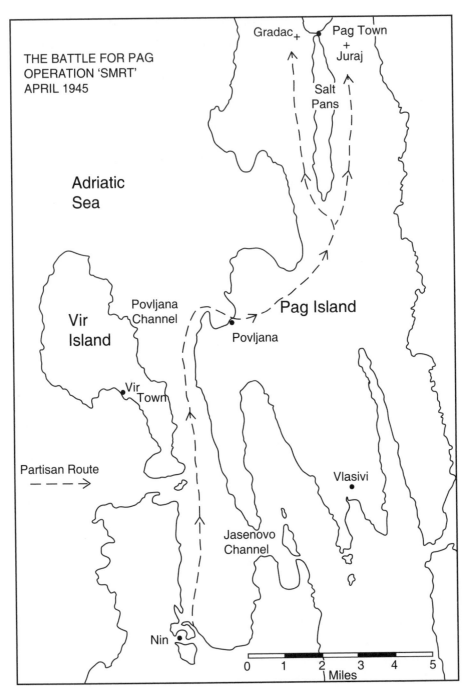

THE BATTLE FOR PAG
OPERATION 'SMRT'
APRIL 1945

Gradac

Pag Town
+
Juraj

Salt
Pans

Adriatic
Sea

Povljana
Channel

Pag Island

Vir
Island

Povljana

Vir
Town

Partisan Route
- - - - →

Vlasivi

Jasenovo
Channel

Nin

0   1   2   3   4   5
Miles

7. The Battle for Pag, Operation SMRT, April 1945

After supper I was shown to a bedroom, where I lay down fully clothed. I was woken in the early hours of the morning. Outside the priest's house, as usual, *rakija* and goat's milk were being passed around. I had got used to the mixture, which was indeed very warming and steadied the nerves.

In the harbour was a veritable armada of fishing boats, assembled from the islands under cover of the preceding night. We boarded the very same vessel which had landed us in the abortive attack in February. To my astonishment, we headed out to sea in the lead. It was flat calm, and once again, the sound of marine exhaust notes echoed over the surface. I thought we had started late and was sure we would not make our landfall in darkness.

As dawn broke, we still had four miles to go. The Germans must have been sound asleep, although their guns already had our range. Wild duck rose in the air in front of our bows. There was high cloud. The whole scene was lit by a grey, cold light. No one spoke. It was a few minutes to H Hour. I was longing to look at my watch but determined not to do so for fear of giving away my anxiety. We listened for the sound of aircraft. Sure enough, dead on time, the RAF were overhead.

The peak of Gradac stood out like a menacing sentinel, and suddenly there was a brilliant orange flash right on the top, followed by a black cloud of smoke billowing upwards. It seemed minutes before the tremendous crash thundered toward us across the sea. The partisans on deck were jubilant; the menace of the observation post had surely been obliterated in that opening attack.

We ran into the bay below Povljana unopposed. There was a scramble ashore, and we started up the rocky hillside path to the now familiar village. As we arrived at the farmhouse, it was broad daylight. The leathery little peasant farmer was hopping about excitedly as he welcomed us for the second time. I wondered where he had been hiding in the preceding six weeks. In any event, he would have been a hard man to catch up with on his own ground. Corporal Knowles soon fixed up the farmhouse as our operations room. We had a lot of heavy equipment as I had to have radio communications with Captain Thompson on the 9th Division front, as well as with the Royal Navy, the RAF and Bethell at the gunsite.

Troops were hurrying through Povljana at the double, after their steep climb up the hill from the bay. They spread out to advance on each side of the rocky road to Pag. The Festungs battalion was now fully awake, and shells burst on the rocks on every side. A second flight of RAF fighter-bombers dropped their load on Juraj.

An hour later, Lord Nelson's forward observation officers arrived. They were Royal Artillery officers with all the skill expected of British gunners. Very soon there was an artillery duel in progress between the guns of the garrison and the gunboats of the Royal Navy now stationed in the Povljana channel.

But I could not raise a whisper on the radio from Bethell. About noon, a partisan runner arrived with a message that he had landed without incident at Vlasivi and was moving up to his gunsite. I told Grubelic of the trouble with the radio. He at once agreed to lay on a telephone line by the crude but effective methods I had already witnessed.

Incredibly, nothing so far had gone wrong.

Soon I heard from Bethell. His guns were now in action. He had a tough job hauling them with their 1,600 shells over the rough going to the gunsite. The RAF Regiment were out in front of him for his protection. They had never been in action before, and I hoped the garrison would not venture a sortie.

The town and harbour were now taking a terrific pounding from the three gunboats and the four howitzers. My radio link to Zemunik was kept busy with calls of support for Second Sector, who were trying hard to scale the heights of Juraj. A report reached me that a Hurricane was missing. The partisans said they had seen it crash into the sea, and I asked them to keep a look out for the pilot.

Bursts of heavy calibre shells began to arrive at random. It was the mainland battery again. I sent a message to Captain Thompson, from whom I had a signal that he was up with the foremost Brigade of 9th Division, to ask him what he could do about it as it seemed the Vidovac battery was absolutely dedicated to the defence of Pag. He replied shortly that it was also firing on him. The commander of that battery deserved an Iron Cross First Class. The RAF were trying hard to seek it out.

A cryptic message arrived from Lieutenant Lloyd Hirst on the gunboat in the Podgorski Channel. It read: 'Do you know the beach opposite you is mined?'

I could only reply that I did not and had no intention of setting foot on it.

The enemy had not recovered from the devastating opening attack by the RAF on Gradac. The survivors had scrambled down the heights to seek safety behind the bunker defences of the town, abandoning the commanding position to the partisans. This was extremely important, as the guns in the cemetery could not now know the position of our gunboats in the Povljana Channel. They were firing at random, but nevertheless, a shell hit the bows of one boat without exploding, taking a gash out of the hull above the waterline.

The enemy's lack of observation now became a deciding factor. The hills rose steeply on each side of the town. Only the strong point of Juraj, on the heights a mile to the north-east, remained in their hands. The defenders behind their wire and in their pill boxes had restricted visibility. But as long as Juraj held, the partisan infantry had to suffer the bombardment of the big mortars, which were being skilfully directed.

As the day wore on, it became evident we were in for a hard fight. The partisans had no experience of orthodox infantry tactics and they were up against the professional soldiers of the Wehrmacht entrenched in a veritable fortress. The stone buildings with their thick walls were standing up to the pounding of the relatively small calibre shells of the howitzers and gunboats. The defences had been built up over the years for just such a contingency as this.

In all honesty, I cannot say that at the time I spared a thought for the valour of the German garrison. When one is young, compassion and admiration are subordinate to one's concern for self-preservation. Nevertheless, the German Commander and his troops were fighting with great courage. Their radio must have told them that everywhere in Europe the German armies were in retreat, yet the little garrison of Pag, hundreds of miles from their homeland, was holding out in the face of the odds against it. There were no white flags here stuck out of the windows. I never met the German Commander, because he died by his own hand on the evening of the following day, 5 April 1945.

As night began to fall, we had got no further. I asked Stocken if his ships could sail into the Podgorski Channel to try to intercept any enemy reinforcements which the Devil's Division might send out from the mainland during the night. Major Grubelic agreed to keep his troops well away from the gunsite, as Bethell had ordered the RAF Regiment to fire at anything that moved in front of his position. He had his guns hitched to the jeeps for a quick getaway if there was a counter-attack.

With the waning light, shellfire ceased. Partisan wounded started arriving through our positions for evacuation to Nin. Behind us there was a first-aid post manned by a Russian doctor; where he came from I never discovered.

We spent an uneasy night, interrupted only by occasional bursts of small arms and machine gun fire. The gunboats had withdrawn to Nin bay during the night but, as dawn broke on the second day of battle, they were back in position. Their guns thundered out, directed by Captain Hill-Smith, who had taken up a position on the heights of Gradac, and soon the howitzers joined in.

Unless we could break the enemy's resistance by shellfire, I began to think the partisans would never take the town.

I had some good news from Thompson during the morning. He thought the Vidovac battery had moved up the coast road towards Karlobag. It had not fired for some time. If his information was correct, then it had abandoned the defence of Pag. Either the pressure of the 9th Division or the RAF attacks had proved too much for it. Could it mean perhaps that the enemy were at last withdrawing to the north?

Incredibly, the 105mm guns in the cemetery were still firing, withstanding all the RAF attempts to silence them. Neither was there a crack anywhere in the perimeter. We kept up the pressure all day.

During the afternoon I had a curious signal from the Navy. It read: 'Could I meet George and David at Vlasivi at 1300 hrs.'

I replied that I certainly could not; and anyway who on earth were George and David? Corporal Knowles searched the codes but could give no answer.

By mid-afternoon the heavy frown across the black brows of Major Grubelic began to lift. Some of his forward troops had got through the wire to occupy several pillboxes on the perimeter. He asked me for one final major attack by our fighters to go in at 1700 hours, and he intended to follow it up by a determined assault to break into the town.

With only half an hour to go, Brigadier George Davey ('George and David') arrived at our headquarters. He had come all the way across the Adriatic to find out how we were getting on, and the Navy had shipped him from Nin.

Within minutes of his arrival, Grubelic sent me a jeep. We were moving up to be in on the kill. I hated being driven on these occasions, so I took the wheel, the Brigadier sitting beside me. Just before we reached the gunsite of the Raiding Support Regiment we saw a young woman standing by the track who saluted us as we passed. She was dressed as a partisan, with her fore and aft cap perched on top of a carefully combed pageboy bob. She might have been a model for a European fashion house. Her presence there was utterly incongruous.

Behind the guns was a vast pile of empty shellcases.

At the foot of Gradac I pulled up. We began to climb the slopes to a vantage point to look down at the enemy, but as we climbed we were exposed to view. George Davey's hat with its red band was conspicuous, so I signalled to him to take it off.

At 1700 hours precisely the fighters dived in, their cannons firing, to drop their last load on the brave defenders. The partisans dashed in now, regardless of the machine gun fire from the pillboxes. We could see them running, outlined against the white walls of the buildings. In a few minutes there was sudden quiet.

We scrambled down the hillside to the jeeps. Major Grubelic and Captain Hrnjak climbed into theirs, motioning me with a gesture of courtesy to precede them on the drive into the town. I politely declined with a sweep of my hat, which I had raised in acknowledgement. I had no intention of testing the road for mines in front of them and I drove carefully in the tracks of the leading vehicle with my valuable cargo, who was certainly holding his breath. There is many a slip 'twixt cup and lip.

In the narrow approach to the town we were held up by a dead German soldier. He was lying across the roadway on his back, his sightless eyes staring at the sky. A little group of children were gazing down at him in wonderment. One hundred and twenty dead lay mostly where they had fallen. We took only 250 prisoners, the Ustaše having deserted by boat during the night. One horse was counted in the booty, still miraculously unharmed.

Very soon we turned and left that sad place.

Karlobag also fell at midnight. Within a few weeks, the German armies everywhere had capitulated.

As I stood on the deck of the ML homeward bound, I felt no elation. After six years and three campaigns I had learnt a trade at which I was never again to be employed.

Chapter 23

A New Life

I had now been overseas for four and a half years, the stipulated period for repatriation to England, and a posting order awaited me at Zadar. Brash packed up our kit, and I took a last look round my room at the villa which had been my home for over three months; at the terracotta stove in the corner before which I had sat with the dog at my feet in the cold evenings of January and February; at the spotless, white, scrubbed wooden floor; at my iron bed against the wall with its clean sheets and neatly folded blankets; and I went out for the last time on to the balcony to look over the blue waters of the harbour, before I called to the dog and shut the door. I had been strangely happy there.

We boarded a Dakota at Zemunik for Bari. The dog was always nervous at take-off and landing and he pushed against me for reassurance as the engines roared and the pilot let go his brakes. Soon there below us lay the beautiful coastline of Dalmatia and, in one panorama, the island of Pag, the town of Preko, the long lines of Dugi Otok, places which were to remain forever in my memory for the strange adventures that had befallen me there.

At Bari we took one of the Mission jeeps and headed for Naples. A dusty haze hung over the city and the bay from the emissions of Vesuvius. It was sad to say goodbye to Trooper Brash, who was not due to go home and had to report back to the regiment. We had been together for a long time and had become good friends and companions, but now I was on my own.

I spent a week in Naples at the Senior Officers' hotel waiting for a passage on a troopship. The streets of the city were thronged with the populace intermingled with the troops of a dozen nations, to such an extent that getting about in the daytime was hard work. I took to going out late at night to walk the dog, whose handsome and rather ferocious appearance attracted the Neapolitan urchins, who never go to bed. They would follow at a respectful distance, taunting us. Husky, for that was the dog's name, was highly trained, and one night when the little urchins were more numerous than usual I let him go after them. To my consternation, he got one and had him down on the pavement, standing over him in the moonlight, his tail wagging furiously. Grimy little faces were soon peering from every doorway and corner at this calamity, but when I called to them, they soon came out of their hiding places to gather about the prostrate figure of their companion, and when I demonstrated that the dog was really very friendly, they were quite delighted to stroke him and make a great fuss over the animal. I returned to my hotel with a large escort of little Neapolitans, and they watched for me every night thenceforth to play the same game over again.

Meanwhile, although I had retired from the scene of action to play nocturnal games with the urchins of Naples, the war had not stopped; but the ring of steel was growing ever tighter about the German nation, and Japan's happy dream of conquest had turned into a nightmare. From the east the Russians had broken the Oder/Neisse line and were advancing on Berlin and Dresden, and from the west the Allies had almost reached the Elbe and the Czechoslovak frontier. Right in the middle, the architect of the Second World War sat in his fortified bunker in Berlin, still directing with shaking hands and frenzied eyes the last defences of the Third Reich.

Laurence Sinclair had designated his dog as the official mascot of Balkan Air Force in order to ensure its safe journey to England on a troop transport, and I was duly informed that a kennel had been installed on the after deck of the *Empress of India*, which lay in the port of Naples to receive us. (Who would not stretch principles a little for the sake of his dog?)

The Mediterranean, which had for so many years been the scene of raging conflict, was now blue and calm and beautiful once more, and the troops lay about the decks almost naked, their bodies turning brown in the brilliant spring sunshine as the great ship headed for Gibraltar.

My fiancée was still at Lisbon, as far as I knew from the few letters which had reached me in Zadar, and it was a temptation to jump ship as we lay at anchor off the Rock. My strictly orthodox upbringing restrained me, although if I had known of the difficulties which lay ahead I might have taken a different view of the matter and another course of action.

Very soon we sailed into the greyer seas of the North Atlantic, and dark thunderclouds covered the sky over the Clyde as we put in to Gourock. I said goodbye to the dog, to whom I had become greatly attached. The Blue Cross kennels were to fetch him for six months' quarantine, and he was to achieve the doubtful distinction of having his picture on the front page of the *Daily Mirror*. (It is really a mistake to look after someone else's dog, because there is inevitably a sad parting at the end of it.)

I am sorry to relate that I felt no thrill at setting foot once again on Scottish soil. I suppose I was suffering from a form of anti-climax, looking over my shoulder at the dramatic events of the last four years; moreover, I badly missed the companionship of my friends. The balloon was deflating with a sigh.

Roosevelt had died on 10 April and Hitler had committed suicide on the 30th, as the Russian armies entered the German capital.

I arrived at Kings Cross on 8 May, on the eve of the capitulation of all our enemies in Europe. There was a busy scene in front of the station as taxis and chauffeur-driven limousines whisked away important looking people with unsmiling faces and fat briefcases. A pretty WAAF officer driving a little van took pity on me, indicating the vacant seat beside her, and I heaved my old scarred bedroll and my scanty belongings into the back and was driven to my mother's house in Knightsbridge.

By midnight the war was over and there were great crowds of people rejoicing in Piccadilly Circus. I took no part in it.

The cable service between London and Lisbon now attracted a heavy increase in traffic, and I applied for leave to go to Portugal which was promptly refused by an unfeeling War Office. Visas to enable my fiancée and her mother to come to England proved extremely difficult to obtain in spite of my future mother-in-law's diplomatic status, and I began to regret my impeccable behaviour at Gibraltar. The smart young men at the Foreign Office, whilst professing great sympathy for my predicament, merely sniffed at their red carnations and raised shocked eyebrows when I began to express my determination in undiplomatic language. However, when I threatened more or less to burn down the building in exasperation, the visas were granted.

Life now looked a little brighter, particularly as I met many friends who had spent four dreary years in prisoner-of-war camps in Germany. I am glad to say that, except for one or two who had been adversely affected by their ordeal, the majority were in good heart but strangely shared with me a curious unexplained depression at their liberation. It was as if we were without positive direction, and this phenomenon was to remain with us for several years. I suppose that, for anyone with imagination, it was unlikely that you could wipe from your memory the dramatic experience of more than six years in a matter of weeks or months, and the readjustment to everyday life proved difficult. John de Moraville, who with his love of luxury had booked a suite at the Berkeley Hotel to celebrate the end of the war, never took up his option, but instead retired to the country. Peter Dollar never regained his usual cynical composure until he sensibly bought himself a horse. Francis Romney fortunately got married. Loopy Kennard, resuming his guise of irresponsibility, gave the impression that he had taken everything in his stride. But he had not. Only my lugubrious Squadron Commander, Major Clements, appeared exactly the same, as indeed he does to this very day, a quarter of a century later.

One day, as I was walking down Jermyn Street, I saw the unmistakable figure of General Freyburg. I resisted a strong temptation to run after him. Under his smart civilian suit his body was riddled with bullet wounds. He had seen the mud and horror of the trenches in the First World War; had taken on his broad shoulders the responsibility for the last stages of the Greek Campaign; had led the vanguard of the Eighth Army in the defeat of the Afrika Korps; had been at Cassino. He was, in fact, a highly professional soldier, almost incomparably skilled in his profession. I wanted to express my admiration, but the English habit of reserve held me back, and the stalwart figure marched down the street no doubt to an appointment with more distinguished people.

Very soon now I went down to Southampton by train to meet Brita, who had at long last got a passage from Lisbon. We had not met for more than a year, and I was in a state of high excitement. I had booked rooms for herself and her mother at the Ritz. She had not been to England since as a child she had stayed at Camberley to learn English many years before, and much to my amusement, she marvelled at the great trees of the New Forest as the train sped towards London.

We married on 9 August 1945 at St Paul's Church, Knightsbridge. Douglas Nicoll was my best man, and Roy Farran kindly consented to be usher, somehow managing to supply the Ritz with sufficient alcohol for the reception party. Many of my friends were present.

Since I had spent very little money during the eight months I had been in Yugoslavia I had saved several hundred pounds in the bank, on the strength of which I rented an expensive furnished house in Astell Street, Chelsea at 12 guineas a week.

Some months later, and after a short spell at Sandhurst and Bovington as an instructor, I was ordered to York to be officially demobilized. A convoy of open three-ton trucks was waiting at the station to take us to the demobilization centre outside the city. As we drove through the streets, a wit amongst us started bleating like a sheep, a lead which was quickly followed by the entire convoy. The people of York stood on the pavements and cheered as we passed. Back at the station we were all presented with threepence for a cup of tea by an embarrassed non-commissioned officer.

I was now ready to face the new world, and like tens of thousands of my contemporaries I had a different sort of battle to fight. But that is another story.

Index

Drapsin, General, 173, 196, 203–4
Duck, wild, 170
Dugi Otok, island of, 137, 144
Dunkirk, 3
Durban, 7

Eden, Anthony, 14
Edhessa, 12
Eighth Army, 60–1, 65, 69, 75, 99, 218
  both sides pause for breath, 70
  fighting hard for supremacy in
      Italy, 178
  has to wait two months for supplies from
      England, 73
  huge quantities of supplies
      reaching, 84
  lands on toe of Italy, 104
  Montgomery takes command and has
      immediate effect, 73–4
  more powerful than ever before, 89
  retreat begins to Sollum, 66
  strikes back to relieve Tobruk, 56
  tired and worn after victory, 52
Egypt, 2, 5, 8
El Adam airfield, 95
El Taqa Plateau, 81
Empire Roach, 113
Epirus, 28
Erithrai, 33
Euboea, 27
Evening Standard, 60

Farouk, King of Egypt, 51, 61
Farran, Roy, 44, 218
Fernie Hunt, 2
Finland, 59
Flying Fortress, 205
Ford 15cwt truck, 36
Free French
  holding extreme left flank, 64
  join 7th Armoured Division, 86

role in Operation Lightfoot, 89
French, 5
Freyberg, General, 40, 43, 45, 218
  comes to the rescue, 67
  is wounded yet again, 67
  regiment under command, 93
Frommer, Leutnant, 146
Fryer, Lieutenant Stuart, 78
Fuka, 93

Garibaldi, 57
Gazala, 60, 64, 95
Geneva Convention, 126
German
  agents in Cairo, 51
  armaments industry, 59
  attack on Crete, 54
  Divisions
    Devils, 122, 169
    90th Light, 89
    1st Parachute, 164
    SS Prince Eugen, 169
    118th, 122
    264th, 140
    369th, 122, 169
    370th, 169
  E-boats, 136
  999th Festungs Battalion, 186
  Fieseler Storch spotter plane, 24
  garrison fights with great courage, 211
  infiltrate into Syria, 54
  prisoners of war, 56, 132
  Schmeisser, 116, 117, 122, 143, 147, 172,
      187, 207
  Sixth Army, 100
  SS Adolf Hitler Division, 18
  Stukas, 19
  Twelfth Army, 15, 21, 24, 31, 45
  withdrawal from Greece and southern
      Yugoslavia, 149
  88mm anti tank guns, 59